What People Are Saying About Guillermo Maldonado

Apostle Guillermo Maldonado is one of the outstanding leaders of the twenty-first century. His prophetic insight into the apostolic foundations of the church and his passion and hunger for the manifestation of the supernatural kingdom of God on earth in our modern times are contagious. His books are destined to become classics for years to come.

—Dr. Myles Munroe
President and Founder, Bahamas Faith Ministries Int'l

I am impressed with the great presence of God that surrounds Guillermo Maldonado 24/7....He not only walks in extraordinary miracles, signs, and wonders, but he also has been supernaturally equipped to disciple others to move in the same supernatural power of God.

—Sid Roth
Host, *It's Supernatural!* television program

The compelling fact of Guillermo Maldonado's life is that he has taken the words of Jesus literally to "go and make disciples of all nations." If your desire is to be a disciple-maker, I encourage you to embrace Pastor Maldonado and his teaching.

—Pastor Rich Wilkerson
Trinity Church Miami and Peacemakers Ministries

Pastor Guillermo Maldonado's preaching is a spiritual banquet that inspires souls....He encourages the brokenhearted and gives them hope. He revives the faith of the sick and helps those who have lost their way to find their path back to the Lord.

—Porfirio Lobo Sosa
President of the Republic of Honduras, Central America

Pastor Maldonado has a worldwide ministry specializing in the miraculous. His books are helpful, contain great revelation knowledge, and most certainly give godly direction. So often, we look at the outward signs of a ministry and admire the fruit of it, but I have seen Pastor Maldonado's ministry inside and out, and I like the fruit of both.

—Marilyn Hickey
President, Marilyn Hickey Ministries

Guillermo Maldonado has challenged both the Hispanic church and the broader church to rely fully on the power of God to transform our lives, communities, and nations through His enlivening Spirit.

—Dr. Carlos Campo
President, Regent University, Virginia Beach, Virginia

Pastor Maldonado is an accomplished and prolific writer whose ministry reaches the faithful throughout the world.

—Dr. Eduardo J. Padrón
President, Miami Dade College

I want to tell you three things about Dr. Maldonado: (1) he has tremendous faith and trust in Christ, (2) he is a powerful minister of the kingdom of God, and (3) he does all of this with great integrity. This combination is hard to find!

—Charles Green, Th.D., Litt.D., L.L.D

I call Apostle Guillermo Maldonado my friend and a man for whom I have the greatest respect. In his ministry, I see Jesus in the now, and the government of God is demonstrated in everything he says and does. There is a demand on Guillermo Maldonado's gifts and calling, and I am thankful that, in this season, the body of Christ is aware that they need to see the demonstration of signs, wonders, and miracles that he is a conduit of.

—Dr. Renny McLean
President and CEO, Global Glory, Inc.

I have known Guillermo Maldonado for several years, and our friendship has grown during this time. His ministry is causing a great impact and influence in Latin America.

—Marcos Witt
Associate Pastor, Lakewood Church, Lakewood, Texas

THE GLORY OF GOD

GUILLERMO MALDONADO

WHITAKER
HOUSE

Cover design by Danielle Cruz.

THE GLORY OF GOD
Experience a Supernatural Encounter with His Presence

Guillermo Maldonado
13651 S.W. 143rd Ct., #101
Miami, FL 33186
http://kingjesusministry.org/
www.ERJPub.org

ISBN: 978-1-60374-490-4
Printed in the United States of America
© 2012 by Guillermo Maldonado

Whitaker House
1030 Hunt Valley Circle
New Kensington, PA 15068
www.whitakerhouse.com

Library of Congress Cataloging-in-Publication Data

Maldonado, Guillermo.
The glory of God / Guillermo Maldonado.
    p. cm.
    ISBN 978-1-60374-490-4 (trade pbk. : alk. paper) 1. Glory of God—Christianity. 2. God (Christianity)—Omnipresence. I. Title.
  BT180.G6M35 2012
  231.7—dc23
                        2011052809

4 5 6 7 8 9 10 11 12 13 **ᴜᴊ** 20 19 18 17 16 15 14 13

Contents

s/19

1

We Are Made for Glory

Did you know you are specially made for God's glory? The glory of God was a gift to mankind in creation, and it is also the inheritance of every child of God. When we enter into God's glory, we dwell in His very presence, receive His love and grace, understand His heart, learn His will, and experience His divine power. That power transforms lives—saving, healing, and delivering—and enacts miracles and wonders that reveal God's majesty. Yet many Christians are not living in this glory. For various reasons, they are settling for far less in their relationships with God as they daily serve Him.

Jesus prayed to the heavenly Father on the eve of His crucifixion,

> And the glory which You gave Me **I have given them**, that they may be one just as We are one. (John 17:22)

Jesus has given believers the *same* glory the Father gave Him. The questions we must therefore answer for ourselves are: What will we do with this revelation? How can we live according to the glory we've received from Jesus?

Experiencing God's Glory

The glory of God is not just a theological concept to be learned. It is a reality that can be continually experienced. Sadly, many theologians, teachers, and preachers consider the glory of God to be a thing of the past, something that was known in

7

biblical times but cannot be experienced today. Yet the glory of God is for this generation. Here is a testimony from a Dr. Coradin, who experienced the transforming power of God's glory with his family when they came to our church, King Jesus Ministry:

> Invited by a friend, we arrived at the church, devastated. Our son David had spent one day in jail because of a drug problem and bad behavior, and, because of this, he had lost his scholarship to Nova School of Medicine. When we arrived at the parking lot of the church, we suddenly felt a supernatural presence invade our car. My son began to cry and sob while asking God and us to forgive him. My wife began to cry and to tremble. I was paralyzed and astonished. If this was happening in the parking lot, the first time we visited the church, then what was going to happen when we entered the church?
>
> About thirty minutes later, we were able to leave the car. As a result of our visit to the church, David was transformed. God delivered him and turned him into an evangelist to drug addicts, a House of Peace [the church's home fellowship ministry] leader, a member of the university evangelistic team, a warrior of intercession, and an example to many of his old friends. As for me, I had neglected my relationship with God and with my family due to alcoholism. The Lord delivered me from this addiction, and I was reconciled to Him. God also began to restore my marriage. My wife, Joy, was delivered from depression and her dependency on antidepressants. This firsthand experience transformed our lives and gave us purpose. It gave new destiny to my family and my future generations.

Jesus lives, and He continues to do miracles among us today. In Medellín, Colombia, there is a woman named Johanna who works with institutions for children who are orphaned, homeless, and infected with AIDS. A year ago, she accepted Jesus as her Lord and Savior when she visited our Miami church. There, she was trained to move in the supernatural power of God. When she returned to Colombia and to the orphanage where she works, she met Xiomara—a four-month-old girl who was diagnosed as HIV-positive. The love of God came upon Johanna, so she began to pray for the little girl, breaking the curse that had come upon her through her bloodline. When she did, she felt the power of God and knew that He had done something supernaturally. Weeks later, after a series of exams, Xiomara was declared totally healed and was placed for adoption. Johanna witnessed the miracle take place before her eyes, and today, that little girl lives in a wonderful home with loving parents. Something similar happened to Laura, a two-year-old girl who had been abandoned by her mother—a sixteen-year-old prostitute. The doctors had declared there was no hope for her recovery, but Johanna prayed for her, also, and the power of God created a miracle by restoring her immune system and eradicating the viral infection. The last three times she was examined, the results came back negative. She was declared healthy by the doctors and was placed for adoption.

Can you imagine these types of miracles taking place on a regular basis? God can do exceedingly beyond what medicine can do! A supernatural power is in operation, and it comes through the glory of God.

Why does the manifest presence of God's glory make such a dramatic difference in people's lives? It is because of the nature of His glory.

The Essence of God's Glory

"Weight"

The word *kabowd* is one of the most significant in the Hebrew language. Its literal meaning is "weight," but the term is used figuratively in the sense of "splendor," "abundance," "honor," or "glory"; it is something "glorious." In the Old Testament, *kabowd* is used variously to describe an individual's wealth, power or majesty, influential position, or great honor. (See, for example, Genesis 31:1; 45:13.) *Kabowd* can also express fame, reputation, recognition, beauty, magnificence, strength, dignity, splendor, respect, excellence, holiness, and greatness. (See, for example, Exodus 28:2; Psalm 49:16–17.) Hence, the glory (*kabowd*) of God expresses all of His attributes.

Today, people commonly use the term *weight* in a similar way. For example, we might say a person has "a lot of weight" (influence) with the particular leader of a country if that leader regularly listens to his counsel. We can also say that a believer has "spiritual weight" (substance) if he possesses a mature, honorable, humble, and just character. This spiritual weight is his "glory," which makes him stand out from others.

The glory of God is the essence of all that He is.

We need to see that God's glory is the realm of eternity. It is infinite, boundless, with no restrictions—it is beyond the imagination of human beings. His *manifested* glory is eternity revealed on earth. Glory revealed is the impact of God's powerful and unforgettable mark, seen and heard in the natural.

"Majesty"

Let's look next at a Greek word translated as *"glory"* in the New Testament. When the first five books of the Hebrew Scriptures (the Pentateuch) were translated into Greek for the first time, the word *doxa* was chosen for the concept of God's glory because it best expressed the meaning of *kabowd*, leading to the notion of reputation, honor, fame, praise, dignity, splendor, and brilliance. This translation, known as the Septuagint, was the first to use the word *doxa* to denote the majesty of God.

Later, that same word was used in some New Testament verses, including certain references to Jesus. (See, for example,

Matthew 16:27; John 1:14.) *Doxa* speaks of the real majesty belonging to God as the Supreme Governor—majesty in the sense of the absolute perfection of His deity. When referring to the Son, it alludes to the majestic royalty of the Messiah—this being the highest level of exaltation and the condition to which the Father raised Jesus after He fulfilled His purpose on earth, defeating Satan and death.

The glory of an individual resides in his intrinsic worth.

If we unite the various meanings of the words *kabowd* and *doxa*, we could say that the glory of God is the total sum of His attributes, character, and intrinsic virtues, the brilliance of His presence, and the splendor of His majesty. Accordingly, we can conclude that the very essence of God is His glory.

The Glory of God Was Manifested at Creation

The glory (presence) of God is the spiritual atmosphere of heaven, like air is the physical atmosphere of earth. Because the glory is the essence of who God is, everything is complete in the glory; nothing is incomplete.

This glory was the life and environment in which the first human beings lived. God created the first man, Adam, in an instant, out of the dust of the earth, and gave him His *"breath of life"*:

> And the LORD God formed man of the dust of the ground, and breathed into his nostrils the breath of life; and man became a living being. (Genesis 2:7)

Therefore, to truly live is to remain continually connected to God's presence—to draw in His breath of life.

In the glory of God, every need is met.

Adam was never an infant, a child, or a teenager; therefore, he did not have to undergo the growth process we experience. The same was true for his wife, Eve. They were created and formed as adults because, in the beginning, God created all things in their finished form, while placing a seed in every kind of species so that it could reproduce.

> *And the earth brought forth grass, the herb that yields seed according to its kind, and the tree that yields fruit, whose seed is in itself according to its kind. And God saw that it was good.* (Genesis 1:12)

In the glory of God—and in His manifest presence—everything "is"; therefore, every need of humanity can be met, so that we are complete. In the glory are healing, deliverance, and miracles (even creative miracles, such as new organs being formed). When human beings were first created, they did not know sickness, poverty, or death because, in the glory, there is no sickness, poverty, or death. They had no knowledge of sickness or death. Yet, as we will see, after human beings sinned by rebelling against God, they had to be removed from His presence, and they began to experience these things. Also, since that time, all human beings have undergone a process of birth, growth, and eventual death.

The Presence of God Is an Environment

To comprehend what it means to live in God's glory, we must first understand the contrast between the environment in which human beings lived in the garden of Eden before the fall and the environment in which they lived on the earth after the fall. In Genesis 1, we see that the first thing God did before creating each aspect of creation was to prepare the perfect environment for it. For example, He created the land and then created plants and trees that would thrive in the soil and its minerals. Likewise, this environment was in place before God created animals that would need to eat the vegetation for food.

Before God created anything, He first prepared the environment that would perfectly sustain it.

God created the oceans and the rivers, and then He created fish and other living creatures especially equipped to exist in an environment of water. God created the firmament of the heavens, and then He created the stars and planets that would be placed in it to function according to gravitational laws and orbital paths. (See Genesis 1:9–25.)

Similarly, when God created the environment of the garden of Eden, He designed the perfect setting for human beings. What was that perfect setting? God put Adam right into the environment of His presence and glory. He never told Adam, "I want you to search for Eden." He placed him there. He didn't give him any choice because that was the only environment in which he could be sustained and thrive. And, in that setting, God revealed Himself and His ways to humanity. (See Genesis 1:26; 2:7–9.)

Let us look more closely at the meanings of the words *"garden"* and *"Eden"* in the original Hebrew to draw out their meaning.

The word *"Eden"* means "pleasure" or "delight." The word *"garden"* signifies "enclosure" or a "fenced" place. It comes from a root word meaning "to hedge about"; it is something that "protects," "defends," "covers," or "surrounds." When we are in the glory, we are surrounded by and protected by God's presence. Therefore, I do not believe Eden was a particular geographical place, but rather a carefully prepared, delightful "spot" of glory that God designed mankind to dwell in.

Significantly, I also believe Eden was a "moment in time" in which the manifestation of God's glory could be seen. Why do I use the phrase "moment in time"? Because God manifests Himself visibly in time (in the natural dimension) for the benefit of human beings, and because God's glory is continually moving. When we are in the presence of the Lord, we go *"from glory to glory"* (2 Corinthians 3:18). No one goes from one place to another without moving. God is active and moving constantly, and He manifests Himself where He desires. And when we are in Him, we move with Him.

Almost all the geographical locations mentioned in the Scriptures have been found by archaeologists. Yet Eden has not been discovered. Why? Because it was a spot, a moment in time, where the presence of God came—and the presence was continually "moving." As the presence was moving, Adam was moving.

The glory of God was the original environment in which mankind lived.

God is everywhere, all the time, but He doesn't manifest Himself everywhere on earth today. He manifests Himself where He is welcomed and where people are in right relationship with Him. Eden was an environment that was a "gate" or "portal" to heaven because God manifested His glory there to human beings who were made in His image and were in unbroken fellowship with Him. God's presence with humanity was truly heaven on earth.

I like to define Eden as "a spot on the earth for a moment in time where the presence of God is a gate to heaven." Jacob caught a glimpse of this type of glory when he dreamed of a ladder ascending into an opening to heaven. (See Genesis 28:12.)

Mankind Fell Short of God's Glory

For all have sinned and fall short of the glory of God.
(Romans 3:23)

Tragically, human beings' existence in glory did not last. Adam and Eve sinned by choosing to go against what God had told them to do and eating from the tree of knowledge of good and evil. As a result, they were disconnected from the life of God and were exiled from Eden—from the glory. (See Genesis 3.) They fell *"short of the glory of God."*

Sin caused man to fall short of the glory of God and to be exiled from His presence.

What fundamental change happened when mankind fell? The Bible says that God sent cherubim to guard the entrance to Eden—to protect the presence—because the glory is not a place; it's an *environment*. God's presence is pure, uncontaminated. Mankind did not fall from a place; it fell from God's presence, from the environment of glory. So, human beings as a whole have been "short" of His glory from that day.

In addition to protecting the presence, God protected human beings. He didn't want us to be doomed to a state of eternal spiritual death, which might have happened if He hadn't intervened to separate humanity from the tree of life until they could be restored to Him. As we will see, God had a plan of rescue and redemption for mankind that would unfold in human history, which He first announced directly after the fall of man. (See Genesis 3:15.)

When Adam and Eve sinned, their spirits—the essence of who they were as human beings made in the image of God—died. They also began to die physically. However, we read that it took more than 930 years for Adam's body to completely stop functioning. (See Genesis 5:5.) I believe that the residual glory that remained in his body kept him physically alive for that long. Likewise, his descendants also lived long lives due to the residual glory of God that remained on the earth in those days.

Life Outside Our Natural Environment

If something is removed from its natural environment, you don't have to actively kill it; it will die on its own. For example, if you take a fish out of water, it will slowly die of dehydration. Likewise, if you pull up a plant from the earth and set it on top of the ground, it will soon wither and die from lack of water and nutrients.

That which is created cannot live independently of its God-given environment; it will die.

In the case of Adam and Eve, they essentially removed themselves from God's presence by choosing to go against His ways and seeking to live outside the parameters of His glory and protection, so that they had to be exiled. Yet God created mankind to live in His glory—that was His plan from the beginning. This is the reason human beings die when they are estranged from His presence. It is the environment we were designed for!

Likewise, today, every human experiences a process of death due to being disconnected from the glory and presence of God. In effect, this process starts from the moment of birth because that is the moment when the curses of living under a "ticking clock" and moving toward the inevitability of death, which are associated with fallen humanity, begin to operate on us and in us.

Human beings' life on earth under the curse of sin is one of lost relationship with God and lost potential of life in His glory. Left to ourselves, we are unable to live in accordance with the high existence we were created for.

"The Glory Has Departed"

Then she named the child Ichabod, saying, "The glory has departed from Israel!" because the ark of God had been captured and because of her father-in-law and her husband. (1 Samuel 4:21)

The loss of God's glory on earth was a tragedy that is graphically illustrated in the account of the death of Eli, the high priest and judge of Israel.

Eli had judged Israel for forty years, and he lived in Shiloh, where the tabernacle (the center of worship) was located. When he learned that the ark of the covenant—the place where the presence of God was manifested—had been taken by the Israelites' enemies, the Philistines, he fell backward and died of a broken neck. Then, when Eli's daughter-in-law heard of his death, as well as the death of her husband by the Philistines, she went into premature labor and gave birth to a son. Before she died, she named him Ichabod and said, *"The glory has departed from Israel!"* In Hebrew, *Ichabod* means "without glory." The manifest glory of God had departed from Israel when the ark was taken. Shiloh had been the center of Hebrew worship until that moment, but it never recovered that distinction.

It is sad when the presence of God departs, and it is pitiful to observe believers, churches, and ministries today that "survive" without it, having only an appearance of holiness and godliness. On the surface, everything may appear to be fine, but the truth is that the presence of God is no longer on the inside. When you see a church in which no one is getting saved; people are not changed or transformed; holiness is not encouraged; miracles, healing, and the power of God are nonexistent; and God's presence is no longer evident, it means that place is without glory—and this is equivalent to death.

Restored to Glory!

The Bible says, *"The Lord is...not willing that any should perish"* (2 Peter 3:9). God provided a way for us to be restored to Him and His glory. He implemented a plan of action to rescue us that included: (1) sending His Son, Jesus, to earth to be born and to grow as a Man who lived a completely sinless life; (2) Jesus dying in our place as our Substitute, taking our punishment for sin; (3) Jesus being raised from the dead and ascending to heaven, thereby conquering sin and death. With the shedding of His blood, Jesus redeemed human beings from sin and sickness; and, with His resurrection, He gave us access to eternal life.

The final objective of Jesus' sacrifice was to restore human beings to the realm of God's glory, for which we were created.

> For it was fitting for [God], *for whom are all things and by whom are all things,* **in bringing many sons to glory**, *to make the captain of their salvation* [Jesus] *perfect through sufferings.*   (Hebrews 2:10)

When we are reconciled to God through Jesus, we receive His Holy Spirit, our spirits are brought from death to life, and we have access to His glory. Spiritually, we can now live in the environment of heaven. We still die physically because our bodies have not yet been resurrected in glory for eternity—an event that will take place when Jesus returns. (See 1 Corinthians 15:42–45.)

The plan of salvation demonstrates that, even though mankind sinned, God's purpose will be carried out according to this cycle: the glory of God was present at the beginning of creation, and it will manifest powerfully in the last days—it will be seen in our time—and we will be returned to living in His presence. The redeeming work of Jesus allows us now to approach, walk in, and live once more according to God's glory in spirit, in soul, and, even to a large extent, in body. It may not be easy, but we will go *"from glory to glory"* (2 Corinthians 3:18) if we believe and persevere. His glory is in us. Jesus' atoning blood gives us access to the Father and once again connects us with His presence while our bodies wait to be completely redeemed from death as well.

We are carriers of God's presence through His indwelling Spirit.

In Christ, we are all carriers of a "portable Eden"; in other words, wherever we go, we carry with us His glory through the indwelling Holy Spirit. We have access to our original environment through the blood of Jesus. When we remain in our true environment, we will have true life. Jesus said, *"I am the way, the truth, and the life"* (John 14:6), and *"He who abides in Me, and I in him, bears much fruit; for without Me, you can do nothing"* (John 15:5).

Remember, you are *made* for glory—for existing continually in God's presence as you live your life. Although the Holy Spirit already dwells within you, you need to actively seek God and His glory through worship, praise, surrender to His will, and faith. Why? Jesus said, *"The spirit indeed is willing, but the flesh is weak"* (Matthew 26:41; Mark 14:38). Until the day when we will once again live in uninterrupted glory, we must seek God's glory daily!

In the next chapter, I will share how God manifests His glory, even in our day, just as He did in biblical times.

EXPERIENCES WITH GOD

- Commit to praise and worship God for a certain amount of time each day, to generate an atmosphere of glory. Prepare your ears to hear, because God wants to talk to you from a "cloud of glory" generated by your worship.

- If you have trouble accepting God as your Father and considering yourself His beloved child, ask Him to reveal Himself to you as Father as you meditate on Scriptures such as Matthew 6:32–33 and Ephesians 5:1.

2

The *Shekinah* Presence

There are countless wonderful facets to God's nature and character. Likewise, there are numerous aspects of God's glory, and He desires to show these dimensions of His glory on earth today to those who love and serve Him.

Where God Manifests His Glory

I have found that the most common pretext used by people who refuse to attend a local church is that "God is everywhere." They do not care to attend church, or they do not care which religion they follow, because, to them, if God is everywhere, then a specific location or religious affiliation doesn't matter. It is true that God is omnipresent—everywhere at once. However, His glory does not manifest "everywhere," because He generally manifests it in only two situations:

- Where He is worshipped in Spirit and in truth

- Where He is continually honored and revealed

In the Old Testament, we see the glory of God manifested among the Hebrew people or Israelites, and, in the New Testament, we see His glory manifested among both Jewish and Gentile believers in His Son Jesus Christ. God's people experienced the manifestation of the glory in close proximity. It often appeared in the form of a cloud known as the *shekinah*. *Shekinah* is a Hebrew word that refers to the "dwelling place of God" or "place where God rests"; it describes the eminent presence of God that transcends the spiritual realm and manifests in the physical world. *Shekinah* is related to the immediate and intimate activity of God—the splendor of the Lord while He is present in the now, in action, and allowing others to know Him.

God is everywhere,
but He does not manifest His presence everywhere.

We can therefore describe the glory of God in two ways: (1) the *kabowd* or *doxa* glory, which is the essence, nature, attributes, and infinite perfection of God—His character and personality, or what He is in Himself; (2) the *shekinah* glory, which is the visible manifestation of His presence to mankind. This is when God's glory transcends the spiritual realm to impact the natural realm.

God will sometimes reveal His *shekinah* glory—His manifest presence—to human beings through physical phenomena, such as fire or clouds. At other times, He will reveal His *kabowd* glory—an aspect of His nature. In His sovereignty, God takes the initiative and decides which aspect of Himself to reveal. Of one thing we can be sure: the will of God has always been to dwell among His people and to manifest Himself to humanity. Let us look at some biblical passages that bear out this truth.

God Manifested His Glory to the Israelites

Then it came to pass on the third day, in the morning, that there were thunderings and lightnings, and a thick cloud on the mountain; and the sound of the trumpet was very loud, so that all the people who were in the camp trembled. (Exodus 19:16)

The above passage illustrates that when God's glory manifested in Old Testament times, physical phenomena took place. His presence was tangible to the senses. All the people perceived it, and their lives were changed. In a similar way, God manifested His holiness and glory to the prophet Isaiah, accompanied by physical manifestations. (See Isaiah 6:3–4.)

We also see that God spoke to His people when He manifested Himself. If a manifestation of God occurs and we don't hear His voice in some way, we are only spectators and not participators. But if God speaks to you, and you receive what He says, it becomes established within you. God sometimes spoke to individuals, such as to Moses through the burning bush, or to Saul (Paul) on the road to Damascus. God sometimes spoke to more than one person, such as Peter, James, and John at Jesus' transfiguration. (See, for example, Exodus 3:1–2; Acts 9:1–8; Luke 9:28–35.) When God speaks to us, He might do so in an audible voice, or He might speak to our hearts.

God Manifested His Glory Through His Son Jesus

The ultimate expression of the manifestation of God's glory in the world was when He sent Jesus Christ to earth to be our Savior.

> *God, who at various times and in various ways spoke in time past to the fathers by the prophets, has in these last days spoken to us by His Son, whom He has appointed heir of all things, through whom also He made the worlds; who **being the brightness of His glory and the express image of His person**, and upholding all things by the word of His power, when He had by Himself purged our sins, sat down at the right hand of the Majesty on high.* (Hebrews 1:1–3)

Jesus *spoke* the Word of God and He *is* the Word of God. (See John 1:1.) He said the following: *"I and My Father are one"* (John 10:30). *"The Father is in Me and I in Him"* (John 10:38). *"He who has seen Me has seen the Father....The Father who dwells in Me does the works"* (John 14:9–10). Jesus led us to know the Father through His character, virtues, and behavior. To see Him was to see the splendor and image of the Father. His substance (essence) was His glory, and to hear Him was the same as hearing the Father.

> *Jesus is the highest expression of God to mankind, the complete revelation and manifestation of the glory of the Father.*

After Jesus ascended to heaven, the apostle John was given a revelation of God's glory similar to Isaiah's revelation. It demonstrated that God is powerful and everlasting (see Revelation 4:8), and it also revealed the majesty of Jesus (see Revelation 1:13–16).

God Manifests His Glory to Us Today

Yet the glory of God was not just manifested in biblical times. Here is one account of what happens when He manifests His glory today. Some time ago, the Lord led me to preach in Rosario, Argentina, with a specific mission: revive the fire of His presence, which a portion of the leadership had lost, and destroy the bondage of religiosity that had replaced the power of God there after the great revivals of the 1980s and 1990s. On the last day of the meetings, while I was ministering to more than 3,500 leaders from all over the country, a manifestation of "fire" descended on the auditorium. The *shekinah* "burned" those who were present. Thousands were crying out to God. In the midst of this experience, a young woman came to the altar to testify. She had been born without her left kidney due to a generational curse that had come from her grandfather to her mother and, finally, to her. To make matters worse, she had required surgery to restore minimum use of her right kidney. Because of her condition, she had been able to go to the bathroom only once or twice a day, even when she drank large quantities of liquid.

The fire of the glory—God's presence—had descended on the first night of our meetings, too, and she had received her miracle then. Intense heat had traveled throughout the left side of her body, making its greatest impact in the kidney area. That night, she'd had to use the bathroom over ten times. The next day, after she was tested, her doctor confirmed that she had a left kidney and that the right one was working perfectly. This was a creative miracle! The indisputable proof that she had two healthy kidneys was her countless trips to the bathroom. God had given her a new left kidney and restored her right kidney to perfect health. So, shocked at her miracle and crying, she came forth and testified on that final night of meetings. Everyone could see her overwhelming emotion and utter joy. The presence of God was all over her. God had delivered her from the curse and completely healed her.

Worship causes God to reveal and manifest His glory or presence.

The city of Rosario, Argentina, was shaken by God's glory. In the midst of His presence, which flooded the place where we were meeting, a pastor was healed of facial paralysis, a woman was identified by name by a word of knowledge and delivered from forty years of depression, several people who had been deaf from birth received perfect hearing, organs were created where they had been missing, legs that had been short grew to normal length, deformed backs and heels were corrected and restored, and Jesus was proclaimed to be the true and living God who continues to do miracles among His people. The glory is God in action; hence, it must be revealed.

We need to understand that a move, revival, or outpouring of the Holy Spirit does not rest upon any particular person but only upon the revelation of God's glory that an individual holds and imparts (communicates) to God's people, who receive it in faith.

"Show Me Your Glory"

While I believe, teach, and practice healthy biblical doctrine, I also know that the glory of God is more than doctrine—it is a reality that we can experience. It is what Moses, David, and other patriarchs longed to experience and what each believer today is a candidate to experience.

And [Moses] *said, "Please, show me Your glory."*
(Exodus 33:18)

Moses knew that the glory of God was more than a theological concept. That is why he asked God to *show* him His glory—the most intimate aspect of His nature. In fact, it was after God showed Moses His glory that He gave him the law. (See Exodus 33:19–34:28.)

Many people have no idea what the glory really is because they have never experienced it, either personally or through a church or ministry. And yet, until they experience it, they will not fully understand what I am describing here. That is why I pray that you will have supernatural experiences even as you read this book. I consider of utmost importance the section at the end of each chapter entitled "Experiences with God." Don't allow reading this book to be only an intellectual act for you. Use it as a guide to bring you into the very presence of God.

Again, the kingdom, the power, and the glory of God are not just theoretical or theological concepts but spiritual truth. I live according to them daily, and I can affirm them to be true. They are heavenly realities that every believer can experience now. Mere "religion" will never produce a supernatural experience with God because it is void of the glory and life of the Lord. Since this distinction is so crucial, in coming chapters we will discuss how "religious" attitudes hinder the manifestation of

God's presence and how you can move beyond practicing religion to having an encounter with your heavenly Father.

If we receive a genuine revelation but fail to obey it or act on it, religiosity will result.

Without a continuous revelation of the glory of God, we will—sooner or later—get stuck in our ways and become *"old wineskins"* (Luke 5:37). In other words, we will not allow God to do something new in our lives that would bring power and healing. We are often so busy trying to keep up appearances and fulfilling norms that we end up trapped in traditions. God wants us to return to His glory. He also wants to take us to new realms of His glory we've never experienced before.

When the presence of God manifests, radical transformations take place in people's lives. Jesus has not changed. (See Hebrews 13:8.) He continues to transform lives and do miracles. People have witnessed the manifestation of God's glory in nations across the globe. Let me tell you about another such example that occurred at King Jesus International Ministry.

A young lady named Jennifer came to our church, and her testimony deeply touched me. In fact, when she shared her story with us, almost the entire congregation broke out in tears. I know that many young people are in situations similar to Jennifer's. She had been rebellious and a drug user, and she had practiced a lesbian lifestyle since the second grade. After she turned eleven, her parents began to purchase marijuana and alcohol for her. She was addicted to the drug Xanax at age thirteen and to cocaine at fifteen. Her parents gave up trying to discipline her and simply threw her out of the house, so she became homeless. At sixteen, she used heroin, until the morning she woke up in a place she did not recognize and realized that she had been raped.

Jennifer's life had been a disaster for as long as she could remember. She could not get through one day without drugs, alcohol, or sexual perversion. She also suffered from bulimia. One day, tired of living and on the verge of ending her life, she visited our church, and the presence of God touched her. She threw herself on the altar and surrendered to Him, and her life began to change. She used to hate her parents, but now she loves them. She was delivered from bitterness, from the shame of her lesbian lifestyle, and from depression. She had actually tried to end her drug addiction by leaving the drugs on the altar several times, but, each time, she returned to the world and to her old habits. This vicious cycle continued until one day, she came back to the church with all her "baggage" and said, "I will never return to that life." She became a new person and has never looked back. Today, she is a leader in the House of Peace and a mentor in our church.

It is easy to see the hand of God upon Jennifer's life and realize that God delivers, heals, and protects us from the world. The love and power of God transformed this young woman on both the inside and the outside when she surrendered whole-heartedly. Nothing and no one else—not psychology, medical treatments, or her parents—can take credit for her new life. It was accomplished solely by the presence and power of God.

Follow the Miracle Maker

While testimonies such as Jennifer's are tremendously moving, I teach my congregation to follow the Miracle Maker, not the miracles. Our priority is to follow Jesus. When we do so, God will confirm His Word with signs. (See Mark 16:20.) I am passionate about seeing signs, miracles, and wonders, but my strongest passion is to know God and His glory in every respect and to become His instrument to impact the earth with the gospel in order to win souls.

When I met pastors José Luis and Rosa Margarita López in 2005, their church—New International Generation in Villahermosa, Tabasco, Mexico—had two hundred members after twelve years of ministry. They were preparing to quit.

Years previously, God had rescued José Luis from alcoholism, drug addiction, and psychotropic medications (medicines that treat the mind), and Margarita had been delivered from bitterness and unforgiveness toward her family. They began to serve Jesus passionately, and, years later, they were anointed and sent out by their church as pastors to establish their own independent church. José quit his profession as an architect and Margarita quit her law practice. They also closed their construction business and sold all the equipment in preparation to serve the Lord. Undoubtedly, God had called them. However, when I met them, they were dealing with a ministry that did not bear much fruit, regardless of how hard they tried. They did not know what else to do. They wanted to serve God and see greater results, but there they were, stuck, unable to move forward! They had also lost their home, and their relationship with their son was not going well. They had reached a point in their ministry where they said, "Lord, this is it. We give up!"

Our priority should be to seek His glory; then, the signs will follow us.

It was then that God brought me into their lives to teach, train, and equip them in the supernatural power and glory of God. They themselves—rather than their circumstances—were the first to change. They surrendered to be delivered from everything that had been hindering them, to be edified, and to receive the impartation of God's supernatural power. God restored their family and then their congregation. By the end of the year, their ministry had grown to fifteen hundred people, and it soon reached twenty-five hundred active members.

What was my role in this? I simply obeyed God. When no one else believed in them, I affirmed them and offered to cover them with spiritual fatherhood, to which they humbly responded. (By "spiritual fatherhood," I mean teaching, training, and equipping them to fulfill God's purpose for their lives.) Their son, Rodrigo, also accepted the call of God on his life and is now the youth pastor. Today, they have a solid congregation of over nine thousand members. The road has not been easy for them. However, choosing to place themselves under the accountability of spiritual leadership, rather than trying to minister independent of any spiritual support or oversight, allowed them to carry out the vision and purpose of God and to manifest His glory in Mexico. They are impacting their nation. This is glorious!

One reason for their impact is that Pastor José Luis began to practice "supernatural evangelism." He no longer relies on man-made methods of evangelizing but allows the Spirit of God to work through him to draw people to the Lord. As a result, a young man named Cresencio visited their church. A short time after learning about Jesus and accepting Him as his Lord and Savior, this young man was kidnapped in front of his home by six men who were armed and high on drugs. These men forced him to go with them to a bar to pay for everything they would consume that night, threatening to kill him if he disobeyed. On their way to the bar, Cresencio was convinced he would never see his family again because he did not have the money to pay. However, the Holy Spirit reminded him of his pastor's preaching on the supernatural power of God. Remembering that message filled him with faith, and he began to pray. While the men drank, he asked permission to go to the restroom. Inside a filthy stall that reeked with urine, he closed his eyes and prayed more intensely than ever, asking God to deliver him from his enemies. He trembled and prayed! Cresensio cannot recall how much time passed, but, when he opened his eyes, he was out of the stench of the bathroom and on the street. God had translated him out of danger! Without hesitation, he desperately ran home and hugged his wife, out of breath and shocked at what he had just experienced. He thanked God for the miracle. This incident reminds me of the miracle involving one of Jesus' disciples, when *"the Spirit of the Lord caught Philip away"* (Acts 8:39).

If this was the extent of the manifestation of God's supernatural power and glory in the life of one individual, we would be more than satisfied. Yet one miracle leads to another miracle, and then another, generating a chain reaction. Days after his miracle, Cresencio visited his sister in a nearby city and discovered that she had been diagnosed with osteoarthritis—a disease that wears down a person's bones until he or she becomes an invalid. His sister could barely walk with the help of a walker. She was in a very delicate state. He was moved when he saw her and thought that if God had been able to translate him from one place to another and deliver him from death, then He could also heal his sister. Cresencio laid his hands on her and prayed, just as he had seen Pastor José Luis do many times, and his sister was instantly healed! She stood up and began to walk by herself without the walker! She could not remember the last time she had walked on her own.

Cresencio is just one of more than four thousand young people who attend the Villahermosa church, and he is not the only one who has astonishing testimonies of the supernatural power of the living God. Since the day that Rodrigo (the pastor's son) accepted the call of God, the youth group has grown exponentially. We trained and equipped Pastor Rodrigo to walk in the supernatural power and glory of God. I placed him with my youth pastors in Miami so he could learn how God has taught me to do things. He is now doing the same in his nation. He is training and equipping thousands of Mexican young people with the tools of the supernatural power of God, and the Lord is responding through miracles and wonders. For example, on one given weekend, Pastor Rodrigo led the youth of the church to visit the hospitals in the city, where they prayed for the sick. Patients who had cancer were healed! Those who had undergone open-heart surgery were also fully healed. People who were waiting in the emergency room were healed. The doctors could not find anything wrong with them. God healed everyone! As a result, the next Sunday, those who had received healing came to the church and testified. This is what the glory of God is doing in the world today.

The Glory in Your Life

Are you experiencing the glory of God in your own life? You need to have a revelation of God's glory so you can experience its manifestation. Then, as you encounter the presence of God, you will be changed, transformed, and ignited by spiritual passion. Don't stay in the same place—there's more for you in God than what you are now experiencing.

Let's continue to explore what it means to enter into God's glory and to live our lives in His presence.

EXPERIENCES WITH GOD

- Keep a daily journal of your supernatural experiences with the living God.

- Share your testimony with others and witness how it becomes a means of "supernatural evangelism" that enables you to reach others for Christ through the power and glory of God.

3

Revelation and Manifestation of the Mysteries of God's Glory

We are living in an age when natural knowledge has increased exponentially, science is making new discoveries, and innovative technologies are being developed; when cures for many illnesses have been found and new ideas and creations in many areas of human endeavor are springing up. At this time, God is also unsealing areas of His knowledge. He has never wanted to be a mystery to His people, and, through the ages, He has manifested His nature and power in various ways. In this new stage of His plan for humanity, He has begun to reveal His glory to the present generation, igniting His final move on the planet to bring multitudes to faith in Him. The apostles and prophets of the Bible spoke of this generation. For example, Peter wrote,

> *Of this salvation the prophets have inquired and searched carefully, who prophesied of the grace that would come to you.* (1 Peter 1:10)

Let me share a testimony about how God is unsealing knowledge to His people. On one of my trips to Mexico, the Holy Spirit guided me to adopt a spiritual son, Pastor Jorge Pompa. At the time, he had 120 people in his congregation in Monterrey, Nuevo León, but he took of my spirit (see Numbers 11:17), and our ministers trained and equipped him with everything God has given us, until the gifts began to flow and growth began to manifest. God led him into a new level of authority and dominion.

The sessions of the Supernatural Fivefold Ministry School, an event hosted by our ministry specifically for the training of leaders and pastors, greatly helped Pastor Pompa. During a class on boldness in the Spirit, I called forth my young people to testify so the leaders could see how they preach and release the power of God in the streets. Later, I ministered and released boldness over the leadership through the Lord's Supper.

When Pastor Pompa returned to his country, God showed him that there would be an assassination attempt on the mayor of the city, which would be carried out no later than February 24. Exercising the boldness he had received, he sent the mayor an urgent message asking for an appointment to see him. In his city, it is very difficult for a common citizen to meet with a mayor, but he was invited to come to the mayor's office. When the pastor arrived at the appointed time, he said, "Sir, I am neither a nobody nor someone guided by emotion. I come to tell you that God said to me there will be an assassination attempt against you before the twenty-fourth of this month." The mayor stayed quiet and very serious, and the pastor warned him that the only way for God to save him would be for him to stop his witchcraft practices because they were an abomination before God. The man bowed his head and began to cry. The pastor prayed for him and declared that he would not die. When he finished, the mayor confessed that he had received a death threat saying that if he did not leave the city before the twenty-fourth of February, they were going to kill him. He never had to leave! The power of God worked in his favor, and, to this day, God protects him and his family. Pastor Pompa's boldness resulted in his being the first Christian pastor to receive the keys of the city. Today, he has a congregation of 1,500.

Another amazing testimony from Pastor Pompa has to do with God's supernatural intervention while he was building his own church in Monterrey, debt free. During the construction phase, one of the workers named Francisco, who was thirty-nine years old, fell thirteen feet to the ground. He suffered a serious head injury with a deep (ten-centimeter) laceration and died instantly. The people at the church called the paramedics and notified the pastor about what had happened. When he heard about Francisco's accident, Pastor Pompa told the people not to allow anyone to take away his body until he arrived. On his way to the church, he began to cry out before the Lord because he did not want the record of a death to be registered in the church. In the meantime, the paramedics did what they could to try to revive the worker, but his heart had stopped, and so he was declared dead.

When Pastor Pompa arrived half an hour later, the worker's body had been covered, and the paramedics were ready to take him away. They said, "Pastor, he has no pulse. There is nothing we can do." But Pastor Pompa prayed anyway, saying, "Spirit of death, I cast you out! I loosen the power of the resurrection of Jesus Christ over Francisco!" Suddenly, the man began to open his eyes and slowly said, "I hear you!" The paramedics could not explain how this man was able to speak and open his eyes when he had no pulse. Finally, when he was fully awake, they took him to the hospital for some follow-up exams and X-rays. On the way to the hospital, his head wound began to close to the point that the X-ray did not show any damage. Apart from this, the man felt perfectly well. He never suffered from contusions or loss of memory. Francisco was released from the hospital on the same day, and, to top it all off, he walked out of the hospital and went back to the church. This was a great miracle—the glory of God residing in His servant brought the dead to life! Pastor Pompa has learned to move in the glory and to manifest it wherever he goes. You can do the same if you receive God's revelation of walking in the supernatural.

Since revelation (spiritual knowledge and understanding) of the glory is an essential step to living in God's presence, let us now look at:

- what revelation is,
- which ministries in the body of Christ are called to restore it,
- how to make the transition from basic Christian doctrine to revelation,
- how revelation relates to the manifestation of the glory of God, and

- how to avoid extremes and abuses in manifestations.

We will learn how to receive, walk in, and manifest revelation through healings, miracles, signs, wonders, and demonstrations of the power of God—the supreme purpose of which is to gather in the final harvest of souls before Christ returns.

Two Types of Knowledge

To understand what revelation is, we first need to distinguish between two types of knowledge: (1) knowledge that comes through our physical senses and (2) knowledge that is revealed.

1. Mental, Sensorial, or Natural Knowledge

The first type of knowledge is the scientific, theoretic, and practical knowledge that comes through the senses—sight, hearing, touch, smell, and taste. It is information or storable data acquired and implemented in the natural world. Mental, sensorial, or natural knowledge must be sought after—an act that demands learning and discipline. People who live only according to this type of knowledge often reason like this: "I believe in what I see, hear, feel, taste, and smell. I believe in material things because they can be understood with my senses. I do not believe in God because I cannot physically see Him and because He does not speak to me."

Miracles are outside the mental, sensorial, or natural realm of knowledge, and science cannot explain them.

One cannot know God through sensorial information alone—though such information is vital for dwelling in the natural dimension of earth. God created the earthly dimension and manifests Himself in it, although He does not belong to it. He is beyond it.

2. Revealed (Spiritual) Knowledge or Revelation

The second type of knowledge is that which is revealed by God:

> Now to Him who is able to establish you...according to the revelation of the mystery kept secret since the world began but now made manifest....
>
> (Romans 16:25–26)

In the above Scripture, the word *"revelation"* is translated from the Greek word *apokalypsis*, and it means "to reveal," "remove the covering," "discover," or "manifest something that was hidden." Revealed knowledge comes directly or indirectly from God's Holy Spirit to the spirit of a person, not to the person's mind or senses. (See, for example, Matthew 16:15–17.) It does not require time to learn, because it is given instantly; it manifests in a blink of an eye. It cannot be researched in a book or in any other source of information. It is something "read between the lines."

Revelation is a fragment of divine knowledge that was not previously known by the person receiving it. For example, a *"word of knowledge"* (1 Corinthians 12:8) is a small portion of the total knowledge of God, given by the Holy Spirit in an instant.

In heaven, things are not learned; they are simply revealed or known.

Therefore, revelation is spiritual knowledge about God and His ways that comes into our spirits as a sudden, impelling force that drives us forward. It induces spiritual motion and stimulates, activates, and accelerates our spirits. It is a window from time into eternity and from eternity into time, bringing God's perspective to us human beings. And revelation always demands change.

Basing One's Life Only on Natural Knowledge

The change from spiritual to natural knowledge as the primary means by which human beings experience and understand life occurred when Adam and Eve decided to disobey God and eat from the *"tree of the knowledge of good and evil"*:

> *But of the tree of the knowledge of good and evil you shall not eat, for in the day that you eat of it you shall surely die.* (Genesis 2:17)

We saw that when Adam and Eve sinned, their spirits died. As a result, they went from having both kinds of knowledge to having only mental, sensorial, or natural knowledge. Sin destroyed their connection to their spiritual Source and to spiritual knowledge. From that moment, they began to consider everything from the perspective of natural knowledge. If you base your life on natural knowledge alone, what you perceive is only a shadow of what truly is. Your vision has become distorted.

Adam exchanged spiritual, revealed knowledge for sensorial knowledge.

To illustrate this point, let us consider the gift of prophecy. To prophesy is to speak from the perspective of God, and the source of that perspective is the Holy Spirit, who reveals what is in the mind or heart of the Father. (See 1 Corinthians 2:10.) Prophecy will always provide *"edification and exhortation and comfort"* (1 Corinthians 14:3) in order to lead people to see what God sees and to walk in a reality that is superior to the natural. It is like taking a leap into the future in God or declaring that glorious future in the present.

A lack of revealed knowledge is a characteristic of spiritual death because we do not live according to spiritual reality. Anytime we try to trust in natural knowledge to operate in the supernatural, we are essentially eating of the tree of the knowledge of good and evil. Natural knowledge offers information about facts or data, but it does not have the ability to effect lasting transformation because it comes from the fallen mind of man, not from the mind of God. Revealed knowledge supersedes every rational analysis and carries with it the intrinsic power to transform.

Revelation Erases the Borders of the Impossible

If human beings had never fallen, we never would have known what it is like to live only according to natural knowledge, and we would have no way of knowing that "impossible" things exist. We would not be able to perceive the limitations of the natural realm. This is the mind-set Adam had before his act of disobedience. *Impossible* wasn't in his vocabulary. However, when intellectual education displaces revelation, we want the latter to fit within the reduced limitations established by reason. Yet this is impossible because revelation is superior to natural knowledge. Although it is good to receive an education and to be a well-prepared professional, a revelation from God can enable us to be more effective in accomplishing our goals than years of schooling can.

Some theologians study God for decades but never know Him because they lack revelation from the Holy Spirit, while others who receive revelation have intimate knowledge of Him, in addition to an understanding of theology. Revelation gives us access to the spiritual world and to the elevated realms of faith, and it erases the borders of the impossible.

In our local church, a woman testified that she had been three months pregnant when she received the devastating news that the baby she was carrying in her womb was dead. The baby's heartbeat could not be heard, even after several attempts by medical personnel to do so. This diagnosis was confirmed by several doctors who said the fetus had to be removed. Yet the woman decided not to accept the diagnosis of death; she appropriated the faith of God within her, believing for a miracle. Although she was afraid, the Holy Spirit filled her with faith. Because she was not willing to lose her child, she started attending our church's early-morning prayer meetings, led by my wife.

One day, by a word of knowledge, my wife perceived that she should pray for a woman who was having problems with her unborn child. When this woman came forward, she immediately felt movement in her womb. The child had returned to life by the powerful hand of God! The expectant mother cried tears of joy and gave thanks to Him. The word of knowledge given by the Holy Spirit to my wife saved the life of that child. The solution presented by the doctors had been abortion, but the solution of God is resurrection and life.

Reason, common sense, and logic serve the soul,
as revelation serves the spirit.

And yet, the story does not end there. The doctors' initial surprise was replaced by new doubts. Near the end of her pregnancy, during one of her last visits to the doctor, she was told again that the baby's heartbeat could not be heard and that the baby would certainly have to be removed this time. Frustration and determination not to give up came upon the woman. Instead of surrendering, she said, "No! That is not true. I believe God, and I know He keeps my baby alive in my womb." New exams showed that the baby was fine and that the heartbeat was normal, but then she was told the baby would be born with Down syndrome due to the periods of time when the heartbeat had stopped. The baby's mother, full of the faith of God, again rejected the negative diagnosis. To the glory of God, her child is now a beautiful and perfectly normal four-year-old boy who is healthy in mind and body. One word of knowledge, given by the Holy Spirit, resolved what the doctors were unable to do.

Prophets, Apostles, and Revealed Knowledge

Many churches, ministries, Christian universities, seminaries, and Bible institutes today are saturated with intellectual education but lack supernatural revelation. Even though knowledge is good, it can become unfruitful if it is sought only for its own sake and never applied in practical ways. For example, in most seminaries and Bible institutes, students preparing for the ministry are taught to preach but not taught to hear the voice of God. How can we offer something fresh that carries the life of God if we cannot hear Him today, in the now? The Bible says that when the prophet Samuel was a boy growing up in the temple, *"the word of the LORD was rare in those days; there was no widespread revelation"* (1 Samuel 3:1). God had called Samuel as an answer to that need.

The roles of prophet and apostle are the two offices of the fivefold spiritual ministry gifts in the church to which God has trusted revealed knowledge to be shared with His people. (See Ephesians 4:11–12.) While some people say these New Testament offices are no longer in operation, there is no biblical evidence to support such a belief. We need all our God-given ministries if the church is to be healthy and fulfilling its purpose. If the role of apostle was limited to Jesus' original disciples, as some people claim, then Paul and James (the brother of Jesus, who wrote the book of James) would not have been called apostles.

The Scriptures do not change. They are the foundation of our belief and practice. However, apostles and prophets are still needed to establish churches, teach and strengthen believers, and give fresh revelation of the ways in which God is working in the present generation.

We must realize that true revelation does not negate foundational biblical doctrine or vice versa. A balance can be restored if we understand and incorporate both doctrine and revelation in the church as we grow spiritually.

Again, I believe, practice, and teach doctrine and theology that support what the Bible teaches. I have a master's degree in practical theology from Oral Roberts University. I am a defender of the sound doctrine of Jesus Christ as Lord and Savior. And, as I have functioned in the role of apostle, I have learned to lay down a solid biblical foundation in the lives of thousands of new believers in the local church and globally. Furthermore, I encourage my leadership to study biblical doctrine and to become established in it. Consequently, most of those who were once new believers in my church are now disciples, leaders, mentors, elders, ministers, and pastors bearing their own evident fruit—all because their spiritual lives were established on proper doctrine. I make this clarification so that no one will mistakenly assume that I reject or belittle doctrine or theology while promoting fresh revelation.

Why Is Revelation or Revealed Knowledge Rare?

I believe that revelation diminishes in the church of Jesus Christ when the ministries of the apostle and prophet are discarded. Paul wrote,

> *By revelation He made known to me the mystery...of Christ...as it has now been revealed by the Spirit to His holy apostles and prophets.* (Ephesians 3:3–5)

The ministries of the apostle and prophet are those of breakthrough, spiritual warfare, and deliverance; they are also responsible for releasing the supernatural power of God on the church. Sadly, apostles and prophets have been replaced by administrators who have an intellectual education but lack the apostolic and prophetic mind-set. By nature, apostles have plans, designs, and projects from God that edify the church and the kingdom and impact their surrounding communities. They have been given the spiritual map that will guide us, showing us the way to accomplish things. They are wise builders of the kingdom, and their hearts are centered on bringing the revelation of God to earth. Paul wrote,

> *According to the grace of God which was given to me, as a wise master builder I have laid the foundation, and another builds on it. But let each one take heed how he builds on it.* (1 Corinthians 3:10)

Prophets express what God is saying and doing at the moment (see Amos 3:7); they also see and speak of the future and of the mysteries of God. Much of the church has denied the ministry of the prophet for years, and I believe one of the consequences has been the rise and popularity of the psychic industry. People have an internal void that they seek to fill with something greater or deeper than themselves. They want direction and knowledge about what the future holds—without realizing that these desires actually reflect a longing to connect with the true God and to experience His supernatural realm. People attend church because they hunger to hear a word from God that makes sense and gives them purpose, but many leave without answers because, in most churches, the voice of the prophet has been silenced.

The Revelation of the Lampstand and the Olive Trees

And he [the angel] *said to me* [the prophet Zechariah], *"What do you see?" So I said, "I am looking, and there is a lampstand of solid gold with a bowl on top of it, and on the stand seven lamps with seven pipes to the seven lamps. Two olive trees are by it, one at the right of the bowl and the other at its left."*

(Zechariah 4:2–3)

Zechariah's vision describes a lampstand with seven lamps, which typifies the church, and two olive trees from which oil flows to the lampstand, which symbolizes the Holy Spirit. The oil—clean, pure, and fresh—keeps the lamps burning in a way that the light emitted by the lamps is bright and clear. And yet, Zechariah did not understand the vision and had to ask God about it.

"What are these two olive trees—at the right of the lampstand and at its left?"...So he said, "These are

the two anointed ones, who stand beside the Lord of
the whole earth." (Zechariah 4:11, 14)

I believe that from the prophetic perspective, the olive trees symbolize Moses, in the ministry of the apostle, and Elijah, in the ministry of the prophet, because the signs of the *"two witnesses"* described in the book of Revelation are similar to what occurred in their ministries when they walked on earth.

And I will give power to my two witnesses, and they
will prophesy one thousand two hundred and sixty
days, clothed in sackcloth. These are the two olive
trees.... (Revelation 11:3–4)

This does not mean the church should continue to be without these ministries until the book of Revelation is fulfilled; rather, it is a reflection of what will come. Both ministries carry out the function of keeping the church alive with revelation and guidance until the final days. Jesus will have a church that awaits His arrival with its lamp burning. How will sinners come to Jesus if there is no light to guide them in the midst of darkness? How will believers be transformed from glory to glory if there is no fresh revelation that enables them to move from one dimension of glory to the next?

Again, the two olive trees standing on either side of the lampstand are the symbolic representation of what is happening in the church today. They represent the apostolic and prophetic ministries. From these flow pure and fresh oil, which symbolizes revelation (revealed knowledge). Guidance and prophecy are the fuel that provides brilliant light to the church. If the oil ceases to flow, the light of the lampstand will end and chaos will begin.

Again, both ministries declare what God is doing and saying on earth today. When the roles of apostle and prophet are rejected by the church, the light is put out and darkness takes over. In contrast, while they are able to carry out their functions, the other three roles of the fivefold ministry also function as they were meant to: the pastor takes care of the flock, the evangelist wins people for Jesus, and the teacher instructs the church—and all, as one, gather in the harvest of souls.

Consequences of a Lack of Revealed Knowledge

Let's look more closely at what happens when the light of revelation is put out and darkness is the norm.

1. People Are Uncontrolled and Demoralized

> *Where there is no vision, the people perish.*
>
> (Proverbs 29:18 KJV)

> *Where there is no word from God, people are uncontrolled.*
>
> (NCV)

> *Without prophecy the people become demoralized.*
>
> (NAB)

The Hebrew word translated *"vision," "word,"* and *"prophecy"* in the above Bible versions is *chazown*, which can also mean "revelation," "oracle," or "divine communication." *Chazown* refers to a fresh revelation from God that declares what He is saying and doing now (fresh oil—always fresh). It is more than just reading and teaching the Bible; it is more than biblical doctrine. It is *rhema*, a "now" word from God; it is the manna that God provides for today—not for yesterday or for tomorrow. There will be another fresh revelation tomorrow that will keep us moving forward so that we don't lose our direction or advancement. This is the revelation of the Holy Spirit. Without *chazown*, the people are uncontrolled, lost, without destiny, demoralized. They perish. We are living in times of darkness, confusion, and insecurity. Now, more than ever, we need the fresh revelation of God.

2. People Are Destroyed

> *My people are destroyed for lack of knowledge. Because you have rejected knowledge, I also will reject*

you from being priest for Me; because you have forgot-
ten the law of your God, I also will forget your chil-
dren. (Hosea 4:6)

Lack of revealed knowledge leads to destruction. The prophet Hosea warned Israel that it was crucial to know, discern, and be wise to choose the path the Lord had placed before them. To reject divine knowledge is to despise or give little value to what God is saying. Any path that does not lead to God ends in an abyss of death. We must learn to choose whom and what to believe.

Ruben, a new member in our ministry, had to choose to believe God's path rather than a path of death. At the time he first visited one of our daughter churches, he had spent the past six years suffering from rare cysts that progressively grew on his face and legs. Each time he took a bath, they would flare up like cauliflower. Desperate over his condition, he was close to accepting the offer of a warlock who had promised to heal him for free, saying that only this type of witchcraft would cure him. Ruben did not accept immediately, but he thought about it because of his desire to end his torment. At that moment, he lacked the revelation that God could heal him.

The enemy will destroy you in any area where you lack knowledge.

That night, as Ruben slept, the Lord gave him a dream in which he saw a giant hand, with its index finger pointed downward, getting closer and closer to him. Then he heard a voice that said, "I am your Healer." Instantly, Ruben believed. In the morning, the cysts were completely dried out—disappeared! They never returned. God had restored his skin to normal. Because he'd said no to the warlock, God healed him in His sovereign way. Today, all you can see are a few scars as a sign of the miracle he experienced.

Did you notice how the enemy almost deceived Ruben because of his lack of revelation knowledge? This is a lesson for every believer. If it had not been for the mercy of God, Ruben would have been lost in the warlock's deception. How many thousands of believers are sick, depressed, and oppressed by the enemy for lack of knowledge?

The Light in the Church Is Dying Out

Now the boy Samuel ministered to the LORD before Eli. And the word of the LORD was rare in those days; there was no widespread revelation. And it came to pass... before the lamp of God went out in the tabernacle of the LORD where the ark of God was, and while Samuel was lying down.... (1 Samuel 3:1–3)

There was no vision in the days of Eli the priest. The fresh word from God and revealed knowledge was rare. The light of the lamp of God was about to go out, figuratively speaking.

Leaders without revelation or fresh knowledge from God for their ministries will become irrelevant.

The same thing is happening today. Many people lack direction, vision, and genuine prophetic revelation from God. They are rampant, not knowing where to go. This is the reason God is restoring the ministries of the apostle and prophet. As we have seen, their roles are to bring revelation and to edify the church, with the ultimate goal of seeing people walk in truth and not be destroyed.

The Purpose and Importance of Revelation

True revelation is in tune with what the Holy Spirit is currently revealing or how He is currently working. Often, it is

From God, through Jan Painter: "I AM Releasing Servant's Heart."

REVELATION AND MANIFESTATION OF THE MYSTERIES OF GOD'S GLORY ⌐ 47

through the spiritual offices of apostle and prophet that heaven reveals the various ministries of the glory of God on earth. Apostles and prophets do not fulfill these roles because they are "better" than pastors, teachers, or evangelists; they simply fulfill their spiritual offices and exercise their gifts. Once God reveals something to an apostle or prophet, nothing can detain it; it must be released. Each time the Holy Spirit brings revelation to the church through these ministries, the revelation will be accompanied by a challenge for people to change, grow, and mature; to rise to new levels; to reach new goals; to take over spiritual territories that had been held by the enemy; and to expand the kingdom.

The purpose of revelation is not to make us complacent. We might not always understand it, but we do not have to understand it to obey it. All we have to do is receive it. Let us remember that, in earlier times, the prophets would announce messages from God that they did not always understand. And yet, they were obedient to declare them, and that which they declared came to pass—or will come to pass—in the Lord's time.

The main purpose of revelation is to lead us to a supernatural experience in God's presence so that we can be transformed.

Some people believe that revelation comes to enable us to acquire more knowledge, to make us look more intelligent or wise, or simply to give us more information about the Bible, but none of these is the case. Revelation comes to transform people and expand the kingdom of God on earth. But we have to obey the revelation to see these results.

> *And lest I should be exalted above measure by the abundance of the revelations, a thorn in the flesh was given to me, a messenger of Satan to buffet me, let I be exalted above measure.* (2 Corinthians 12:7)

The apostle Paul did not have this *"thorn in the flesh"* for being a good preacher or for helping the poor and the widows—although these are good things. I believe he had the thorn not only to humble him but also for the revelation he carried. The devil hates it when believers seek fresh revelation from God. He wants us to remain stagnant, rather than moving forward spiritually. We cannot be common people if we carry a revelation from God because the revelation makes us different. It distinguishes us from the multitudes in our generation. We must decide: are we going to be "religious" people with only the appearance of holiness, or are we going to be people who hear, obey, and have firsthand experiences with the revealed knowledge of God? If we decide to live according to revelation, we must also be willing to be persecuted for it. (See Matthew 5:10–12.)

Today, more than ever, we need breakthroughs in all areas of our lives: personal, family, social, professional, and ministry. Many believers are at a standstill; they are not advancing or growing, not possessing the blessings, and not taking over new territories that God has given us. We must say, "Enough!" and begin to ask for a divine *rhema* to pull us out of our ruts and thrust us far beyond our limitations.

EXPERIENCES WITH GOD

- Is your knowledge of God based on natural knowledge or on revelation? If it is based only (or mainly) on natural knowledge, you are missing a vital spiritual connection with Him. Pray that God would give you a fresh revelation of Himself so that you can enter into a deeper relationship with your heavenly Father.

- Ask God to give you a divine *rhema* to pull you out of any "ruts" you may be experiencing in various areas of your life: personal, family, social, professional, and ministry. Remember, He can take you farther than you ever imagined!

4

From Foundational Doctrine to Revelation

How can we move from merely knowing doctrine to living in God's "now" revelation? The first step is believing and acting on what we already know. The Pharisees were a prominent Jewish group in the days of Jesus who were knowledgeable in theology and theory and kept their own practices very strictly. They interpreted the law of Moses but had a major problem: they did not often practice what they preached about that law; this made them "religious" people. They had an appearance of piety—frequently praying, fasting, and paying tithes—but they lacked moral authority. Jesus rebuked them and called their actions hypocritical. (See, for example, Matthew 23.) Since such behavior can easily spread to others, defiling them spiritually, Jesus told His disciples,

> *Beware of the ["yeast" KJV] of the Pharisees, which is hypocrisy.* (Luke 12:1)

Live in the Reality of Scripture

If we take a close look at ourselves as a church, we will find that things have not changed much since those days. Many people claim to believe in the supernatural; they say they want to see miracles, witness the power and the glory, and have revival, but they hardly ever go beyond theory because they refuse to accept, live in, and experience the true power of God. This makes their conduct very similar to that of the Pharisees in not practicing what they preach.

Having intellectual knowledge of any biblical truth does not imply that we have experienced it.

For example, I have met hundreds of pastors and visited countless congregations who claim to believe in healing and miracles but rarely pray for the sick. They claim to believe in the gifts of the Holy Spirit, but they seldom see the manifestations of the Spirit. They claim to believe in deliverance, but they don't practice casting out demons. They claim to believe in the baptism of the Holy Spirit with the evidence of speaking in other tongues, but most of their members do not speak in other tongues.

—And yet there are healings And MIRACLES

What they have is pure theory—information—without experience. They do not obey the voice of God. If you doubt me, ask yourself, "When was the last time a blind person received his sight or a deaf person had his hearing restored in my church? When was the last time a person was healed of cancer?"

A pastor living in Honduras who is under the umbrella of King Jesus Ministry is a faithful witness of the point I am making here. I will allow him to share with you his transition from doctrine to revelation.

> My name is Alejandro Espinoza. I am a medical doctor and pastor of Misión Internacional El Shaddai in San Pedro Sula, Honduras. Together with my wife, Julissa, who is also a doctor, we practiced our professions for over ten years. God has given us two precious children, Julissa and Isaac. We were pastors in another denomination for ten years, and we served God because we loved Him. We are extremely grateful to God for that experience; it was a good one, but I must admit that it was a religious atmosphere. There were marked preferences for the structure, programs, and regulations of the denomination, which generated only order and human government while ignoring

the supernatural power of God—replacing it with routine, tradition, and passivity. The manifestations of the kingdom of God were seldom seen, and miracles were rare, without relevance or revelation. The supernatural was ignored, rejected, and criticized.

And yet, I am thankful to God that we were transformed through the spiritual fatherhood of Apostle Guillermo Maldonado and his wife, Prophet Ana Maldonado, so that this revelation came to us. They gave us identity and an inheritance and imparted gifts, fire, passion, and vision. We stopped working in our strength and being guided by our reason and began to follow the guidance of the Holy Spirit and His revelation. The evidence of this is the fruit produced in our ministry. When we were first adopted under the spiritual covering of King Jesus International Ministry (Ministerio Internacional El Rey Jesús), we had eighty people in our congregation. Today, five years later, we have a church family of over two thousand people and ten churches under our spiritual covering throughout the country. We purchased our own land to build our church, in the best location in the city, and we acquired a radio station that covers the entire territory and reaches almost a million homes. The creative miracles, healings, and salvations are continuous. We have seen leg bones grow, the blind see, the deaf hear, the lame walk, cysts disappear, and the demon possessed delivered. We have witnessed marriages restored and people delivered from drug addiction. Carlos, a spiritual son whose past includes drugs and violence, decided to change his life the day he was shot five times with a 9 millimeter gun and survived. He surrendered his life to the Lord, and he is now free of drugs and winning souls for Christ. This is the manifested kingdom of God! Everything that takes place at Ministerio El Rey Jesús also happens in our church. The same anointing and glory flow because we apply the training we continually receive. I can say, using Jesus' phrase, that we were *"born again"* (John 3:3). Religion had held us back, but the kingdom of God gave us life, in addition to the ability to produce and multiply the fruit of our efforts. We used to live in darkness; our lamp was off. But today, with revelation, the glory of God has manifested! Religion appeals to the external, but the kingdom of God transforms the heart. We hunger and thirst for God, and we have passion for change and radical transformations. God is doing something new in our city!

Build on the Foundation of Basic Doctrine

Therefore, leaving the discussion of the elementary principles of Christ, let us go on to perfection, not laying again the foundation of repentance from dead works and of faith toward God, of the doctrine of baptisms, of laying on of hands, of resurrection of the dead, and of eternal judgment. (Hebrews 6:1–2)

The author of Hebrews outlined the foundation of Christian doctrine that should be taught to those who have entered into a relationship with Jesus. The purpose of doctrine is to establish and affirm believers, enabling them to be solidly rooted in the faith. Once we lay down the foundation of doctrine, we begin to build on it. Believers are to be skilled in the *"word of righteousness... [and] by reason of use have their senses exercised to discern both good and evil"* (Hebrews 5:13–14). If we want to grow in faith, we need revelation or revealed knowledge. Revelation is the meat of the Word because, again, it is a word for today in one's life. It is not learned by studying alone but by the Holy Spirit illuminating it.

Doctrine is the foundation we lay down to build a new believer; this prepares him to receive revelation.

You do not buy land in a residential area, only to look at it each Sunday and then ignore it for the rest of the week. No! After you buy the land, you lay a foundation because you want to build a house—a dwelling place or habitation—so that you or someone else can live there. A similar process occurs in the spiritual realm. Jesus paid a high price to redeem people from sin and death. He calls the church to lay down a foundation of doctrine in each person in order to build a dwelling place there for the presence of God, according to the revealed plans of the Holy Spirit. Remember that God does not dwell in buildings of cement or brick. He dwells in earthen vessels—us! (See 2 Corinthians 4:7.)

Yet many people do not actually begin to build. They remain on the foundation of Christian doctrine, setting aside revelation—not because they reject it but because they are terrified to move from one place to the next, to commit, and to pay the price. Doctrine, in and of itself, does not produce spiritual movements or revivals. Revelation does produce a movement of the Holy Spirit because, again, it reveals what God is currently saying and doing in our midst.

Keep Moving to New Levels

Every transition implies risk because it involves moving from a known location to an unknown one. Most people fear the unknown; therefore, they prefer to stay in one place where it is comfortable and convenient. However, people who do not move—those without revelation—may never experience the power of God flowing through them. We must desire to go to other levels, other dimensions; to expand into new territories; to move to higher realms of faith, anointing, glory, maturity, and growth. Christian living is designed to be an adventurous daily walk because we must meet every new challenge with faith. If we conform—settle—we become stagnant, and this does not please God.

Doctrine is the milk of the Word, and revelation is the meat of the Word.

Several spiritual transitions are taking place right now: the church is crossing over from doctrine to revelation, from biblical fundamentals to the move of the Spirit, from root to fruit, from anointing to glory, from spiritual deafness to hearing the voice of God, from church to kingdom, from old wine to new wine, from theory to experience, from theology to demonstration, from knowledge to manifestation, from simple words to concrete works, and much more. As I said earlier, when we make the transition from one to the other, this does not negate the former or indicate that it is bad or insignificant. What it does mean is that God wants to lead us into newer, deeper, and more extensive territories in Him—and only a solid foundation will ensure the stability and firmness of the building.

> *For do I now persuade men, or God? Or do I seek to please men? For if I still pleased men, I would not be a bondservant of Christ.*　　　　　(Galatians 1:10)

Many movements and revivals of the Spirit have been lost because leaders sought to please people more than they sought to please God. Revelation challenges people to rise to new levels and territories, but, again, we cannot stop at a certain level and become stagnant. God is calling every believer to grow and mature. He is pushing us to make the transition. On this particular point, today's apostles have a big job to carry out because they are meant to ignite the fire that generates the new moves and revivals. The apostles light the fire because they are not willing to compromise principles, and they are always in the forefront of what God is saying and doing. Apostles position themselves on the front lines as they expand the kingdom forcefully, win souls for Christ, do miracles, and bring vision and direction to the church. They mobilize the believers to evangelize. They are advanced in revelation within their generation. This is also the reason why they are often not well received but are often persecuted and rejected. Many people do not understand them because they were the first to see what others have not yet seen and to understand what others have not yet understood.

Whenever a truth based in Scripture was revealed to the church for the first time, it was often classified as false.

People who are stuck in the basics are not very open to receive revelation or revealed knowledge. Many believe there is nothing else to know or experience. Others do not support the idea of learning more; they lack sufficient humility to receive anything new. Because they stay on the foundation of the faith without moving on, they remain spiritual "infants."

These believers are usually the ones who criticize the movements and revivals of God and those who ignite them. Only when it is too late—after they have rejected, persecuted, betrayed, and morally annihilated those who have been anointed by God—do they sometimes realize that these were authentic movements. When I witness such things, I ask myself, *Could there be anything false in a movement that leads thousands of people to salvation? Where countless marriages are restored and thousands are healed and delivered from depression, alcoholism, and drug addiction? Where thousands of young people walk away from their gang affiliations and the streets and return home to their parents, repentant of their actions? Could the movement or revival be false when thousands of people prosper lawfully? Is there anything wrong in any of these things?* I do not think so. There cannot be anything false when Jesus is glorified and exalted. Unfortunately, leaders and other believers who have mental strongholds and rigid ideas—"old wine" people full of theories without supernatural demonstrations—find such occurrences false and deny that God is behind them.

There is a difference between (1) wanting to correct false/ inaccurate theology or disorderliness due to unscriptural conduct and excesses, and (2) stifling a genuine move of God because of our presuppositions and entrenched ways of thinking and acting. We must learn to discern between these different situations if we are to keep pace with what God is doing among His people today. If we don't, we may hinder not only our own spiritual health and growth but also that of others.

At one time in my life, I made the mistake of throwing out the good with the bad. I didn't believe that prophets were valid for today because I had been hurt by one of them. A prophet came to my church and started "prophesying," yet it caused confusion among the people, and so I told him to leave. (See 1 Corinthians 14:33.) But when you merely react to an error without putting it into biblical perspective, you make another error. Instead, you have to respond to truth. You do this by asking yourself, "What does the Bible say about prophets (or any other matter)?"

Later, I learned to discern between a false and a true prophet. For example, we built our current church for $27 million—debt free—and it was the result of a prophetic word. The prophet said to me, "This is the place, and you will build it debt free," and I took the word from God and walked in it. If I had said, "No, I don't want to listen to any prophet," do you see what a blessing my church would have lost? So, we can respond to all situations by knowing the full Word of God.

You cannot create a doctrine based on experience, but all doctrine that comes from God will lead you to have an experience with Him.

The Word of God says:

If anyone wills to do His will, he shall know concerning the doctrine, whether it is from God or whether I speak on My own authority. (John 7:17)

I grew up in a church that qualified as having sound doctrine. The pastor continually warned the congregation to be careful of false doctrines, false prophets, and merely emotional experiences. His intentions were good. He wanted to protect the people and keep them from being deceived because he was a man who had a reverential fear of the Lord and a zeal for sound doctrine. However, his overprotectiveness also blocked the supernatural—healings and miracles were nonexistent. A fear of being deceived prevented the people from experiencing the supernatural power and presence of God. This often happens in churches with pastors who have great theological knowledge, concepts, and theories but little or no experience with the person of the Holy Spirit. Let us ask ourselves, "Who is deceived, the one who preaches on supernatural experiences, or the one who, out of fear of being deceived, deprives himself of having them?" Those who fear being deceived may think they have the right motivation, but they're missing a wonderful part of what God wants for them in having a close relationship with Him and receiving power for serving Him.

Those most reluctant to receive revelation are believers whose heads are full of theory but who lack experience.

As Hebrews 6 indicates, I believe that once the foundation is in place, we must move toward the revelation of the mysteries, toward new realms of faith, toward anointing and glory, until we are impacting the world. Fear of being deceived cannot detain us, because, if our hearts are pure and we hunger for what is genuine and fresh from God, the Lord will stand by us.

I have met believers and leaders who constantly ask, "Is this all God has for me? Where is the God of power and miracles? Is Jesus a historical figure or the living Christ? Can the Lord still do the same miracles the Bible talks about? Where is the God of Moses who parted the Red Sea? Where is the God of Joshua and Elijah who parted the Jordan River?"

God has not changed. He is the same yesterday, today, and forever. (See Hebrews 13:8.) I can testify from firsthand experience that God exists and continues to do miracles in our time.

If we do not have supernatural experiences with the presence of God, we are already deceived about His will for us.

Some time ago, I met Luis, a minister of a local church in Miami. His health was deplorable. He had diabetes, and his blood-sugar level had risen from 200—already high— to 600, a condition that was life-threatening. The doctors treated him with insulin therapy four times a day, up to a maximum of thirty-six units. His pancreas and other organs began to deteriorate, and he started to suffer intense pain in his kidneys. The disease reached the stage where he was urinating blood. His interior was like an open sore. His diet was restricted, and his mobility was greatly limited because of the chronic pain he suffered. He felt like the "living dead." The most optimistic prognosis was that he had no more than three years to live.

One day, his daughter, who attends our church, gave him my book *How to Walk in the Supernatural Power of God.* Luis testified that after he had begun to read it, he prayed, "Lord, I want to meet this powerful God mentioned in this book. I want to see miracles, signs, and wonders. I want to see the living God who exists in me." And, before he had finished reading the book, he experienced the glory of God in his body. In an instant, his blood-sugar level went down to 96—a normal reading. Since that moment, he has not needed insulin therapy, and his pancreas and kidneys have been working perfectly. That is the glory of God! Jesus does continue to do miracles. Are you ready for your miracle today?

People who love the truth cannot be deceived. Do not listen to people who have only an opinion and have never had supernatural experiences.

What Is the Connection Between Revelation and Manifestation?

It is common to find people who seem to have deep revelations but no manifestations or demonstrations of what they teach. The teachings may be profound, but there is no accompanying move of the Holy Spirit in their lives or ministries. This seems to indicate that the revelations did not come from God but from the intellect of man, because knowledge, revelation, and teaching that come from God produce supernatural manifestations and life transformations. The kingdom, power, and glory of God do not consist just of words but of power to manifest what is being taught. (See 1 Corinthians 4:20.) Therefore, in addition to knowing the meaning of revelation, it is necessity for us also to understand manifestation and what that entails.

When God Is Revealed, Some Aspect of Him Will Manifest

Manifestation is a supernatural demonstration that can be perceived by our senses. When God is revealed, some invisible aspect of Him will manifest or make itself known to the human senses, causing great impact and transformation. Miracles predispose the hearts of people to the reality of the existence of God; they experience reverential fear when they are confronted with His power and love.

> *And one* [seraph] *cried to another and said: "Holy, holy, holy is the Lord of hosts; the whole earth is full of His glory!"* (Isaiah 6:3)

The Bible declares that the whole earth is full of God's glory. Therefore, someone may ask, "If this is true, why can't we see continuous manifestations of that glory around the world?" In other words, why can't we see God doing miracles, signs, and wonders in a tangible way?

It is easy to preach or teach something we do not have to demonstrate or prove.

As I wrote earlier, God is everywhere—He is omnipresent—but He does not manifest everywhere. His glory manifests in visible and tangible form only where He is worshipped in spirit and in truth (see John 4:23) and where revelation exists—and is received by faith. We must understand this reality if we are to make the transition from revelation to manifestation.

> *For the earth will be filled with the knowledge of the*
> *glory of the* Lord, *as the waters cover the sea.*
> (Habakkuk 2:14)

The above verse is a wonderful promise of God for these last days. The Lord promises us so much knowledge of His glory that the manifestations will fill the planet we inhabit. Great miracles—both unusual and extraordinary—that have never before been seen will begin to take place. Why? Because humanity is receiving the revealed knowledge of the glory of God.

Our Faith Is Strong Where We Have Revealed Knowledge

When we have knowledge or revelation from God and move forward with it in faith, we see continuous manifestations of His presence because we transcend the laws of time, space, and matter and because the perspective of God is enacted on earth. There is a basic principle in the manifestations of the glory in our lives: our faith will always be the strongest in the areas where we have the greatest revealed knowledge. Therefore, if your faith is weak in a specific area, it is because you lack revelation for that area. Your ignorance—lack of spiritual light or revelation—gives the enemy access to you, and he begins to build one or more mental strongholds there to enclose you, isolate you from God, and destroy you. But the situation will change after you receive revelation.

> *And they went out and preached everywhere, the Lord working with them and confirming the word through the accompanying signs.* (Mark 16:20)

Revelation introduces us to the manifestation of the glory of God; without it, the glory cannot be seen.

You don't have to be a preacher or a leader in your church to begin to receive revelation and to act on it. As He did with the early church, the Lord is doing in the twenty-first century: He is using common people to carry out His will on earth.

Franklin is one of the thousands of disciples in our church. He learned that one of his coworkers, who had been struggling with deep depression, had put a gun to her head and shot herself. She survived and underwent surgery to have the bullet extracted. Franklin felt led by the Lord to visit her at the hospital and pray for her, but he did not think he would be allowed to enter the intensive care unit where she was. When he arrived, he saw people crying; everyone feared the worst. A nurse intercepted him and asked, "Who are you and what are you doing here?" He answered, "God sent me. I have come to pray for her, and then I will leave." The nurse said, "Go ahead and pray. And, if possible, anoint her with oil."

Where genuine revelation of God exists, there must be visible manifestations that confirm its divine origin.

2/17/14

The young lady had been in a coma for a week without reacting to any stimuli, but, after Franklin released words of life over her, she began to recuperate rapidly. Suddenly, she started to move her hands and feet; she even tried to remove the tubes that connected her to the monitors and other machines. Everyone was amazed! The next day, this woman was disconnected from the machines and released from the hospital. She accepted the Lord and was delivered from depression and the spirit of suicide. God rescued this young woman from the grip of death! I repeat: God will use anyone who makes himself available to Him. Where the revelation of the will of God abounds, His glory will manifest!

Extremes and Abuses of Manifestations

As wonderful as manifestations of God's glory are, we must be careful not to lose our focus. Truly, we must follow the Miracle Maker rather than the miracles. Let us therefore look at several extremes and abuses in relation to manifestations, and learn from them, so that we always give God the glory.

1. Failing to Maintain Spiritual Soundness

In the body of Christ, we have seen leaders move in the power of God and exhibit great manifestations of His glory but then fall due to moral failure or an acceptance of counterfeit doctrine. This type of situation can happen for a number of reasons, such as lack of sound character, not being accountable to spiritual authority or having adequate spiritual covering, or making manifestations the only priority, going to extremes, and setting aside the fundamentals of the Word of God. Yet, if we avoid making these same mistakes, or if we immediately correct them when they begin to happen, there is no excuse for not moving in the supernatural. Let us remember those men and women in the Bible, as well as believers through the centuries up to our current times, who have moved in the supernatural and ended their spiritual walks on a high note.

2. Fixating on Manifestations

Another extreme occurs when people fixate on manifestations, but mainly because they want to disprove them. They want to know exactly where to find examples of specific signs or demonstrations in the Scriptures. But what if the specifics aren't there? For example, there is no biblical account of someone overweight suddenly losing pounds after being prayed for, which has happened in meetings I've been in. The only references we have for these kinds of phenomena are (1) the confirmation of the Holy Spirit within us that a manifestation is from God, and (2) a *rhema* word—a word from God that speaks to the present circumstances—and a *rhema* will never contradict the Scriptures. The Lord would not do anything against His Word. We need to ask ourselves questions such as these: "Is losing weight a good thing for people?" "Did the experience promote a love for God in the person who experienced it?" "Do I have peace about this situation?"

Focusing on the glory apart from the Word of God leads to unbalance.

Earlier, I gave examples of two prophets who visited my church. When the first prophet came, he brought confusion among the people. However, when the second prophet came and spoke about our having a new sanctuary debt free, I had peace about it. We must keep in mind that manifestations such as sudden weight loss are *signs*; they are not doctrines. After this manifestation occurred, I didn't proclaim that everyone had to experience weight loss in order to be saved or to experience the genuine presence of God. The real question is: Is God taking the initiative? Is He doing the work? We will know this is the

[handwritten marginalia: We should ask God what He wants for... the intended...]

case if the work is consistent with God's nature and character and produces the same in the people involved.

3. Giving In to the Temptation to Prove One's Spirituality

An abuse of manifestations occurs when we try to use them to prove how "spiritual" we are. In the following passage, note how the enemy tempted Jesus to do a miracle in order to prove His identity as God's Son.

> *Now when the tempter came to [Jesus], he said, "If You are the Son of God, command that these stones become bread." But He answered and said, "It is written, 'Man shall not live by bread alone, but by every word that proceeds from the mouth of God.'"*
>
> (Matthew 4:3–4)

The devil wanted Jesus to react in a sinful way and demonstrate His powers to prove He was the Miracle Maker. The Son of God not only had the power to turn stones into bread, but He also had the power to turn water into wine, multiply bread and fish to feed thousands, heal multitudes, and even raise the dead. Yet He knew who He was and the power that was within Him, and this kept Him from falling prey to the trap of vanity and narcissism presented by the tempter.

[handwritten marginalia: ? Is there a difference between ... to prove yourself and let God show through yourself to His glory?]

The temptation to prove yourself is not a valid reason to manifest the power and glory of God.

When Jesus did miracles, it was not to prove a point but to glorify the Father and to bless people. He never did anything to exalt Himself, as Satan tempted Him to do. Therefore, we must be extremely careful when demonstrating the power of God, so as not to be led by incorrect motives that would only serve to please our egos. Those who decide to satisfy their egos will fall as a result of pride, and they may be destroyed by the weight of their mistakes.

In my walk with Jesus, I have traveled to places where people would subtly insinuate, "If you are a man of God, why don't you raise that person from that wheelchair?" Others have openly criticized me because I have called ten deaf people to the platform to pray for them but only five were healed. They judge me, saying, "Prove that you are a genuine servant of God and heal them all!" My job is to pray for the sick, but their healing is between God and them. When people say these kinds of things to me, my answer is always the same: "I did not come here to prove anything about me but to do the will of God and to demonstrate that Jesus lives. He sent me to bless His people, and that is all I will do." That is how I avoid falling into the temptation of the enemy.

Every time we use our gifts or anointing to exalt our egos, to seek gain, or to obtain a position, we are commercializing the anointing.

By affirming my identity in Christ, I frustrate every perverse plan to win followers for myself or to open doors that God has not opened for me. I refuse to fall into that trap! We should never succumb to peer pressure to manifest the power of God or to take any other action.

Balance Between Theology and Manifestation

Everywhere I am asked to preach, I take the time to carefully teach the Word. I instruct the people on theology, knowledge, and revelation based on what God is about to manifest. I have found that, otherwise, the impartation will not remain in them, and they will lack the ability to repeat what they have seen me do. God has taught me that when the people are not given knowledge and principles that support the manifestation, they will not see the need to practice it.

Let me restate that I am a firm believer in and practitioner of both scriptural knowledge and manifestation, and I consider the gifts of the Spirit to be important. I know that revelation (revealed knowledge) and theology (intellectual knowledge) must walk together to produce spiritual manifestation. I always make certain that the Word supports every experience and manifestation that occurs. I encourage the youth in my church to study theology, but only at institutions that believe in the manifestations of the Holy Spirit and do not have teachers and theologians who reject these manifestations and have not had the experience of being baptized in the Holy Spirit.

Revelation or knowledge of the Holy Spirit activates people.

My apostolic calling is to teach, train, and equip believers. My heart's desire is not to be one of a small number of vessels God uses to perform His miracles, signs, and wonders but to equip thousands of leaders to train and guide others on the same path and to win souls. I have invested myself in the new generation that God is raising up, and I am witnessing amazing results. I want you to have the same results by combining your scriptural knowledge with revelation and allowing God to manifest His glory through you!

The Glory Is with Us

God's glory is with us on the earth, just as the Scripture says. (See Habakkuk 2:14.) The only thing we need to access and manifest the glory is the knowledge of God as revealed by the Holy Spirit. Men and women who have moved in God's supernatural power and have been used by Him to do miracles, signs, and wonders have had a revelation given by His Spirit; this is what made them different from others. In the next chapter, we will see how to move from the anointing to the glory and how to receive revelation from God.

EXPERIENCES WITH GOD

- In what past manifestation of glory might you have become stagnated? Perhaps it is the Azusa Street revival, which emphasized the baptism in the Holy Spirit. Maybe it is the Word of Faith movement. These and other movements were given by God, but He is continually moving, and we need to move with Him to receive a fresh word for today. Ask God to reveal a "now" word for you.

- Remember that reacting to an error can cause us to make another error. If you have been fearful or overly cautious of supernatural manifestations because of abuses you have seen, study the Word of God, asking the Lord for discernment to bring you to a greater biblical understanding and balance in relation to them.

5

Transitioning from the Anointing to the Glory

Without a continuous revelation of the glory of God, we will become spiritually stagnant. As I wrote earlier, we will become "old wineskins." Entering into God's glory requires revelation, and receiving revelation requires understanding the interrelationship between three dimensions of the supernatural: (1) faith, (2) anointing, and (3) glory. We will now look at each of these areas, and then we will discover essential steps to transition from the anointing to the glory.

Three Dimensions of the Supernatural

1. Faith

Romans 12:3 tells us that everyone has been given a *"measure of faith"* by God. He gave us this measure of faith to enable us to interact with the spiritual realm while physically living on earth. Faith is the believer's spiritual antenna to "hear" beyond the natural dimension; it is the *"substance of things hoped for, the evidence of things not seen"* (Hebrews 11:1).

Just before raising Lazarus from the dead, Jesus said to Martha, Lazarus' sister, *"Did I not say to you that if you would believe you would see the glory of God?"* (John 11:40). Faith is a prerequisite for seeing the glory because having faith means you believe in what God can do. It is the ability to believe the "unreasonable" or "impossible."

Faith was given to us so we can reach beyond time into eternity.

There is a difference between believing for something with the measure of faith that God has given us, and God exercising His own faith. The realm of "glory" is the latter—God Himself in faith and action—what He believes and does on His own, compared to what we believe based on our faith and what we are able to do based on our anointing. But there's a prerequisite to seeing God Himself in the dimension of glory, and that is our faith.

2. Anointing

There are several aspects of the anointing for us to consider. First, just as each believer has been given a measure of faith, he or she has been given a measure of anointing, or a particular gift or gifts to fulfill God's purposes. (See, for example, 1 Corinthians 12:4–11.) The anointing is the power of God, provided to enable believers to carry out the work of the ministry. It is also used to send men and women into the ministry. (See Ephesians 4:11–13; Acts 13:1–3.) In the Old Testament, the glory of God fell on the tabernacle after the priests, the altar, and the utensils had been anointed. (See Exodus 40.) So, the anointing is God's power working through us to do what He wants done on earth. He may say to one person, "You are called to be a missionary, so I will give you a portion of My power, as well as the necessary faith, to enable you to fulfill this calling."

It has been my experience that each measure of anointing given to a believer is made up of various levels. One level is equivalent to a "step" that must be taken or ascended as we progress in our ability to move in that anointing and grow spiritually in relation to it. No step can be skipped, because each step represents an essential aspect of maturity in spiritual matters. We must go from step to step, or from level to level, without missing one, until we reach the level at which we have fully developed the measure of the anointing we have received. When we reach the last level, we can do nothing further in terms of our anointing— we have reached the fullness of that measure. At this point, the only option available to us is to enter into the glory.

Another aspect of anointing is that the faith of one believer can draw out the anointing of another believer. In other words, a person can exercise faith that puts a spiritual "demand" on the anointing of another person to operate in that anointing. For example, suppose I am preaching when, suddenly, I have to stop in the middle of my message and pray for someone in the audience because that person is exercising faith, thinking, "I believe that he will come now and lay hands on me for healing because I need a miracle." Faith attracts the anointing. So, we see that faith and the anointing work together.

A minister of God cannot force the anointing on people— they have to appropriate it by faith.

Having the anointing is not the same thing as moving in the glory, which includes all of God's attributes. The anointing is a *part* of God, operating through us. Also, it is only one aspect of His power because there are many aspects to the power of God. For example, God's power in the area of ministry is called the *anointing*, the power of God in the area of law is called *authority*, and the power of God in the area of spiritual warfare is called *might*. The power of God in the area of territory is called *dominion*, which is the highest level of power. That was what Adam received when he was created. Therefore, we can't really refer to "the power of God" as if it were all the same.

Finally, let me say that in 2 Corinthians 5:4–5, we learn that God has given us the Spirit as a *"guarantee,"* *"deposit"* (NIV), or down payment for the glory. It is the mark of our destiny. (See Ephesians 1:13–14.) The anointing (as well as faith) prepares us to receive the glory, which is God's manifest presence. In short, faith calls the anointing, but the anointing calls the glory.

3. Glory

We can operate in the gifts of the Holy Spirit by faith and the anointing if we know how the principles that activate them operate. However, the glory of God is different. The glory is the manifest presence—*shekinah*—of God. It testifies of heaven and the *"powers of the age to come"* (Hebrews 6:5). The manifest presence operates according to God's sovereignty. He does what He wants, when He wants, and in the way He wants, without depending on our faith, gifts, or anointing. It is God doing His works without bringing in the participation of human beings. I strongly believe that the last move of God upon the earth will not come through a man or woman but directly from God.

When the glory of God manifests, it operates according to the initiative and sovereignty of God, not of man.

The presence of God cannot be provoked, stirred up, or manufactured. Yet His presence can be attracted through worship. God has often healed, delivered, and transformed people during a church service without the use of my faith or anointing; these were sovereign acts of our heavenly Father. When the glory of God is present, we don't think about the person who may be imparting to us an aspect of that glory. God takes the initiative and works according to His will. The glory or presence of God supersedes all gifts, anointing, faith, or ministerial functions—though, of course, all these things come from Him and are used by Him to build up His church.

Operating Under the Anointing Versus Experiencing the Glory

To help you better understand the glory, let me describe for you the contrast between ministering under the anointing and experiencing the glory.

Cooperating with God

When I am operating under the anointing, I feel power coming out from me. Remember when the woman with the flow of blood touched the hem of Jesus' robe, and He said, *"Who touched Me?...I perceived power [dunamis] going out from Me"* (Luke 8:45–46)? It is similar to that. This is because it is God's power working *through* me, using my cooperation. When I minister under the anointing, I am very tired by the time I finish, because it is God using my humanity.

As believers, we know the anointing is in operation when we feel virtue and power coming out from us, as Christ did. Preachers often experience this. In the realm of faith, people put a demand on the anointing, or mantle, of a man or woman of God and receive what they desire.

Resting in God

Yet, when we experience the glory; when God, in His sovereignty, chooses to work alone, this is the realm of rest because we don't "do" anything. We just worship. I've been with fourteen thousand other people in a stadium, worshipping God, crying out to Him, where we were touched by Him as He came among us.

We work under the anointing but rest in God's glory.

When I was preaching at one of our daughter churches in Orlando, we started worshipping God. Suddenly, His presence came. Many people saw the *shekinah* cloud. I didn't see it then, but I perceived it. It was moving in a certain section of the audience, and people in that section started weeping and being healed and delivered. I hadn't touched anyone, and nobody else had touched them. Then, people started coming forward to testify about what had happened to them. People were being healed and delivered continuously for two-and-a-half hours. There was a woman in that audience who'd had her womb removed due to cancer. But she came up to the altar, saying over and over, "I felt something!" She went back to the doctor two weeks later, and it was confirmed that she had a brand-new womb. This is what happens in the glory!

The anointing was given to heal the sick, but in the glory, we are covered with a supernatural immunity to sickness.

Now, when the glory is present, I still feel fresh at the end of a service, rather than tired. That is because God isn't working through me but is working independently.

Should I Wait for God in His Glory or Take the Initiative by the Anointing?

Since God has given us the anointing but also acts independently, we need to learn how the two situations are distinct and how they work together. Some people say, "I never minister unless God tells me to do so," believing they are imitating Jesus, who said, *"The Son can do nothing of Himself, but what He sees the Father do; for whatever He does, the Son also does in like manner"* (John 5:19). What happens is that these people keep waiting for God to show up in His glory to speak to them, specifically, and they end up doing nothing. What they don't realize is that hearing from God in that way is only one dimension, or aspect, of the way He works. For example, there are certain things that we have already been instructed to do, such as spread the good news of the gospel to those who have not heard it. Luke 9:2 says, *"[Jesus] sent [His disciples] to preach the kingdom of God and to heal the sick."*

We don't say, "Well, I'm just waiting on God before I go evangelize." That's taking things to an extreme. Of course, we must be listening for His guidance as we tell others about Jesus. And we should wait on God to see if He chooses to manifest His glory. But if He doesn't, then we are to operate according to the anointing He has given us. There are certain things He's already told us to do and anointed us to do, and we are to move forward in them if He doesn't take the initiative.

People know they are moving in a dimension of the glory of God when they no longer need to use their faith or anointing.

Then, some people go to the other extreme by not giving God *any* room to work. They don't wait for Him at all. For instance, some pastors already have a concrete plan for the order in which their services should go and what elements should be included, and they never consider the fact that the Holy Spirit may want to move in a different way. They leave God out of their plans, when God is saying, in effect, "I want to visit you; I want to come and demonstrate My glory. I want to move among you in healing and deliverance." Tragically, He is hindered from doing any of those things if the pastor and congregation have left no room for Him to work. So, we can see that we need to have a balance between operating under the anointing and allowing God the freedom to move in the way of His choosing.

Respecting the Glory

While most believers have never experienced the glory of God, many of those who have experienced it have not known what to do when it was present. And, sadly, some do not recognize His presence when it manifests. These situations can cause people not to respond to the glory as they should. This happened to Uzzah, who touched the ark of God (ark of the covenant) when it was being brought to Jerusalem by King David.

> *And when they came to Nachon's threshing floor, Uzzah put out his hand to the ark of God and took hold of it, for the oxen stumbled. Then the anger of the LORD was aroused against Uzzah, and God struck him there for his error; and he died there by the ark of God.*
>
> (2 Samuel 6:6–7)

There is an important warning in these verses. Uzzah, whose name means "strength," fell dead because he disobeyed the instructions given by God. The ark never should have been transported on a cart pulled by animals. (See verse 3.) Instead, it should have been carried by the Levites (see Deuteronomy 10:8), raised upon their shoulders by wooden poles (see Exodus 25:13–15). In the Old Testament, not even the priests were allowed to touch the ark or to examine its contents. Although Uzzah did belong to the tribe of Levi, he failed to respect the presence of God represented by the ark by trying in his own strength to keep the ark from falling. This should demonstrate for us that we are not to become too casual about the presence of God in our lives or in our midst when we gather together as believers; that is an atrocity! Uzzah's fate teaches us to be reverent toward God. He is the only One worthy of worship and all honor. These verses ultimately reveal the importance of knowing and understanding the glory of God so that we can walk in it, live in it, and experience it without offending Him. Otherwise, we expose ourselves to discipline and punishment, including death. *We can't bring in God's glory with our own flesh (or at that stuff)*

Essential Steps to Transition from Anointing to Glory

Since many believers are familiar with the anointing but know little of the manifestation of God's glory, we will look next at some fundamental steps to moving from one dimension to the next.

1. Understand the Revelation of the Three Supernatural Dimensions

As we have seen, it is not the same for us to exercise a measure of faith, to operate in a measure of anointing, or to use a spiritual gift as it is for God to do as He wills with His power and majesty. Time does not exist in the glory of God; therefore, when we stand in His presence for an hour, it seems like only

Mid 76 -
3/24

minutes. By the same token, what took us a decade to build with the anointing can be finished in a year or less when we consistently dwell in the glory. I can personally testify of the effects of this transition in my life. But, first, I had to actively receive the revelation of the three supernatural dimensions, and the same will be true for you.

For lack of revelation and knowledge, many believers have never experienced the glory of God.

For many years, I had written about, lived in, and walked in faith and the anointing. I had seen many healings and miracles in my ministry, and this had been powerful. However, a time came when I felt I had reached a peak where nothing happened beyond a certain level, and I was hungry for more of God. I hungered for creative miracles, supernatural provision, signs, wonders, and radical life transformations. I had the faith required for these to happen, but nothing like them ever did. I believed that God could create new organs and heal any type of disease. I started to look for people who needed new organs, who could not walk, or who had incurable diseases. However, when I prayed for them, nothing happened. I have concluded that my dimension of faith was greater than my level of anointing.

We just discussed the fact that each believer has received a measure of faith and a measure of anointing. Yet I had reached a level that required more than the anointing, so I began to search for a higher realm in God. In the meantime, the Lord had led my wife to Isaiah 60, which describes the glory of God and His blessings coming upon us; she had been praying for it for three months. During that time, an apostle friend of mine shared with me the revelation of the three dimensions of the supernatural. As I said, I had written about and preached on faith and the anointing, but I had never seen them connect and work together. This completed the revelation so that I could make the commitment to enter into the dimension of glory. In this dimension, it would be God, not my faith or anointing, in operation.

Revealed knowledge introduces us to the dimension of glory, but hunger and thirst for God are what maintain us in it.

Once I understood this revelation, I learned to let God be God, to flow with Him, and to allow Him to "give it all He had." The glory began to manifest in visible ways! People were healed of incurable diseases. Creative miracles took place: people received new organs, such as kidneys; they received new bones and cartilage and even new hair growth where they had been bald. There were radical transformations in people's lives, as well as supernatural provision of money. When I realized that God could take the initiative, I concluded, "Why not let Him operate directly?"

After I received the revelation of the three dimensions of the supernatural, I learned to discern when to take the initiative with the anointing and when to let God do so by the glory, as we discussed above. I also learned to identify when it was faith, when it was the anointing, and when it was the glory in operation. In a similar way, trust God to take you through this process as you make the transition from the anointing to the glory.

2. Renew Your Mind According to God's Perspective

To move in the supernatural power of God's kingdom, we need to renew our minds, because it is only through this renewal that we can see according to His perspective. For us to be useful in the kingdom, we must be transformed or transfigured by a redeemed mind-set. Believers often pray for nations to be transformed, but the Bible teaches that we should first have a changed outlook.

> *Now after six days Jesus took Peter, James, and John his brother, led them up on a high mountain by themselves; and He was transfigured before them. His face*

*shone like the sun, and His clothes became as white
as the light.*   (Matthew 17:1–2)

The Greek word translated *"transfigured"* in the above passage is the same word used in Romans 12:2 for *"transformed"*: *"Be **transformed** by the renewing of your mind, that you may prove what is that good and acceptable and perfect will of God."* That word is *metamorphoo*, and it means "to change or transfigure into another form; to undergo a metamorphosis or change of form." When Jesus was transfigured, He reflected the reality of the world to come and manifested His glory. The disciples had seen Him live and walk under the anointing, but on that day, for the first time, they saw His true glory—the glory He left behind when He came to this world. And, as we renew our minds according to His nature, we will reflect the reality of His glory.

The renewed mind is the essential tool needed to bring the reality of the kingdom, the power, and the glory to earth.

Having a renewed mind makes us more useful to God because it means that our thoughts are aligned to His. It also allows what is in heaven to continually manifest on earth in miracles, signs, and wonders. A mind that has not been renewed can experience the supernatural only from time to time. When that occurs, it is God's way of giving people a taste of the supernatural in order to awaken in them a yearning for it.

Are you ready to renew your mind? Are you prepared to make the transition from the anointing to the glory? Do you wish to experience the glory of God? Since this process of transforming our minds is essential, we will explore in greater detail how to go about it in chapters 8 and 9.

3. Allow God to Be God

Third, we must let God do as He wills rather than try to do everything ourselves.

Be still, and know that I am God; I will be exalted among the nations, I will be exalted in the earth!
                                                    (Psalm 46:10)

One of the major problems we have as human beings is that we always want to be in control. We have created religious structures and rigid denominations (either by design or default) that cut off the flow of the Holy Spirit. But what would happen if we decided to wait on God? If we allowed Him to take the initiative? If we simply learned to rest in His glory?

Allow the Holy Spirit to move as He wants, when He wants. Learn to trust in Him because He already is in control of all things!

How to Receive Revelation from the Holy Spirit

To conclude this chapter, I want to give you some guidelines for receiving revelation as you draw closer to God and His glory.

1. Let Your Heart Be Filled with a Reverential Fear of the Lord

The secret of the LORD is with those who fear [reverence] *Him, and He will show them His covenant.*
                                                    (Psalm 25:14)

God shares His secrets only with those who reverence and respect Him, not with His enemies, who despise and reject His secrets, and not with those who are complacent toward Him and His ways. Intimate communion with God is part of the covenant we have with Him in Jesus Christ, and He gives His revelation to the humble in heart. When people do not reverence the Lord, they are not able to receive truths taught from the Word of God. In such cases, their receiving the truths does not depend on the preachers or teachers presenting them but on the state of their hearts. Therefore, if you want to receive revelation, you must commit to cultivate an intimate relationship with God and develop a reverential fear of the Lord.

This is the only way to obtain results such as Cecilia and her husband did. This couple went to the Lord for help when their two-year-old son was diagnosed with autism, which causes children to have difficulty communicating and interacting with others and is accompanied by other physical challenges.

The neurologist told them that he would prescribe medication to calm their son's anxiety when the time came for him to start school, but, for the moment, he could prescribe something that would only help improve his quality of life—nothing more. But Cecilia believed Jesus and brought her son to a miracle crusade. She went through personal inner healing and deliverance and started attending early-morning prayer at our church. As she fasted and prayed, she was guided by the Holy Spirit and received revelation about how she was to pray for her son. By faith, she began to anoint him with oil every day, declaring the Word over him.

Cecilia began to see the healing of her son through eyes of faith until it became a reality. She declared that his neurons had to align themselves to the perfect design of God. She prophesized that his vocal cords were loosened to preach and to pray for others, and she established that he would have supernatural intelligence. Since then, things have changed radically. The year he should have been promoted to first grade, he was promoted to third grade! He does apparently have supernatural intelligence. Even though he is now only seven years old, he speaks and reads better than a ten-year-old. And, while he formerly had difficulty eating, today he eats normally—he even likes spinach and carrots!

This is an example of life under the glory of God. Revelation came to this boy's mother through her reverential fear of the Lord and her commitment to seek Him. Although there is no cure known to man for autism, nothing is impossible for God!

2. Know the Fundamental Truths of the Gospel

As we have seen, basic Christian doctrine must be well established in our hearts. This doctrine includes, for example, the nature of the triune God—Father, Son, and Holy Spirit—the divine inspiration of Scripture, the virgin birth of Jesus, new birth through repentance from sin and faith in Jesus' sacrifice on the cross on our behalf, the resurrection of Jesus from the dead, ongoing faith in God through Jesus, baptism in water, the baptism of the Holy Spirit, the laying on of hands for healing and commissioning, the second coming of Christ, eternal rewards and judgment, and the new heavens and earth. When these truths are engraved on our hearts, then the foundations of our "spiritual buildings" will be prepared, and God will release revelation to us.

Treasuring basic truths and living according to them edifies the foundation for God to dwell in us and give us revelation.

3. Practice, Value, and Obey the Truths You Already Know

From God's perspective, if you are not willing to do something, you are not ready to know it. As we have seen, we are not to learn biblical knowledge just so we can accumulate information about God; rather, the Word is an invitation by the Holy Spirit to have a supernatural experience with Him.

No knowledge or revelation becomes ours until it is obeyed and practiced.

Many people who live according to the mind-set of the world might say that "knowledge is power," but that is only a half-truth, because knowledge becomes power only when it is put into practice.

4. Understand That Revelation Is Only for Those Who Hunger and Thirst for God

> [Jesus] *answered and said to them, "Because it has been given to you to know the mysteries of the kingdom of heaven, but to them it has not been given."*
>   (Matthew 13:11)

In this verse, Jesus presents two types of individuals: *"them"* (the Pharisees—and everyone today who is similarly "religious") and *"you"* (the disciples—and everyone today who actively and sincerely follows Jesus). Most of the Pharisees accumulated knowledge of the Scriptures only for the sake of vanity; they had no intention of obeying the spirit of the law or being transformed by it, so Jesus did not reveal the *"mysteries of the kingdom"* to them. Likewise, many believers in the church seek to fill themselves with biblical knowledge yet have no intention of obeying the Word. In short, they are motivated by pride rather than love for God. (See 1 Corinthians 8:1.)

If the motivation to seek knowledge is not love, then the acquired knowledge will lead only to vanity.

In contrast, Jesus' disciples hungered and thirsted not only to hear and learn the Word but also to obey it, and therefore He gave them a revelation of the kingdom of God. The same will be true of everyone today who hungers and thirsts for Him. Best of all, God promises that His mysteries will be revealed both to those who deeply desire to see the kingdom advance on earth and to their children.

> *The secret things belong to the* Lord *our God, but those things which are revealed belong to us and to our children forever, that we may do all the words of this law.*   (Deuteronomy 29:29)

What is a mystery, spiritually speaking? It is something that cannot be perceived or known through natural means; it must be revealed by the Holy Spirit. A mystery is knowledge that God alone has, and, again, it is unveiled only to those who hunger and thirst for Him; it is withheld or hidden from those who do not want to know Him. If we sincerely seek God's mysteries because we want to understand Him and His ways, we will receive them with the help of His Spirit. He will guide us in our search and unveil them before us.

Knowledge of the glory belongs to the realm of the mysteries of God.

Call to Me, and I will answer you, and show you great and mighty things, which you do not know.
(Jeremiah 33:3)

When we cry out to God from the bottom of our hearts, He reveals the great and hidden things, as long as we truly want to use them to further His purposes. The church needs to know these hidden things in order to manifest God's glory on earth and to gather the souls that are ready to be harvested for Him.

As it is written: "Eye has not seen, nor ear heard, nor have entered into the heart of man the things which God has prepared for those who love Him." But God has revealed them to us through His Spirit.
(1 Corinthians 2:9–10)

In this day and age, it is not strange to find a generation that yearns for these mysteries—for the wonderful, hidden things that have been promised in the Word. People are desperately crying out day and night, saying, "Lord, I want the 'new.' I want to see Your glory. I want to see the great manifestations of the Lord of Israel." This attitude motivates God to release such revelations and knowledge of His glory as have never been seen before. (See Habakkuk 2:14.) A revival will spring up in every city, nation, and continent, and the kingdom of God will expand throughout the earth.

The transformation of an individual can also transform families, cities, nations, the world.

---

5. Pray for the Spirit of Wisdom and Revelation

...making mention of you in my prayers: that the God of our Lord Jesus Christ, the Father of glory, may give to you the spirit of wisdom and revelation in the knowledge of Him. (Ephesians 1:16–17)

We need to pray daily for *"the spirit of wisdom and revelation."* In this regard, it is important for us to understand the difference between wisdom and knowledge. What is wisdom? It is the ability to know how and when to apply the knowledge we possess. Wisdom is useful when guiding others.

If the ax is dull, and one does not sharpen the edge, then he must use more strength; but wisdom brings success. (Ecclesiastes 10:10)

The tongue of the wise uses knowledge rightly, but the mouth of fools pours forth foolishness. (Proverbs 15:2)

Although wisdom and knowledge are different, they work together. Wisdom provides direction while knowledge provides information. You can have the wisdom to do something, but if you lack knowledge, you will not accomplish much. On the other hand, if you have knowledge but lack the wisdom to apply it, you will also be incomplete. Many people possess knowledge but use it incorrectly, not understanding how to relate it to their daily lives. The wisdom of God is practical and simple.

It provides instruction and guidance regarding how to live and how to apply the knowledge of God effectively.

The spirit of wisdom and revelation illuminates our minds and hearts as it transforms us. While Jesus walked the earth, He operated in the spirit of wisdom and revelation. He taught His disciples that signs and wonders do not belong to the realm of the natural or the common but to the supernatural dimension. Each miracle Jesus did was the result of a revelation unveiled by the Father and the Holy Spirit. Many people today seek miracles, healing, provision, and answers to their problems in the natural realm, without ever realizing that they are seeking them from the wrong source. We need revelation from God to find new healing, provision, and answers.

When the spirit of wisdom and revelation is absent, the church imparts only information and natural knowledge, and people are not transformed.

When the spirit of wisdom and revelation are imparted to us by God, we discover a dimension of His glory and are immediately activated in it; we receive the ability to do what God revealed. The Lord is willing to reveal and manifest His glory on earth! However, we must again remember that revelation comes only when we are well-rooted in the basic truths of Christian doctrine, are obeying these truths, and yearn to know God. Nothing will happen if we try to obtain revelation in any other way.

Allow me to ask you some questions: First, what has God revealed to you in the past that you have not yet obeyed? If you are aware of some specific knowledge He has given to you that you have failed to apply, ask God for forgiveness and obey it immediately. Second, can you honestly answer yes to the following statements?

• I yearn to know more of God.

- I truly want to see His glory manifest.

- I am willing to cry out to the Lord continually for Him to reveal the *"mysteries of the kingdom of heaven"* (Matthew 13:11).

If your answer to each of the above statements is yes, then all that's left to do is to commit to cry out to God! If you answered no to any of the statements, ask God to create a hunger and thirst within you for Him and His glory.

I would like to pray for you right now:

Heavenly Father, on behalf of my dear readers, I pray that You might open the eyes of their understanding and illuminate them with the spirit of wisdom and revelation, which will enable them to comprehend the mysteries of Your glory. I ask You to confirm this revelation by supernaturally manifesting in their lives right now. If they are sick, I ask that You heal them. If they are depressed or emotionally oppressed, I ask that You deliver them. If they need a creative miracle, I ask that they receive it right now. Manifest in their lives with miracles of supernatural provision. And for those who yearn to be transformed and to enter a greater dimension of glory, I release Your presence upon them right now! Manifest as the living and resurrected Christ. I believe with all my heart that You will do this. In the name of Jesus, amen!

Take time to meditate upon all that the Lord has revealed to you through these pages. These first five chapters are the theological foundation of what is to come in the following chapters. From now on, you will receive the training to know with what attitudes to receive the glory of God. Additionally, you will discover the benefits of seeking His manifest presence, and much, much more.

EXPERIENCES WITH GOD

- Pray that God would manifest His glory, that His revelation would penetrate your spirit, and that your mind would be transformed, so you can move from the anointing to the glory.

- Increase your prayer time to an hour of crying out to God wholeheartedly, so that revealed knowledge can come and His glory can manifest.

- Practice what you learn. Go and pray for the sick, evangelizing and teaching others the revelations you have received.

6

Passion and Thirst to Seek God's Presence

Anyone who has truly known God in any of His qualities cannot stop the passion to know Him more. One question I am frequently asked is, "What motivates you to seek the presence of God more each day?" My answer is always the same: "It is the passion I feel for Him, the reverent fear I have for Him, and my hunger and thirst for His presence. I recognize my need for God. I know that without His presence, I am destined for failure. I know that without Him, I am nothing and can do nothing. I remember from where He rescued me. I recognize my smallness as a human being, and I admit my absolute need of and dependency on God. I am who I am because of Him. I am where I am because of Him. Nothing in my life would have been made possible without His favor, grace, power, and presence."

I deeply love my Savior, and I passionately desire to see all the kingdoms on earth surrender to the dominion and lordship of the one and only God, the King of Kings and the Lord of Lords. Every morning, I wake up with greater passion. My thirst for Him is insatiable! I thirst to see millions of souls come into the kingdom, and, every day, I focus on serving God with that purpose in my mind and heart. It is a fire that burns in me, a flame that never dies out. From the Bible, I have learned that the only ingredient we need to experience calamity is to separate ourselves from God's presence, as happened to Adam. If I am successful, it is because I live my life bound to Him. I say, as Moses said when he was about to lead the Jewish people out of captivity from Egypt, *"If Your Presence does not go with* [me], *do not bring* [me] *up from here"* (Exodus 33:15).

The Bible tells us about various people who were passionate about God's presence. Let's look at three of them: Moses, David, and Paul.

Moses' Greatest Passion

Moses was unable to live without the presence of God from the moment he recognized it in the desert. He cherished His presence to the point that he would not take one step without first consulting Him. On several occasions, God was ready to destroy Israel, but Moses interceded, and God held back His judgment. God listened to Moses because He knew who he was—and they enjoyed an intimate relationship with each other.

> [The Lord said,] *"My servant Moses...is faithful in all My house. I speak with him face to face, even plainly, and not in dark sayings; and he sees the form of the* LORD.*"* (Numbers 12:7–8)

It was common for Moses to speak face-to-face with the Lord, but it was not like that for the rest of the Israelites. I think God knew that if He showed Himself to them, they would raise up a figure or sculpture in His image to worship, instead of worshipping the true God. (See Deuteronomy 4:15–19.) Idol worship occurs today in the form of anything we put ahead of God in our lives. But as we allow Him to uproot the idolatry from our hearts, He begins to reveal Himself to us at a personal, intimate level.

Everyone in the Bible who saw God "face-to-face" had to pay a price and submit to major changes in his life. I think it is safe to conclude that many people today reject the "fire" of God's glory because experiencing it exposes their true spiritual conditions. (See Deuteronomy 5:4–5.) Furthermore, it produces holiness and purity, which are two qualities a great number of people reject because they do not *want* to change. Submitting to major changes in our lives is not easy; it is costly. It is the reason the Bible calls very few people "friends of God."

David's Zeal for God

Another man who had a passion and thirst for the Lord was David, Israel's second king, whom the Word calls a man after God's own heart. (See 1 Samuel 13:14.) He had great zeal to constantly seek the Lord and to be in His presence. The first king, Saul, apparently never thought about bringing the ark of the covenant to Gibeah, where he reigned. Instead, the ark remained for twenty years in the town of Kirjath Jearim, where it had been brought back after having been captured and returned seven months later by Israel's enemy, the Philistines. Yet, when David took over as king of Israel, one of his first royal acts was to bring the ark—and, with it, the manifest presence of God—to Jerusalem, where David had established his residence and seat of government. (See 2 Samuel 6.)

David was a man after God's own heart because of his thirst and passion to seek His presence.

One pattern in his life is easily distinguishable: almost every time he faced a difficult situation, when he needed to make an important decision or face an enemy in battle, he first went before the Lord, seeking God's face. (See, for example, 1 Samuel 30:6–8.) He had great passion for worshipping the Lord. In the Psalms, we read about his great thirst for God's presence, which led him to seek God without ceasing.

Paul's Intense Desire to Know God Intimately

That I may know [Christ] *and the power of His resurrection, and the fellowship of His sufferings, being conformed to His death.* (Philippians 3:10)

The apostle Paul also had a passion for God and for knowing Christ. In the original languages of the Bible, we find several words that describe the verb "to know": *Gnosis*—a Greek word that alludes to informative, mental, theoretical, and scientific knowledge. *Epignosis*—a Greek word that indicates experimental knowledge or knowledge acquired by practice or experience; at the personal level, it refers to having intimacy with another individual or knowing that person intimately. *Yada*—a Hebrew word that means to have intimate knowledge of or to know someone at the intimacy level. The will of God is for every believer to have an experience of Him, or an intimate, face-to-face encounter with Him.

> *[That you may really come] to know [practically, through experience for yourselves] the love of Christ, which far surpasses mere knowledge [without experience].* (Ephesians 3:19 AMP)

What Paul was expressing in the above verse is that we should reach the *epignosis*, the love of Christ that exceeds all *gnosis*. To know God is to experience His love. Regardless of what we do, how many books we read, or how many university diplomas we obtain, if we never have a practical experience with God, we will never understand the love of the Father or the life of Jesus. I truly desire for you to know firsthand that the kingdom, the power, and the glory of God are not just theological concepts; they can be experienced here and now, in the present. To know Jesus is to bring His reality, His dominion, His life, and His power to earth. That is why we need more than theology; we need experience. Every person who has truly known God has experienced Him, and every believer today can also aspire to experience Him.

Theology without experience or without a divine encounter is not spiritually profitable. If we never experience or receive Jesus as our Lord and Savior, we will be lost, even though we have the correct theology or theory about Him as such. Sadly, this is why thousands of religious people are now in hell.

Knowing God in All His Facets

Moses asked God to show him His ways so he could know Him. In essence, what Moses said was, "If You give me the revelation of who You are, I promise to seek You wholeheartedly until I have an encounter with You." I believe we cannot settle for just the initial encounter that we had with Jesus as our Savior; we must continually seek Him to have more encounters and experiences with Him and come to know Him more fully in all His various facets. We cannot be content knowing *about* Him. We must know *Him*. For example, many people know God as a provider, but they have yet to know Him as *their* Provider. We gain little by knowing that God provides for others if we do not know Him as *our* Provider. Do you know Him as your Provider? You need to have a personal encounter with Him as your Provider to receive His supernatural provision.

For a period of two months, I taught my church on knowing God as Provider, and people received both supernatural provision and jobs as He revealed Himself in this way. Provision is just one aspect of His glory, because the glory encompasses who God is in His *totality*. There are many names of God, though most believers know very few of them. Remember that the glory of God is the environment of God Himself. And the various facets of His glory correspond to His names and His ways. Each name of God reveals a specific promise of who He is for His people, an aspect of His nature and character. That is how we know that every manifestation of God comes from the very nature and character of God Himself. When God manifests an aspect of His glory, we are to receive from Him accordingly.

Many people miss out on divine experiences and encounters with His presence. They are satisfied with the theory, theology, and knowledge they have, but that should never be enough for us. Jesus promised that He would be with us every day of our lives. (See Matthew 28:20.) Affirming this truth should not be just a doctrinal declaration on our part. We should receive His promise by faith every day, knowing that He is with us—now with us! Then, we can experience His wonderful love, grace, strength, and power.

> *A satisfied soul loathes the honeycomb, but to a hungry soul every bitter thing is sweet.* (Proverbs 27:7)

The modern church has many resources: study Bibles, books, teachings on CD and DVD, dictionaries, computerized programs, online Bible studies, and the preaching of the Word through satellite, which reaches much of the world. These resources are easily accessed by many Christians, especially in Western nations. We have every available resource to help us grow and mature spiritually. Yet, we have so much knowledge that we have become selective to the point that some of us place our personal interests above the living and transforming Word of Jesus. As a result, some of us also often reject sound doctrine and adopt beliefs that seem to be more acceptable to our own lifestyles; in essence, we have become so self-satisfied that we "loathe the honeycomb." And yet, even though many people reject divine revelation, there is a "generation" of people—of all ages and nations—who genuinely thirst and hunger for God, people who have the mind-set of a disciple or dedicated student or apprentice of God and who humbly serve others in His name. This multitude yearns to learn more of Him in order to make a difference in the world. To them, even that which is bitter tastes sweet. (See verse 7.)

Being aware of our need for the presence of God keeps us hungry and thirsty for it.

A few years ago, I ministered to thousands of pastors and other church leaders in Trujillo, Peru. During the conference, I kept seeing a flag in one section of the meeting place that read, "Sons of the kingdom in the Peruvian jungle." That section was the most boisterous in their praise; they danced and jumped nonstop! After the service, they asked to speak with me, so we met in the hotel where I was staying. What I heard from them moved me beyond words. I called my team to hear what they had to say, so they could value what they have at home.

In the middle of the Peruvian jungle, where there are minimal economic resources, and where medical care is scarce, these people were mounting a spiritual revolution. The group had traveled over twenty-four hours by land to get to Trujillo for the opportunity to request spiritual covering by our ministry. They told us how hard they had to work to gather enough money to buy our material. They shared how our teaching on religion versus the kingdom was liberating the people from religiosity. They had been able to purchase our music and, through it, had revolutionized praise in their churches. Through our books, they had learned to hear the voice of God. They are radical, and the signs of the believer follow them! They find drug addicts where they are hiding, lead them to Christ, and deliver them. They minister healing to the sick and deliverance to the demon possessed. The hospitals send them their hopeless cases! They had never met me or seen me, and yet they were doing the same things through God's power that we do in our ministry. Their hunger and thirst for God and His power were releasing His hand of justice in their favor.

Since then, we have trained them further, providing them with spiritual resources and instructing them on the supernatural work and fatherhood of God. Every time I see them, Pastor Benito Risco shares testimonies of what God is doing in the Peruvian jungle. For example, a mayor in his area had skin cancer, to the degree that when he would lie down, his skin would peel off on his clothes. His body was one great boil. He had used up all of his resources seeking a cure, but the doctors gave him no hope of recovery. Pastor Benito and his people shared the gospel with him, and he received Jesus in his heart and attended a deliverance retreat where he was freed from unforgiveness, among other things. The following week, he noticed his skin looked new. He had been completely healed! Where there had been one boil after the other, now he had normal, healthy skin. Jesus had healed him! The doctors could not explain what had happened.

We think a miracle must be instantaneous.

Here is another testimony from Peru: A twenty-three-year-old man who was in the last stage of AIDS had been sent home from the hospital to die and was suffering with convulsions. Pastor Benito visited this young man, led him to Christ, and prayed for healing, and the young man felt a little better. I teach people to work out miracles, even when they do not manifest instantly, so they returned two more times to pray for him. Today, this young man is completely healed! When Pastor Benito first came under the umbrella of our ministry, he had twenty churches; now he has thirty, with over five thousand believers—in the middle of the jungle! We have trained and equipped these believers with every resource God has given us, and they are producing great fruit, manifesting the same miracles and signs that we see in our ministry. Even though they had experienced problems within their denominations and had suffered persecution for manifesting the power of Jesus, they chose to obey the voice of God because they wanted to see people saved and to provide answers to their needs. Their thirst for God keeps them seeking more and more of Him, and signs follow them!

Benefits and Blessings That Jesus Won at the Cross

I have said all of this to awaken in you a passion to know God intimately. This can be accomplished only through Jesus, who has made a way for us to go "behind the veil" of the Holy of Holies to enter into the presence of God. Through the following benefits and blessings that Jesus won at the cross, and which belong to those who receive Him as Savior, we can pursue our passion to know God.

1. The Holy of Holies Was Opened to Us

And Jesus cried out again with a loud voice, and yielded up His spirit. Then, behold, the veil of the temple was torn in two from top to bottom.

(Matthew 27:50–51)

Under the law, in the old covenant, only the high priest could enter the Holy of Holies in the temple once a year on the day of atonement to make restitution for the people's sins. In the Holy of Holies was the ark of the covenant, or the ark of God's presence. Yet, because of the death and resurrection of Jesus, we now have direct access to His presence, to His glory, in the heavenly Holy of Holies. The barrier that limited our access and kept us from penetrating the glory was sin and our sinful nature. But Jesus—God the Son, the Lamb of God—destroyed the stronghold of sin and death. When He died on the cross, the veil of the temple ripped from top to bottom so there would be no doubt that this was God's doing and not man's. Jesus alone granted us access into the presence of God. And, the moment the veil ripped, God's Son entered the Holy of Holies—the presence of the Father—as our High Priest and forerunner.

2. We Have Access to God's Presence by Jesus' Blood

Having boldness to enter the Holiest by the blood of Jesus.... (Hebrews 10:19)

God gives us access into His presence through the blood of Jesus, the perfect Lamb. When Jesus entered the heavenly Holy of Holies, He presented His blood on the heavenly altar, and His blood continually speaks in our favor before the Father. Without His blood, we would have no freedom to enter. In the above verse, the word translated *"boldness"* is the Greek word *parrhesia*, which means "freedom of speech; unreserved in speech; to speak openly and with honesty." This definition helps us to understand that merely "believing" in what Jesus did for us is not enough. We must say it, declare it, decree it. This is why the redeemed must testify saying, "I am redeemed." (See Psalm 107:2.)

The right to freedom of speech in America is granted to citizens by the United States Constitution, and it is granted in many other countries around the world by their governing documents and laws. We must realize that, through the blood of Jesus, God grants us freedom of speech in His presence;

we can come with confidence, without having any doubts, and speak openly to Him. God also wants us to declare out loud and with absolute freedom what the blood of Jesus did for us in defeating Satan and breaking his bondage over us.

3. We Have a New and Living Way to Enter Into God's Presence

...by a new and living way which He consecrated for us, through the veil, that is, His flesh. (Hebrews 10:20)

Jesus lived a life of obedience and self-denial, culminating with His sacrificial death on the cross for us, which opened the way into the Holy of Holies. He also set an example for all believers to follow in His footsteps.

- *Self-denial:* Jesus had to deny Himself to go to the cross and fulfill the Father's purpose for salvation. (See, for example, Matthew 26:39, 42.) He had to set aside His own will to do the will of the Father. This was the zenith of all His self-denial. Similarly, we must deny ourselves to say "no" to our rebellious, sinful nature. When the ego says, "I want," we respond, "No." What the ego thinks or feels is not important. The important thing is what our heavenly Father wants us to do. We cannot negotiate with the ego. It must be executed. It must die so that Jesus can live through us!

The first step to following Jesus as His disciple is to deny the ego.

- *Obedience:* Jesus showed us the way of obedience as the only path to reach maturity and enjoy eternal life; no rebellious person will enter the kingdom of heaven. Afflictions that come because of disobedience usually do not purify or mature, but the ones that come through obedience do. (See Hebrews 5:7–8.)

98 ⌣ *The Glory of God*

- **Suffering:** All of God's children must follow Jesus' example to be perfected in holiness through suffering. (See verses 8–9.) In the church today, the concept of suffering is rarely mentioned; in many cases, it is even rejected. Some people have reached the extreme of labeling it as a bad word because they refuse to accept the suffering that accompanies full obedience to God and His Word.

- **Death:** Jesus surrendered His life as a sacrifice to show us the path we are to follow: the way of death to ego, self, or the "flesh." We must choose to walk on this path of self-denial, suffering, obedience, and death on a daily basis so God can be glorified and manifested through us. (See, for example, Matthew 16:24–25.)

4. We Were Given a High Priest

And having a High Priest over the house of God....
(Hebrews 10:21)

In the heavenly Holy Place, we have a High Priest who welcomes us and gives us access to the presence of God Almighty—the Supreme Authority of the universe and of all created things. It is important to reemphasize that all of this is possible thanks only to Jesus; without Him, we would not have access to the presence of the Father—we would not be accepted, allowed to enter, or welcomed. Jesus is the center of everything.

Some years ago, I met President George W. Bush. When we shook hands, I sensed the authority that was upon him. At that moment, he was the most powerful man in the world, and being in his presence made me feel nervous. Seeing him face-to-face generated great emotion in me; it was the weight of governmental authority and political power that rested upon him. If this type of reaction can happen when we meet a human being who is really no different from other human beings, then imagine the impact of being in the presence of the living and all-powerful God, the King of Kings and Lord of Lords! Can you imagine having total access to Him, all of the time, everywhere? Jesus entered the Holy of Holies as High Priest to present the perfect sacrifice of His blood so that you and I can enter into the presence of the Father, anywhere, at any time, and under any circumstances—as many times as we want to. Praise God! Thanks to that access, God transfers His power and likeness to us, so we can do His works on earth. (See 2 Corinthians 3:18.)

For example, during one of the services in our local church, I called forth those who had been delivered from spirits of homosexuality, bisexuality, and transvestism to share their testimonies, and Raul came forward. The members of the congregation were deeply moved as they heard his testimony. He said that from the age of thirteen to the age of forty, he had been a homosexual and had practiced transvestism. He had also used drugs, consumed alcohol, smoked cigarettes, and practiced witchcraft. As time went by and he became older, he felt more and more drawn to feminine clothing; the desire was so strong that he began to carry a purse and to wear jewelry, makeup, high heels, skirts, blouses, and dresses. He even colored his hair blond and let it grow down to his waist.

This curse had likely come because his mother had practiced sexual relationships with a bisexual man while Raul was still in her womb. Raul also said he had been sexually abused by his uncle and his cousin when he was a child. When he came for deliverance, there was a moment in which the demons furiously manifested and shouted, "What are you doing here? I have been with you since you were a child!" But the power of the Lord delivered and restored him, giving him back his manhood and identity as a man of God. His received a total transformation!

In time, he met a woman in the church, fell in love with her, and married her. Today, he rejoices because he is free and has a beautiful family. He testifies that he no longer has homosexual desires. The blood of Jesus paid the price for him and gave him access to His grace and favor to activate the power of God and be delivered from the curse of sexual immorality.

Keys to Living a Life of Passionate Thirst for God

Would you like to have a thirst and passion for God? Let me share four keys that will help you to develop such a lifestyle.

1. Ask the Holy Spirit for the Desire to Drink of Him

On the last day, that great day of the feast, Jesus stood and cried out, saying, "If anyone thirsts, let him come to Me and drink." (John 7:37)

We must ask the Holy Spirit to give us the desire and thirst to drink from God's water of life. When we are filled with the Holy Spirit, with the evidence of speaking in other tongues (see Acts 2:4; 19:6; 1 Corinthians 14:18), the rivers of living water will begin to flow in us. However, there is more. The Bible teaches that we should be *continually* filled with the Holy Spirit. (See Ephesians 5:18 AMP.) However, we cannot walk in the Spirit until we experience being gloriously filled that first time. To be baptized by the Holy Spirit is the initial infilling by which we begin to experience the supernatural power and life of the Holy Spirit. But afterwards, we must seek to be continually filled. This filling enables us to walk in the Spirit at all times—for the long run.

Now, what benefit do we (or others) gain when we testify of how the Holy Spirit filled us many years ago if, today, we are dry rods? This is the condition of many people who, at one point, received the infilling of the Holy Spirit but never learned to drink of Him continually. So, to be baptized by the Spirit of God is only the first step. Then, we need the fire that will ignite us to carry out His plans on earth. After all of this, we also need to live exposed to His glory and fire in order to be continually filled. Otherwise, we will dry up, regardless of how great and powerful that first infilling was. We should never stop seeking to be continually filled by the Holy Spirit.

If you have only a remote desire to seek God but want to exchange it for true passion, the solution is to pray for the Holy

Spirit to descend upon you with His fire and to fill you with *His* passion! We will look more closely at this process in later chapters.

2. Let God Fill All in All

> *I saw the Lord sitting on a throne, high and lifted up, and the train of His robe **filled** the temple....*"*The whole earth is **full** of His glory!*"*...and the house was **filled** with smoke.* (Isaiah 6:1, 3–4)

Several times in these verses, we see the word *"filled"* or *"full."* I see the action as continuous, never ending. In other words, the train of His robe filled and continued to fill the temple. The smoke filled and continued to fill the house—the infilling never ended. The Bible says that Jesus fills *"all in all"* (Ephesians 1:23). God can fill all things with His fullness—our churches, cities, nations—the whole universe! He can fill and continue to fill. He is the only One who can fill the universe with His presence. The question is, how much of God do we want? How much we are filled with His fullness depends on how much of Him we desire. Some people think they are already sufficiently "full" of God, but God continues to live, continues to fill. Therefore, there is always more of Him to have; there is always something new and greater to receive. The glory of the Lord used to fill the tabernacle made by human hands (see, for example, Exodus 40:34), but today, He wants to fill the temple that He built and fill us with His fullness. (See, for example, Ephesians 1:22–23; 1 Peter 2:5.)

Thirst is a compulsive force that makes us forget our reputations and do "crazy" things.

If you thirst for God, stop living on past glories, like the Israelites did when, for example, they recalled their forefathers eating manna in the desert. They did not recognize that the

End 4/28/14

manna from heaven represented Christ, the Bread of Life, and that the *"true bread from heaven"* was living among them. (See John 6:30–35.) Today, Jesus lives in our hearts. Therefore, we do not have to live in the past—relying on former glories—or wait for tomorrow for something to happen. Just believe!

> *If anyone thirsts, let him come to Me and drink. He who believes in Me, as the Scripture has said, out of his heart will flow rivers of living water.* (John 7:37–38)

Again, let us read this in the continuous present: "If anyone thirsts and continues to thirst, let him come continually and drink continually. He who believes in Me, and follows Me continuously, as the Scripture has said, out of his heart will continuously flow rivers of living water." It is not enough to be touched by the Holy Spirit or to receive a blessing from Him. We need the continuous flow of the rivers. Once our thirst has been quenched, we can pray for the sick, testify of Jesus, and become effective instruments of God that will bless many people. But to maintain these ministries, we must keep returning to drink.

The key to being continually filled is to passionately seek God through worship, including singing hymns and other songs. We must constantly worship and commune with Him.

3. Be Willing to Take Risks

When we pursue the glory and choose to believe God for the supernatural, not only do we take the risk of moving into a new arena in our lives, as we discussed earlier, but we also risk other people's disapproval. Yet, we must take risks to minister God's grace to others, just as Jesus did. (See, for example, John 5:1–17.)

What are some of those risks? Many people in the church do not believe in the manifestations of the Holy Spirit, such as healing and miracles, because they think these things occurred only in the days of the apostles. We might therefore be misunderstood. We might face excommunication from a denomination, or experience criticism, ridicule, or even the loss of employment because of manifestations, such as laughing or "falling down" in the Spirit. If you are a pastor, you may lose members of your congregation and even some of its leaders. And yet, I ask you, "Are you willing to take the risk?"

Pastor Javier Aguilar of Málaga, Spain, is associated with our ministry. He used to belong to a denomination that does not believe in the supernatural. However, not long ago, he began to thirst for God. One day, while he was praying, he heard God say, "Guillermo Maldonado." He knew nothing about me, so he searched for me on the Internet. On our Web site, he noticed my book *Inner Healing and Deliverance*. Even though he did not believe in these things, he ordered the book, and, as a result of reading it, he was delivered from senseless jealousy that had been destroying his marriage. He continued to read my teachings and decided to take risks by preaching and demonstrating the power of God, which he did, even though he was excommunicated from his denomination.

Before this happened, he was diagnosed with hepatitis C—a potentially fatal disease that damages the liver. The doctors had given him only ten more years to live, but, full of faith, he rejected the diagnosis. He chose to believe the Lord, appropriated the power of the blood of Jesus, and declared himself healed. He even refused the idea of a liver transplant, saying, "Apostle Maldonado teaches that I have the authority to break and destroy all generational curses, in the name of Jesus." A month later, he returned to the doctor, who confirmed that all the tests had come back negative! The doctors told him that he was a lucky man, but he knows it was not luck. It was Jesus who healed him!

Pastor Javier's congregation has multiplied, and he is equipping and training his people. The Lord uses him and the members of his congregation to deliver the captives and heal the sick. For example, a child was suffering from a pulmonary sickness that kept him from growing and gaining weight. Pastor Javier sat the boy down and held his legs out straight while he prayed, and God manifested in such a magnificent way that the child's legs instantly grew five centimeters in the presence of witnesses. God is doing amazing wonders in Málaga, Spain, because one individual decided to take a risk! He launched himself in faith to see the glory of God descend upon his nation. He paid the price, and today, hundreds are reaping the benefits.

4. Change Rigid Mental, Religious, and Denominational Structures

Previously, we have talked about how established structures within the church—while not necessarily bad in themselves—can block the move of God in our lives and dull our passion for Him. For instance, some churches never deviate from a predetermined order of service. They start with prayer, sing three fast "praise songs" followed by three slow "worship songs," collect the offering, present the message, and end with an invitation to accept Jesus as Lord and Savior. Yet, what if the Holy Spirit wanted to change the order on a particular day to have the call to the lost occur before the presentation of the message? We must be ready and willing to break any structure that would keep Him from moving among us as He desires. The program is not as important as allowing the Holy Spirit to flow when He is ready to save souls.

Religiosity kills our passion and thirst for God.

Another example of following a rigid structure is not allowing the public ministry of tongues and interpretation during a service. We must break with human regulations, yield to the Holy Spirit, and trust Him for the results. We can be assured that if He is in control, nothing will get out of control. He is always orderly, never disorderly. The question is, do we please the Holy Spirit, or do we surrender to pressure from other people and follow an agenda created by men? If our priority is to please Him, then we must be willing to take risks and demonstrate that God still speaks to us and does miracles today and that the Holy Spirit should not be limited by the rigidity of our religious structures. We must allow the Spirit to give the glory and honor to God and to advance, extend, and establish His kingdom everywhere.

Religiosity is unfortunately prevalent in the church, killing our passion and thirst for God. A survey conducted by George Barna revealed that the average believer spends more time watching television, listening to music, or reading other books than reading the Bible. Most people die without ever winning a single soul for Jesus. In addition, "eight out of ten believers confess to never having entered into the presence of God, or experienced a connection with Him, during a worship service." In effect, these people follow a religion but don't really have a true relationship with God. They attend church and observe the norms, precepts, rules, rites, and traditions but do not experience His living, real, and tangible presence.[1]

Earlier, we talked about the Pharisees, who were the theologians and highest religious authority in the days of Jesus. Their logical and philosophical training, their knowledge of the law, and their theology were deep and extensive. Yet their carnal minds, which were bound to religiosity, blinded them and prevented them from experiencing their heavenly Father, who became flesh in Christ Jesus. They thought they were justified by works and personal sacrifice, and most of them never became aware of their need for Him; in fact, the opposite was true. They accused Jesus of being a heretic and tried to silence everyone who was willing to testify of His power. While they kept vigilant to ensure that the rites, traditions, doctrine, discipline, and law were observed, their religiosity destroyed their hunger and thirst for experiencing the true power of God. It kept them from having a supernatural experience with Him and from seeing that Jesus was the fulfillment of prophecy. Most never recognized Him as Messiah.

---

[1] George Barna, *Revolution* (Carol Stream, IL: Barna Books [Tyndale House Publishers], 2006), 31–37.

Busying ourselves with performing religious acts makes us forget our need for God.

By contrast, consider the following examples of people who were perhaps not as scholarly but had a greater awareness of their need for God. There was Simeon, an elderly man who recognized Jesus as the Messiah when He was only a newborn baby. His hunger for God's presence brought him the revelation of the Holy Spirit. (See Luke 2:25–32.) There was Zacchaeus the tax collector, who was small in stature but had a passion to know God. He risked his dignity and his source of wealth, and Jesus forgave his sins and transformed his life. (See Luke 19:1–10.) There was the despised Samaritan woman who risked talking to a Jew, dared to confess her immoral lifestyle, and learned to worship the true God. (See John 4:5–42.) Finally, consider the demon-possessed man who lived in the area of the Gadarenes. He desperately ran toward Jesus and was delivered of all demonic torment. (See Mark 5:1–20.)

All these people demonstrated a thirst for God, and they were blessed by Him in return. Religion is guilty of creating theologies, practices, rules, and norms that separate us from the blessings of God because they produce formats that, in the name of God, hinder us from receiving the true gospel. Christian living is not complicated if Jesus is first in our hearts. The religious people in His day did not recognize Him because they were comfortable in their positions, knowledge, training, and discipline, and in the ways they worked for God or offered great sacrifices to please Him. These things separated them from the truth; their ears were not ready to receive it.

On the other hand, those who recognized Jesus were aware of their needs. They desired change. They were tired of their situations. This leads us to the conclusion that, often, the people who are ready to be transformed are those who are deeper in sin; they are those who have tried everything else and have realized that nothing they've tried has worked or will work. They need a miracle!

Others who are ready to be transformed are sick and tired of religion. They may not be involved in blatant or deliberate sin, but they recognize that they are stagnant and need something new from God. They need to grow!

A hunger and thirst for God activates His provision. He will not manifest where there is no need.

If we do not feel we need anything—if we are comfortable where we are, with our works and rituals—then we will likely consider ridiculous or even heretical anything new that God is doing.

Every time I preach outside the United States, the greatest demand for the anointing of healing that is upon me comes from areas where the people hunger and thirst for God; they live in countries where they know that if He does not heal them, they will die because they lack health insurance or resources to visit a doctor. They are very aware of their need for God. All they have is their faith in Him for a miracle. This leads them to take risks and to travel great distances to receive healing or deliverance, either for themselves or for a loved one.

Not long ago, in a South American country, I met a woman who had traveled hundreds of miles to seek deliverance for her demon-possessed daughter. I had finished preaching and was spending time talking with people, and the crowd surrounding me was almost impenetrable. Yet this woman took her daughter, pushed the ushers aside, made her way through my personal security, and came up behind me. She was unstoppable! When she reached me, she was crying, sweating, and screaming. Security tried to take me out through another door, but I could feel the pain she was experiencing. I felt compassion for her need, and so I stopped. The woman desperately told me what was happening to her daughter, who was terrified. I rebuked the demon that was tormenting the girl and anointed her with oil, and she was instantly delivered! The expression on her face radically changed. The woman started to cry while embracing me and giving thanks to God. What happened? This mother, strongly aware of her need, risked everything to receive help and was rewarded.

Recover Your Passion for God!

Some people have an intellectual desire to seek the presence of God, but they have no passion for it. This type of "desire" is a passive mental attitude; it is merely a wish or a yearning to reach something without any accompanying action to attain it. Passion, on the other hand, is a driving force, a spiritual energy, that shapes our lifestyles, mentalities, and actions, leading us to fight to achieve our dreams. When a person is passionate about obtaining something, every thought and every ounce of his or her energy is dedicated to seeking and achieving that desired objective. Our mind-sets, our conversations, and our priorities are based on our hearts' true passions. Simple desire has never led anyone to accomplish anything. We need spiritual passion!

Avoid the Extremes of Lasciviousness and Lethargy

When we do not release our passion through fulfilling God's vision—expanding His kingdom on earth and winning souls—the tragic result is that we often (1) release passion in an unhealthy way by satisfying the desires of the flesh (lascivious behavior), which is actually the opposite of true passion, or (2) become lethargic toward spiritual matters.

The Greek word for "lasciviousness" is *aselgeia*, which means "excess," "sexual debauchery," "unbridled lust," and "indecency." Lasciviousness does not refer only to sexual immorality but also to other negative attitudes and behaviors, such as gluttony toward food, wasteful consumption of goods, hoarding of material things, and other manifestations of selfish desires in areas of our lives that have not been surrendered to Christ. Lasciviousness is unbridled living for self-centered and evil purposes, but true passion is unrestrained living for reaching the vision and purposes of God.

Lethargy is a mortal weapon on which the enemy relies to prevent the army of God from fulfilling God's intent. Its purpose is to cause us to lose our passion for Jesus and His kingdom. Apathy comes like a blanket, covering us in deep slumber. This is the state of much of the church today. Jesus warned the passive-minded,

> So then, because you are lukewarm, and neither cold nor hot, I will vomit you out of My mouth.
> (Revelation 3:16)

A serious problem in the church today, especially in the United States, is that as people grow spiritually and are blessed by God, they become less aware of their need for Him—for His presence and power. Many ministers are comfortable with their salaries, membership, and routine, and they do not appear to have a need for change. And when believers are healed, free, and prosperous, many of them become comfortable and stop seeking God. We cannot hunger and thirst for something if we are unaware that we need it. And if we do not believe we need something, we will not look for it with passion.

Strangely, when believers do seek God through fasting, prayer, and intercession, they are often regarded as fanatics. Yet many of these seekers understand that multitudes of people in the world are lost, and they desire to help them, through the power of the Holy Spirit. They know that some people are trapped in addiction, some are confused, some are despairing, some are suffering from broken homes, and some are on the verge of committing suicide. And still, much of the church does not respond in compassion. People who have been sedated by the spirit of lethargy lack the desire to serve God, and they cannot fight back against this passivity because they have no energy with which to do so. But once they are freed from lethargy through the power of the Holy Spirit, nothing will be able to stop them from doing the will of God and defeating the enemy! The Spirit of God can break the spirit of lethargy.

Be a Passionate Pioneer

Individuals who have passion cannot be stopped. They don't lose their focus or become discouraged. They always display strong convictions because they are dedicated to fulfilling their obligations and responsibilities. Those who are passionate for Jesus are consumed by a divine vision, which helps them to rise above daily opposition, struggles, and mere routines. Their passion leads them to break human patterns and rigid structures. They are pioneers of great changes. They have a sense of destiny and are moving toward specific goals. They are visionaries who live uncommon, irrepressible lives. They manifest their passion when they praise and worship God, give Him offerings, and serve Him wholeheartedly. They recognize the urgency of the times and desire to have a close, intimate relationship with the Holy Spirit. They want to tell others about Jesus and His kingdom, and they know that the spiritual harvest is ready for gathering. They love lost souls and are motivated to action by the purpose of God; hence, they work with excellence for Him.

God is using men and women, young and old—people of all races, languages, and professions—to further His kingdom. This is why the following testimony, which was shared by one of our House of Peace leaders in Miami, has touched me deeply. Rosslynn is only twenty-one years old. She had an ear infection that turned into meningitis, which then became more complicated through hydrocephalus (water and pressure in the brain). An operation reduced the pressure, but not before her optic nerves had been irreversibly damaged, so that her vision diminished until she was declared legally blind. She went to several doctors throughout Florida and even to the leading eye institute in the United States, but the diagnosis was that she would never see again. Then, during one of our church services, the Lord showed me that He wanted to heal the blind, and after I prayed for healing, Rosslynn's sight was supernaturally restored!

The power of God began to flow so mightily through her that many others were also healed after she prayed for them. This is the river of God that never stops flowing, and its current only becomes stronger. She started to evangelize everyone who crossed her path, telling people her testimony of healing. One afternoon, before her House of Peace meeting, she went to the mall to evangelize. There, she noticed that the vision center had a sale on eyeglasses that included free eye examinations. Boldly, she approached a group of eight people standing in line and asked for their names and prescriptions. In turn, she gave them a card with an address where they could go and claim free eyeglasses! At 7:00 p.m., the people were knocking on her door, demanding their eyeglasses. She welcomed them and said, "Please, give me thirty minutes to teach this lesson, and, at its conclusion, you will have what you came looking for." When she finished, she asked if she could pray for them, and they said yes. After presenting the plan of salvation, she took hold of the truths about healing and miracles that I had taught at our church, and she prayed with faith. The supernatural power of God came upon their eyes, and, to the glory of God, everyone's eyesight was restored!

Using the Bible, she had each person do what he or she could not do before—read without the aid of glasses—proving each person's healing. Imagine the people's surprise! And yet, interestingly, they still demanded their free eyeglasses. So, she said to them, "Let us return to the mall, which is only three minutes from here, and have your eyes checked for free." After they were examined, they were all told that they had 20/20 vision; they no longer needed glasses. The doctors could not get over their surprise, because, according to these people's medical histories, some had been diagnosed with -2 and -3 myopia and astigmatism; even a young man who had -5 myopia and had been declared legally blind in one eye was completely healed. (The orders for new eyeglasses were then canceled.) By the end of the evening, everyone had not only been healed but also saved! Praise the Lord!

The key to getting something you really want is to risk anything to get it.

Rosslynn is also the protagonist of the "craziest" testimony of evangelism I have ever heard. She was so excited over her miracle that she began to do many things she had not been able to do since losing her sight, including driving her car. One night, while driving, she was stopped by a police officer. I would like you to read what happened next, in the words of the officer, who e-mailed us:

On the night of March 21, I stopped a young woman, her last name was Rodríguez, for driving over the speed limit in a construction zone. She was under great emotional stress, crying and yelling excessively. She did not have a driver's license, and her documents showed that she was legally blind, for which reason she was arrested, handcuffed, and placed in the back of the police car. She never stopped talking while we waited for the tow truck to pick up her car. I told her to calm down, but she just kept on talking. Her tone of voice was so bold and sincere that I had no choice but to hear her out. She said her documents stated that she was legally blind because her optic nerve had died and could no longer receive information from her brain—she had the proof signed by her doctor—and yet, she could see perfectly well because God had healed her. She shared with me what she called the "Good News." In my patrol car, the presence of God touched me, and her testimony pierced my heart, while she said that she would demonstrate the power of God. She first guided me to confess what she called the "sinner's prayer." Then she prayed for my health, not knowing the doctors had diagnosed that I had gout and an accumulation of uric acid, which had produced cysts and tumors...and an inflammatory process that causes arthritis and renal damage that could become irreversible. When she finished praying for me, she asked me to check myself and find signs of my healing. In silence, I examined the places where the cysts and tumors had been, including my neck and legs. I could not find one cyst or tumor! I started to cry. I could not stop. God had healed me! I immediately opened the door of the car, removed the handcuffs, and told her to leave. But instead of leaving, she hugged me and said that Jesus loved me, and that He had saved and healed me. She deserved to pay over $300 in fines and spend at least three days in jail until the judge signed her bail, but I let her go. I will never forget that night. God completely transformed my life! [Rosslynn did renew her license after this!]

Think about the level of your zeal for God. Has it waned, so that you have turned toward lasciviousness? Are you obsessed with your job, sex, material goods, or a hobby? Then, recover your true passion for Him! Or, have you turned passive, so that you are not motivated or impressed by anything? Wake up and come out of your spiritual lethargy! Return to your first love. (See Revelation 2:1–5.) A needy world thirsts for the true God!

Dear friend, I would like to ask God to release His presence and cause you to hunger and thirst for Him like never before:

In the name of Jesus, I pray that the veil and bondage of religiosity be removed right now. I declare that your eyes are opened to understand and receive the truth. Lord, release hunger and thirst in the one reading this book, so that his or her desire to seek Jesus, in the power of His resurrection, will increase more each day. Amen.

EXPERIENCES WITH GOD

- Spend time in God's presence, seeking Him, even when you don't feel anything toward Him. Just making this effort will make a difference. *"Draw near to God and He will draw near to you"* (James 4:8).

- Always come thirsty to the Source of life—Jesus. During your personal time with God, read several psalms (such as 42, 63, and 84). Notice how David prayed with a passion for God, even during extreme trials. Use these psalms as prayers, and then continue talking with God in your own words.

7

Conditions, Rewards, and Benefits of the Glory

A passion for God is foundational for experiencing His glory. An essential way in which we can develop this passion is by recognizing and fulfilling four spiritual conditions for God's blessings, which are described in the Scripture passage below. When we do, we will receive rewards and benefits connected to these conditions. The Lord tells us,

> *If My people who are called by My name will humble themselves, and pray and seek My face, and turn from their wicked ways, then I will hear from heaven, and will forgive their sin and heal their land. Now My eyes will be open and My ears attentive to prayer made in this place.* (2 Chronicles 7:14–15)

Four Conditions for Receiving the Blessings of God's Glory

The above passage reveals the conditions God required of the Israelites to receive His blessings. They are the same conditions He places on us for His justice, revival, and glory to descend on our cities and nations—the same conditions that will establish and expand His kingdom on earth and bring salvation to millions of souls. Let us learn and fulfill these four conditions.

1. Humble Ourselves Before the Lord

Humbling ourselves is a freewill action. It means we bow before God, recognize our spiritual condition, and turn our

115

backs on sin. This is not an emotional experience as much as a decision. It is a way to remember who we are and from whence we came, to admit that only God can change our hearts because we are unable to do so in our own strength. Very often, I humble myself before my Father by prostrating myself on the floor. There, I am able to recognize that everything I have and everything I am are from Him. I know that this is my place: bowing before Him, with my face to the floor, in a position of humility.

Jesus illustrated our need to always have a humble attitude before the Father by calling a child to Himself and then telling His disciples, *"Unless you...become as little children, you will by no means enter the kingdom of heaven"* (Matthew 18:3). His statement depicts a child who believes what he is taught without questioning or argumentation.

2. Pray

It is not just about humbling ourselves, however; we must also pray, spending time talking with our heavenly Father. The disciples recognized that all Jesus was and did was the result of His prayer life; this is why they asked Him to teach them to pray. (See, for example, Luke 11:1–13.) Later on in this book, we will learn more about how we can pray in order to experience His presence.

3. Seek God's Face

To seek His face means to want to see Him face-to-face, as Moses, David, and Paul desired. This practice is similar to what we do when we want to know and understand another person and so position ourselves to see his or her eyes. When we seek God in this way, we will become one with Him in spirit and allow Him to shine through us.

The right motivation for seeking God should be to know the Lord intimately out of love for Him and for who He is. It is not enough to know about Him. We must know Him intimately. Jesus said,

And this is eternal life, that they may know You, the only true God, and Jesus Christ whom You have sent. (John 17:3)

God wants to reveal Himself to us as we come to know Him as a Person and have experiences and encounters with Him. If an individual is saved but does not seek to have a close and continuous relationship with God through Christ Jesus, then God is still like a stranger to that person; He is merely a doctrine, a religion—in other words, information! But God is so much more than that. He is a Person! We need to grow in our relationship with Him, day by day, from *"glory to glory"*— or, in this case, from intimacy to intimacy. Abraham walked with God and, in the end, became His friend. (See, for example, Isaiah 41:8.) The Lord called him a friend because they had continuous, intimate fellowship.

Each time I purpose to seek God's face, I do so with reverence, perseverance, and dedication. Some people have a very casual attitude about their relationships with God, seeking Him only when they have time to spare—or starting to develop a relationship with Him but not continuing in it. The Holy Spirit has taught me to have an attitude of worship, respect, and commitment when in His presence. This means that I seek His presence despite the consequences or the cost, and that I seek Him at all times.

And you will seek Me and find Me, when you search for Me with all your heart. (Jeremiah 29:13)

The above phrase *"with all your heart"* indicates fervor and passion; it raises the search to a new level, intensifying it beyond habitual prayer. To seek God with all your heart implies seeking Him with your totality—spirit, soul, and body—making yourself available to Him at any time, regardless of the place or circumstances. It also suggests yielding in His presence, being needy and desperate for Him. We can conclude, therefore, that seeking His presence cannot be done halfheartedly. To seek

God diligently means to do so with enthusiasm, fervor, passion, effort, and readiness. We must be prepared to overcome any barrier to make seeking Him a priority in our lives.

Sadly, I believe that the church as a whole has lost these attitudes and qualities. And yet, God is calling us to reinitiate our search for Him. The Word exhorts us to seek Him through fasting, prayer, and worship. In my church, we participate in seven-day and twenty-one-day fasts throughout the year. The main goal of these fasts is to seek God's face. The types of results we have experienced after these fasts include salvations, signs, debts paid off supernaturally, deliverances, healings, and all types of creative miracles.

4. Turn from Our Wicked Ways

The idea of "turning" includes repentance, and repentance means changing our old mentality and actions; it often means making a 180-degree turn to stop pursuing our wills and do the will of God. Changing the way we think allows our way of life to change. We acknowledge we were formerly going in the wrong way. We were friends of wickedness, of bad habits, of things that offended God. We ask His forgiveness for governing our own lives. We alter our direction and allow Jesus to take total control. We repent of our sins of commission and omission, change any behaviors that do not reflect God's character and ways, and turn to Him to become established in His ways.

Three Rewards of Seeking God's Face

If we will meet the above conditions, the Scripture says the following three results will take place:

1. God Will Hear Us

God is committed to hear our prayers. Therefore, if our prayers are not answered, one of the reasons may be that we are not keeping these four conditions. Wholeheartedly humbling ourselves and seeking God through prayer, as well as walking on the right path, releases many of God's promises. By faith, we know He hears our cries, and we can begin to declare that we receive what we have asked for. Then, whatever we bind on earth is bound in heaven, and whatever we loosen here on earth is loosened in heaven, also. (See Matthew 16:19; 18:18.)

2. God Will Forgive Our Sins

The forgiveness of God comes as we turn from our wicked ways. When we surrender to God and repent of all our sins, the first One who forgives us is God; then, a whole process of mutual forgiveness can be initiated with other people. It is only when God forgives us and fills us with His love that we are capable of forgiving ourselves and others. And forgiveness has an incredible healing effect in our lives.

> *But without faith it is impossible to please Him, for he who comes to God must believe that He is, and that He is a rewarder of those who diligently seek Him.*
> (Hebrews 11:6)

The kingdom of God is one of rewards. There are qualities and attitudes in our lives that will be greatly rewarded, such as faith, faithfulness, good stewardship, and seeking God, among others. Only the Lord can reward us for seeking Him. Our rewards will come in the form of healing for our bodies, deliverance for our souls, forgiveness, restoration, financial blessings, direction to carry out our purposes in God, and more.

During a retreat for inner healing and deliverance for new believers, a young man testified that he had grown up with much anger toward his father due to his psychological, physical, and verbal abuse of his mother. For as long as he could remember, he had witnessed his father abuse his mother. He therefore experienced disappointment, resentment, and hatred toward his father. His hatred became so strong that he decided to kill him. He found a knife, sharpened it, then waited for his father to provoke him. But someone else killed his father before he had the opportunity to do so. Losing his father in that way led to increased disappointment, guilt, and pain, as well as to additional anger because he had not been able to kill his father. His heart had been corrupted by hate and vengeance.

In addition, everything that had happened to him in his youth had led to his involvement with gangs. While he was a member, he used drugs, and his life was going from bad to worse. Then, he visited our church. This broken young man went to the altar, received Jesus, had an encounter with the presence of God, and was totally transformed. During the retreat, the presence of God touched him, and he cried like a child. A leader ministered deliverance, and he was freed from guilt, resentment, and pain. He forgave his father, and now he is completely free! The root of bitterness was removed from his heart, and he can now enjoy life.

3. God Will Heal Our "Land"—Our Total Being

"Land" in 2 Chronicles 7:14 represents one's personal life, family, ministry, job or business, community, and nation. In each of these areas, there is a great need for human beings to have a personal encounter with God. People yearn for healing in their bodies and souls, but they also want financial and spiritual prosperity. God wants to heal our "land" and end the consequences of sin and separation from Him: confusion and lack of direction, frustration and depression, discord, injustice, drug addiction, the shedding of innocent blood, and much more. However, the healing will not take place until we humble ourselves, pray, walk away from wickedness and ungodliness, and seek His presence. People who live in darkness (those who do not know God and His Word) are not able to do these things, but those of us who have learned the truth are obligated to do so. I have seen thousands of men and women who have obeyed these principles, including myself and my family, enjoy the shower of blessings the Lord sends. We are healthy, prosperous, and happy. Do you want to experience the same things? Decide now!

The young lions lack and suffer hunger; but those who
seek the LORD shall not lack any good thing.

(Psalm 34:10)

In my experience, people who truly seek God do not lack anything. God is faithful to keep His Word. Let us continue to study, work, and care for our families, but let us also seek God because He is our true Provider. We may experience moments in which things do not work out the way we want them to— in our finances, our health, or other life circumstances—but these situations are only temporary. In the end, God will work all things out in our favor. (See Romans 8:28.)

I sought the LORD, and He heard me, and delivered me
from all my fears.   (Psalm 34:4)

When we live in God's presence, fear cannot control us, and the dangers of this world cannot harm us. His perfect love casts out all fear. (See 1 John 4:18.) A young man who came to our church had been terribly afraid of failure and had never had a vision and direction for his life. He had grown up without a father, and although his mother had tried to fill the void in his heart, she had been unable to because she, also, was in great pain. Her divorce had led to years of depression, a condition that she had passed on to her son. He told me, "I suffered with depression for over twenty-nine years. I had no faith in myself and felt abandoned and rejected. I felt I had no future or plans. My life was sedentary. My thinking was limited, and I had no interests or aspirations."

This young man came to our church one Sunday when I was preaching on the spirit of fear and the boldness we need in order to take action and be brave, and the message impacted him. When I finished, I ministered deliverance from the spirit of fear and imparted the boldness of the Spirit. He testified that, since that day, his life has been completely transformed. He used to think he would have to deal with depression for the rest of his life, but now he dares to do things he had never imagined being capable of doing. The perfect love of God cast out all fear from his heart.

We Must Seek His Glory "Until…"

Sow for yourselves righteousness, reap the fruit of unfailing love, and break up your unplowed ground; for it is time to seek the LORD, until he comes and showers righteousness on you. (Hosea 10:12 NIV)

The Word is clear: the time has come to seek His face, His power, and His presence—His glory—*until* He descends and *until* His justice overflows in our lives. We cannot stop *until* it happens. This verse implies that we should pray *until* we experience the breakthrough. Revivals will not take place in ministries or churches *until* we seek His glory with passion and zeal. We will not see His righteousness prevail *until* His kingdom is established. Our cities and nations are full of sin and iniquity; hence, it is imperative that we cry out with all our might in prayer and intercession for a revival and a visitation from God. His justice will not come *until* there is a manifestation of the glory—of the presence of God and His kingdom.

Some people give up too soon, when the miracle is around the corner. They become discouraged and neither seek His face nor intercede "until." If you have been praying and seeking His face but have not received an answer, I encourage you to persevere. God will hear you! Keep seeking, and you will find; keep knocking, and it shall be opened to you. (See, for example, Matthew 7:7–8.)

If we do not know how to hear from God, we will have nothing relevant to say.

A husband and wife in our church were experiencing great financial difficulty and were on the verge of losing their home. They were taken to court, and foreclosure was a certainty. In such difficult circumstances, they decided to seek the favor of God through fasting and prayer during our congregational fast at the beginning of the year. They chose to completely trust in God. One night, while they were presenting their petition in the House of Peace, their mentor gave them a prophetic word, saying, "No one is going to force you out of your home." They took hold of God's promise, and, a few days later, they received a notarized letter from the bank stating that their debt had been paid in full and their case was closed. No one knows how this happened. No one they knew had paid the debt, and the bank had not forgiven it. It simply appeared paid. This was a supernatural provision allowing them to stay in their home. God did the miracle! This couple still does not understand how it happened, but miracles do not have natural explanations.

> And in every work that [King Hezekiah] began in the
> service of the house of God, in the law and in the commandment, to seek his God, he did it with all his heart.
> So he prospered. (2 Chronicles 31:21)

The word translated *"prospered"* is the Hebrew word *tsalach*, and among its meanings are "to advance," "to make progress," "to succeed," or "to be profitable." Prosperity is always connected to seeking God's presence because prosperity is more than financial stability—that is only a very small part of it. Prosperity goes hand in hand with being able to do the will of God, with having life in our spirits, and with enjoying health in body and soul. When we passionately seek the glory, or the manifest presence of God, He releases His favor and grace upon us, which leads to the provision of all our needs. We are transformed in His presence—so much so that we will never be the same again. Furthermore, we are equipped to carry the same blessings to our circle of influence.

Seeking God's Presence Releases His Blessings

The most important thing to understand is that we must passionately seek Him. If there is one thing I want to engrave on your heart, it is that the earnest seeking of the presence of God releases all of His blessings.

Who is able to be used by His glory? Every believer! The only prerequisite is to be constantly aware of our need for God. Our hunger and thirst will produce a fire that will continually consume us and fill us with the passion to see miracles, signs, and wonders manifest through us at any time of the day or night.

Are you satisfied with just reading about the powerful works of God related in the Bible or in books about past revivals? Are you content with the ministry you are in right now? Are you truly passionate for His presence? Are you sufficiently desperate for the salvation of the lost, to the extent that it keeps you awake at night? Do you hunger and thirst for God to bring a revival to your church and city? If so, you must be feeling a clamor within that says, "I must have it! I cannot live without it! I need to have it now because it is a fire that consumes me!"

He will be very gracious to you at the sound of your cry; when He hears it, He will answer you.

(Isaiah 30:19)

God will not intervene in our personal lives, families, ministries, cities, or nations until His people have reached a state of total desperation and realize there is no hope apart from Him. We know that salvation comes through Jesus, because He is the only path to take to escape eternal hell. No one knows how much time he or she has on earth. Therefore, we need to be sure of our salvation. Today, many churches speak little about hell, but salvation is a matter of urgency. Hell is real!

Prayer with a sense of desperation and urgency must be made *until* God has mercy. What is God waiting for? He waits for you and me to cry out in utter dependency, like a drowning man, "Help me!" God is waiting for His people to come to this point. Our prayer of desperation must be made with the aid of the *"Spirit of grace and supplication"* (Zechariah 12:10). This term refers to the supernatural intervention of God that goes beyond our abilities. God says that when the Spirit of grace comes, we will be given the ability to cry out like never before. (See Romans 8:26–27.)

If we have yet to experience a breakthrough in an area where we need one, it could be that we lack hunger and thirst for God.

It is time to pray for an outpouring of the Holy Spirit, for revival, for the manifestation of the glory of God, so that our lives, families, ministries, cities, and nations can be transformed. God is seeking committed people who are willing to make themselves available to Him as vessels through which He heals and delivers. Seek His face *until* His glory—His presence—manifests!

EXPERIENCES WITH GOD

- Pray this prayer with desperation, and God will hear your cry, forgive your sins, and heal your land: "Heavenly Father, I humble myself before You in the name of Jesus. I repent of my sins of commission and omission and turn from all ways that do not honor You. I declare myself free from them, and I will passionately seek You and experience Your presence."

- Near to where you live, there are many desperate souls crying out for God. Go to them and give them a word from Him. Pray for them, and teach them to seek His face with passion. Lead them to the Source where they can drink and quench their thirst for Him.

8

Changed and Transformed
by His Glory

In the past, there have been men and women of God who had memorable seasons in their lives; they walked in the glory as their ministries impacted cities and nations and strongly influenced various areas of society—political, educational, economic, health, and more. What happened to them? Where are they now? Some continued on their paths, while others simply disappeared from the public eye, never to be heard from again. Some lost their ministries because of sin in their lives, while others simply decided not to continue in them.

Many began in the right way, and some even had the appearance of being giants in the faith, but they did not allow God to continue transforming their lives. Perhaps they felt they had reached the peak of their ministries and therefore settled for maintaining their big congregations as they adapted to the surrounding culture, to the norms of their denominations, or to religious rules. Basically, they accepted and settled for the level they had reached, and they went on to preach lukewarm motivational messages that sounded nice but lacked the power to change lives.

Whatever We Conform to Becomes Our Reality

As we have seen, spiritual stagnancy begins when the presence and power of God cease to operate in our lives. From then on, everything becomes repetition—mere routine. The first warning sign of stagnancy is when we remain at a particular level of faith or manifestation of God's power. The men and women referred to above once flowed in the Spirit; they ministered during God's appointed time for them, but then they let it pass.

The greatest tragedy in life is to lose the presence of God and not even know it.

Becoming stagnant or settling for less than God's best because of various circumstances is the unequivocal sign that the glory of God has gone. The most incredible part of this state of affairs is that most people do not realize when it is happening to them. It is easy to perceive when the presence of God descends upon us, but we often fail to realize when it is gone.

When We Are No Longer Transformed, We Lose Relevancy

Stagnancy is evident not only when we become frozen in a particular state, unable to move forward, but also when we begin to move backward and fall to a prior level of faith. Sadly, that level of faith no longer works because challenges, obstacles, and adverse circumstances are often greater each day. Therefore, we need an actualized faith that comes through the continuous flow of revelation from God.

When we stop being transformed, we lose relevancy and can no longer be active members of the body of Christ. This is what happened to the leaders whose ministries died out or no longer flourished. They became "old wineskins," obsolete, so that they lost their spiritual influence and were unable to ride the next wave—the next move—of the Holy Spirit. They became religious, like the Pharisees described earlier.

When Christians cease to be changed, they lose their power and return to religion and formality.

In much of the church today, the gospel of the kingdom—the gospel that produces transformation rather than conformity—is no longer being fully preached. That is why many believers are no longer experiencing transformation. Over two thousand years ago, Jesus came as a Man to teach us the path to transformation. God took the form of a human being (see Philippians 2:5–8) so that humanity could be remade in His image.

> *For He made Him who knew no sin to be sin for us, that we might become the righteousness of God in Him.* (2 Corinthians 5:21)

At the cross, Jesus became the recipient of all the sins committed by humanity. He became like every other human being—carrying our iniquity and rebellion. Though He was born without sin and never sinned, He became sin of His own free will because of His love for us, in order to conform to our nature, so that we could *"become the righteousness of God in Him."* He left His heavenly glory behind to reach us in our fallen nature. Yet, when He was resurrected, He reclaimed His glory and then gave it back to His people, the church, so they could be transformed and shaped according to the glory of the Father.

Jesus conformed to our image so we could be transformed into His likeness.

Since we need to be continually transformed from glory to glory, there is a problem when we are not in the process of being changed—it means we do not currently walk in the glory of God. This is the reason for the lack of transformation we observe in the lives of many believers: they are not being regularly exposed to the glory of the Father.

God's Design for Christian Living

But the path of the just is like the shining sun, that
shines ever brighter unto the perfect day.
                                                    (Proverbs 4:18)

When we are born again, God places His presence in our spirits so that we receive the divine "breath of life" and His spiritual "DNA." God's DNA contains His glory, enabling us to become the same image of glory as His Son Jesus. Before being born again, we had Adam's sinful DNA, but now we have God's sanctified DNA. The Word encourages us to leave our pasts behind and to move toward perfection. (See, for example, Philippians 3:13–14.) Christian living was never designed to become stagnant. We were never to become comfortable at any stage of the way and settle there, but to go from faith to faith, from glory to glory, and from victory to victory, until we are transformed into the complete image of Jesus.

Spiritual maturity is measured by the change produced by the presence of God and His Word in our lives.

If we choose not to change, we hurt not only ourselves and the people in our lives but also future generations. We might even lose our ministries, marriages, jobs, or friends. However, when we choose to change, we can bless multitudes, even though we must be prepared for persecution and loss, as well. Change affects the way we hear the Word, and it influences our approach in our search for God. When we want to be transformed, we hear the Word attentively in order to receive its wisdom, and we apply it to our lives with an attitude of obedience.

Obstacles to Change and Transformation

Even when we yearn to be changed and transformed, we often discover certain character traits and behaviors within us that block the process. Let us uncover some of those obstacles so that we can effectively remove them.

1. Rebellion, Stubbornness, and Idolatry

For rebellion is as the sin of witchcraft, and stubbornness is as iniquity and idolatry. (1 Samuel 15:23)

Rebellion is resistance to divine authority. To be rebellious means to reject instruction, discipline, teachings, and correction, to resist obeying God and His delegated authorities. In the eyes of God, rebellion is the same as divination and witchcraft.

Rebellion says, "I will not do it," while stubbornness says, "I will do it my way."

Many believers and church leaders, influenced by the spirit of rebellion, reject fresh moves of the Holy Spirit—such as revivals and supernatural manifestations of God—because they do not understand them or simply do not care to understand them. Stubborn people persist in doing something, even when it is obviously wrong. (See, for example, Acts 9:1–5.) Idolatrous people worship their own ideas and tightly close themselves off to new thoughts.

2. Pride

When the spirit of pride influences people, they are unable to perceive their need to change (see, for example, 2 Corinthians 4:3–4), and they lose their fear of the Lord. Pride may be the only sin for which Satan will never make you feel guilty. I do not believe there is anyone in this world who has never dealt with pride. The only solution to pride is to develop a humble spirit.

Humility is a decision of the will expressed through an action.

We cannot ask God to make us humble. The Word commands us to humble ourselves. (See 1 Peter 5:6.) Although God has the power to humble us or to create circumstances that will do it for us, in the end, we are the only ones who can decide to humble ourselves. However, we can do so only through the grace given to us by the Holy Spirit. If we allow pride in our lives and never deal with it, we will eventually destroy ourselves.

3. Denying the Need for Change

Many people reject the transformation God wants to do in their lives because it proves painful for the self, or ego. The ego is the first to deny its need for change. This fact confirms that a genuine transformation begins with an adjustment of one's mind-set and attitude, and this type of adjustment is often difficult to achieve without humility, such as we just discussed—humility like that of a child. (See, for example, Mark 10:13–16.)

At the beginning of my pastoral ministry, I did not believe in deliverance, casting out demons, or generational curses. I understood the theory behind deliverance but never practiced it because I came from the school of thought that teaches that once a person is saved, there is no need for deliverance. However, one day, I realized that two years had passed and the membership of the congregation had not grown. We had become stagnant at two hundred members, and I could not understand why. It was then that the Lord used His prophets to make me realize what was happening: the people needed deliverance from generational curses and bondage from their pasts, such as unforgiveness, depression, addictions, and immorality.

Once I recognized this truth, I decided to change my attitudes and actions. I began to minister deliverance, and the growth of the congregation was released. What led me to make this change was knowing that many believers who were filled with the Holy Spirit, spoke in tongues, and served and worshipped God, still kept falling into depression, sexual bondage, and other sins, over and over again, and this touched my heart. Even though I had not been taught to minister deliverance, I received the revelation and trusted that it would be beneficial for the people.

The result was the release of such great blessings that we quickly became the size of a "megachurch." My emphasis here is not on the number of people who attend our church but on the quality of their faith. I also want to call attention to the fact that deliverance accelerates spiritual transformation, attracts unbelievers, and releases multiplication. Thousands of men and women have been delivered from the bondage of immorality, generational curses, unforgiveness, hate, witchcraft, and much more, all because I made the decision to kill my ego and to obey the revelation, rather than persisting in what I already "knew."

4. Religion and Legalism

Therefore, if you died with Christ from the basic principles of the world, why, as though living in the world, do you subject yourselves to regulations: "Do not touch, do not taste, do not handle," which all concern things which perish with the using according to the commandments and doctrines of men? These things indeed have an appearance of wisdom in self-imposed religion, false humility, and neglect of the body, but are of no value against the indulgence of the flesh.
(Colossians 2:20–23)

We have previously seen that "religion" comes from erroneous concepts that lead us to observe and obey sets of laws, norms, and man-made doctrines in order to gain favor with God; in short, it involves our personal efforts to please Him. There are numerous religions in the world today, such as Buddhism, Scientology, Kabbalah, Hinduism, Jehovah's Witnesses, Christian Science, Islam, Confucianism, and Mormonism. Unfortunately, many Christians have reduced Christianity to one more religion by following a set of rules or impositions. For example, they may believe women should not use makeup or wear jewelry. They may observe certain rituals, such as allowing the Lord's Supper to be taken only once a month or strictly keeping the Sabbath (I wholly believe in taking time to rest, which God calls us to, but I do not think that, under the new covenant, we have to forgo all activities on Sunday in order to be saved). They have turned faith into legalism. It is shameful for a preacher to teach about Christianity without demonstrating God's power or miracles, because what he is teaching is no more than another dead religion. Religious people convert doctrine into oppressive rules and then impose them upon people as the standard that should govern their lives.

Without the manifestations of the supernatural power of God, Christianity is like any other religion.

The following characteristics are evident in people who are religious or legalistic: (1) They observe all the rules but are rebellious toward the foundational principles of the Word of God, as well as the fresh move of the Holy Spirit. (2) They want to live *for* God rather than *off* God. The emphasis here is that our strength comes *from* God, not from doing things *for* Him. This is not just about living *for* God but allowing Him to live *through* us. (See, for example, Galatians 2:20.) Religious people obey the Word out of fear, insecurities, and pride in order to achieve acceptance, to attain a higher perceived level of holiness than others, or to feel superior, rather than doing so out of love and obedience to God. (3) They have a well-developed Christian "language" that they seldom or never practice. They confess Jesus with their lips, but their hearts are far from Him; they talk about serving God, but their actions differ from their words. (See Isaiah 29:13.) (4) They have an appearance of spirituality but lack the power thereof. (See 2 Timothy 3:5.) They are sick but lack the power to heal; they are depressed but lack the power to deliver; they suffer anger and bitterness because they lack the life of the Holy Spirit, which would produce spiritual fruit in them. (See Galatians 5:22–23.) (5) They are full of pride, contentiousness, bitterness, envy, and a competitive spirit. (6) They have not received the revelation that holiness is attained in God's presence and not by self-effort or good works; hence, they struggle in their own strength to become what God already has accomplished through Jesus. They try to be worthy of approaching Him through their own merits when they have been made worthy through Jesus' blood.

Are You Producing Fruit or Religion?

Now in the morning, as [Jesus] returned to the city, He was hungry. And seeing a fig tree by the road, He came to it and found nothing on it but leaves, and said to it, "Let no fruit grow on you ever again." Immediately the fig tree withered away. (Matthew 21:18–19)

A fig tree with foliage but no figs represents the religious spirit or religious activity—it has the appearance of holiness but lacks the power to give life. This is why it does not produce fruit for the kingdom. Something significant happened in this incident, and to fully understand what it represents, we must return to the account of Adam and Eve in Genesis. When the first human beings sinned, they became aware of their nakedness and hurried to cover themselves with fig leaves, thinking that this might make them acceptable in the eyes of God. They went before the Lord with contaminated souls, believing that the leaves would cover up their mistake.

When people feel guilty before God, they try to cover themselves externally with religious actions. Yet the Scriptures are clear about this fact: only the blood of Jesus can make us acceptable before the Father. (See, for example, Matthew 26:28.) In Genesis, God gave Adam and Eve coverings of animal skins rather than fig leaves. These sacrificed animals may represent the first symbol of Christ's sacrifice and shed blood on the cross to atone for our sin.

In the church today, there is a vast variety of "fig leaves"; some "leaves" may be found in Pentecostal churches and others in charismatic or evangelical ones; some may be found in Baptist congregations and others in Methodist ones; some may be found in Catholic houses of worship and others in Adventist ones, and so on. However, it is worth noting that within various Christian denominations or organizations, there are genuine believers who are producing fruit and are not religious. Regardless of what we call ourselves or what new denomination we may belong to, if we do not produce fruit for God, all we have is religion.

Fruit represents an interior life that pleases God. Fig leaves represent an external appearance that displeases Him.

Jesus went to the fig tree because He wanted to eat figs. He wanted to taste of its fruit. If Jesus came to eat of your fruit today, what would you be able to offer Him? What fruit would you give the Lord to eat? Do you have fruit of love, peace, and patience in your personal life? Can you offer Him the souls you have won for His kingdom, the marriages that have been restored, or the sick who have been healed? Or, are your life and ministry like the fig tree that Jesus cursed—having much foliage but no fruit, religious in appearance alone? If you have no fruit to offer Jesus, then, again, all you have is religion. Let us ask God not to curse us, as Jesus cursed the fig tree, and to enable us to allow His glory to transform us so that we can bear much fruit. (See John 15:5–8.)

The Word clearly teaches that we are saved by grace, not by laws or practices. (See Ephesians 2:8.) The Holy Spirit does not impose religion on us. Our obedience and love for God are expressed voluntarily, from the inside out.

Satan is God of This World
Let The Mind be in you that was also in
Christ Jesus

Conformed Versus Transformed

And do not be conformed to this world, but be trans-
formed....   (Romans 12:2)

The Greek word for *"conformed"* is *suschematizo.* This
term comes from two root words: *sun*, which means "with," and
schema, which means "figure," "form," "shape," "appearance,"
or "external condition." Thus, "to be conformed" refers to adap-
tation and accommodation, or taking the form, shape, or appearance of the pattern of this world.

When we conform to someone or something, we stop being transformed.

Suschematizo highlights a change in external—not internal—appearance. Sometimes, this term is translated as "disguise." The idea here is that the world is pushing to give us
form according to its pattern, similar to wearing new shoes that
rub against the natural shape of our feet—giving us an external and transitory appearance that does not transform us from
within. It does not remove sin, depression, or bitterness, or give
abundant life. It works through *"the lust of the flesh, the lust of
the eyes, and the pride of life"* (1 John 2:16). In essence, what
the world gives is only a disguise; it is not what we are meant to
be or can be in Christ.

When we look at ourselves in the light of these revelations,
certain questions arise: Am I truly transformed? Am I still the
same, or have I changed? Have I stopped being transformed?
Are the power and presence of God in my life? If not, when
did I lose the supernatural? Have I become irrelevant in the
advancement of the kingdom of God? When did my church services become routine?

God is calling every believer to change because He wants to
take us to another level. He wants to do a *"new thing"* (Isaiah 43:19)!

What Is Transformation?

...be transformed by the renewing of your mind.
(Romans 12:2)

In an earlier chapter, we noted that the Greek word for "*transformed*" is *metamorphoo*. *Meta* means "among," "with," "after," or "behind," and *morphoo* means "to form" or "to fashion." *Metamorphoo* therefore means "to change into another form," "to transform," or "to transfigure." The same term is used in Matthew 17:2 in regard to the transfiguration of Jesus. The main idea of the verb is to die to one form of life in order to be born into another.

For example, a caterpillar "dies" to its old, primitive form in order to transform into a beautiful butterfly. This is a natural process that the caterpillar must enter into to experience a better life. Likewise, it is natural for a baby, after nine months in its mother's womb, to come out and be born. The baby must enter a new realm through the birth process; otherwise, it will die and even endanger the life of its mother. Similarly, if we do not renew our minds spiritually, we will not be transformed, and, ultimately, we may lose our lives because stagnancy brings about spiritual death.

No transformation is permanent until we renew our minds.

God wants us to die to our old self (our old thinking processes and ways of life) and extend our minds toward the greater things He has for us. The renewal of our minds is like a door that gives us access to the supernatural because a total transformation, inspired by the Holy Spirit, will manifest in our character and behavior.

Morphoo indicates an internal structural transformation that results in an external change of our actions. *Schema*, on the other hand, which we saw was a root of the word translated *"conformed"* in Romans 12:2, shows merely an outward and superficial change, or a disguise. God wants us to have a total transformation and transfiguration so we can become like His Son Jesus. Are you conformed to your surroundings? Are you conformed to your denomination? Are you conformed to your sickness, poverty, or sin? Are you conformed to your circumstances?

What you conform to defines the way you think and live.

Right now, let us decide to change. Let us ask God to deliver us from everything to which we have conformed so that the Holy Spirit can begin to transform our lives, families, and ministries from within.

> *For do I now persuade men, or God? Or do I seek to please men? For if I still pleased men, I would not be a bondservant of Christ.* (Galatians 1:10)

To conform to the world is to show that you do not have hope for a better future. To be content is to rejoice in your present situation with the hope that it will change and that something better will come. Many people resist transformation because they have conformed. They are in bondage to man-made traditions and are afraid of change because they believe it could affect their positions, status, respectability, lifestyles, and even finances. On the other hand, they are also greatly dissatisfied because they know God has something more for them, but they do not know how to define or describe it, much less reach it. They feel trapped by their surroundings and socio-religious paradigms. They realize it has been a while since they felt the presence of God. And yet, they feel they owe their loyalty to men. They are emotionally bound to their leaders, pastors, ministries, systems, and organizations.

Please allow me to remind you that our loyalty is first and foremost to God, His kingdom, and His Word. Now, let me ask you: Do you seek to please men or God? Do you want to be conformed to one religion and to formalities, or do you want to be transformed from glory to glory to manifest the supernatural power of God in your family, church, city, and nation?

A generation that does not embrace change will not impact the world.

Stagnancy leads to frustration because what used to work no longer works. We need to break through the routine. Change must begin with us. It is our choice. We must ask the Holy Spirit to give us His grace to change. It will be a painful process, but remember that a change is not really a change until it is genuine and lasting. It is time to decide! Do we conform to please men, or do we transform to please God?

The Greatest "Weight" of the Glory Is Transformation

I have firsthand knowledge of what the glory of God has done in the lives of thousands of people. However, the most extraordinary manifestation of His presence—the greatest weight of His glory, the absolute demonstration of His power—takes place when the heart of an individual is transformed. This begins when a person is born again, and it continues with the ongoing transformation of his or her soul (mind and character). It is in the heart that we can trace the line that divides what religion cannot do, with its man-made regulations, and what the only true God can do. He alone can change a heart. This ability will never be surpassed by religion because religion lacks the authority and power to do it. Religion does not change anyone; only the manifest glory of God can change the life of an individual.

The only movement able to generate transformation in society is the outpouring of the glory of God.

A few years ago, a man began to attend our meetings whose testimony demonstrates the power of transformation through the glory of God. Eugenio was involved in Satanism, and he did not visit our church at first because he wanted Jesus. He came to kill me. For several years, he had been trained by five diabolical organizations in preparation to take my life. Satanists taught him by giving him strategies for how to reach me; they even told him how to kill me. His goal was to end the prosperity of King Jesus International Ministry.

The day he decided to carry out his mission, he came to one of our services with a gun hidden under his clothes. On that particular day, I was ministering deliverance and had no idea of this man's plans. I saw him run to the altar, crying, to receive Jesus. He was unable to harm me because God "disarmed" him! Thirty-five years of satanic involvement ended by him yielding to God. The plan of the devil against me was destroyed when it was confronted by the weight of glory that changes hearts. Eugenio later testified that, on several occasions, he had wanted to leave the cult and the evil he was doing, but he did not know how. He used to hate Jesus, but today, he feels alive and free. He feels human once more. He now realizes how much God loves him, and this love has turned him into a passionate believer in Jesus. Now he knows that people *can* walk away from Satanism because the power of Jesus is much greater than the power of Satan.

The glory of God, or His presence, exposes the spiritual condition of an individual.

Eugenio's full deliverance was difficult and lengthy, but his life has been completely transformed. He sees my wife and me as his spiritual parents, and he is now an instrument in God's hands to save souls. He prays for the sick and casts out demons. God healed him, and now Eugenio uses his life to heal others. God delivered him, and now he delivers others. If you want, you can become an instrument of God, like Eugenio is. (See 2 Corinthians 4:17.)

When we speak of the glory or presence of God, therefore, we are talking about transformation. Every time I see the manifest glory of God, I also see changes take place in people's lives. Many people desire the glory because they want to be transformed, but others reject it because, deep down, they really do not want to change.

It is interesting to note that many things in the world change, while the church prefers to remain stagnant or to take steps back. We isolate ourselves from the new things God is doing. Later, we realize that where there used to be life, blessings, and virtue, there is nothing left because God is no longer there. The cloud of His glory has moved to another location. Let us not be deceived. It is very dangerous to stay behind where the glory or presence of God no longer manifests.

Let us now see how transformation takes place in the manifestation of His glory.

The Purpose of Jesus' Transfiguration

And [Jesus] was transfigured before [Peter, James, and John]. His face shone like the sun, and His clothes became as white as the light. And behold, Moses and Elijah appeared to them, talking with Him....Behold, a bright cloud overshadowed them; and suddenly a voice came out of the cloud, saying, "This is My beloved Son, in whom I am well pleased. Hear Him!"
(Matthew 17:2–3, 5)

Why was Jesus transfigured? What was the purpose of His changing in this way, since He was perfect? Let us remember that Jesus had laid aside His glory before He came to this world to be a human being. Therefore, He experienced the same temptations that any of us experience. He had a mortal body, and His human nature was able to sin. Otherwise, the temptations He endured would have been meaningless. Until the moment of His transfiguration, Jesus had operated under the anointing of the Holy Spirit, but through this manifestation, He showed three of His disciples the glory that was available to them. When Jesus was transfigured, they were able to see Moses and Elijah with Him. I believe that Moses represents the Torah (the law) or the *logos* (the written Word of God); Elijah represents the church, God's power, and the *rhema* word; the cloud represents the glory; and Jesus represents the kingdom of God, as well as both the former glory and—through His forthcoming resurrection—the latter glory. (We will discuss the former and latter glory in chapter 12.)

In essence, Jesus revealed to these three disciples that He would bring His kingdom, His power, and His glory. Otherwise, how would the disciples have known that the two figures standing next to Jesus were Moses and Elijah? In the presence of God, people are known as they are, regardless of any time that may have separated them.

At the moment of Jesus' transfiguration, the disciples were able to see who Jesus was on the inside in a physical, visible, and tangible way. Likewise, the expression *transfiguration* reveals the fact that what is contained within us—His glory—can no longer be hidden or held back. It must explode, burst forth, and overcome the flesh.

We are transformed or transfigured by the renewing of our minds, and the transformation never stops. It is what should be taking place as we spend time in the presence of God. We are constantly being made into His image. We can no longer continue to be the same people we were in the past.

If the glory always produces change, then we are able to understand why many individual believers and leaders, as well as many ministries and churches, continue to be full of religion and reluctant to seek the manifest presence of God. The glory reveals the truth of who they are and the conditions of their hearts, and they know the instant they enter into it, they will have to submit to many changes—including those of renewed minds and character, as well as approaches to worship, preaching styles, and manner and length of church services, with the removal of rigid structures that impede the Holy Spirit from freely moving.

To avoid dealing with the glory, many people choose to preach a gospel of conformism rather than of transformation.

In the Spirit, we do not learn—we know! This is an instantaneous knowledge, one that comes quickly and without study. With this in mind, we can say that the transfiguration or transformation of Jesus demonstrates what you and I can hope to experience. It shows that we are on our way to becoming believers *transfigured* by God's glory. He has opened the way for us to walk in glory. This is not a theory or abstract theology. It is real, and it can be practiced today. It is available to us right now!

In one of our services, while we were singing, a spirit of worship descended. I shared this fact with the congregation and allowed it to flow freely. That day, we worshipped for an hour and a half, nonstop. Suddenly, three waves of the manifestation of God's glory began to take place: first, transformation—people were crying out to God in repentance; second, deliverance—people were being delivered without anyone touching them; and third, fire—people began to shout, "I'm burning up!" When I gave the altar call for salvation, many people went forward. I had prepared a solid message for that service, but when God's presence manifested, I set it aside and just worshipped with the people, and His glory descended. At the end of the service, people came to me and shared the changes they had experienced. It was glorious, and absolutely different from any protocol, format, or program we could have prepared.

How Does Transformation Take Place in a Believer?

Now the Lord is the Spirit; and where the Spirit of the Lord is, there is liberty. (2 Corinthians 3:17)

In the verses leading up to the above, Paul compared the glory that Moses experienced under the law with the glory of Jesus in the New Testament. The glory of the law was seen on Moses' face with a temporal splendor. Yet the glory of the Father is the face of Jesus, whose splendor is permanent. The Word teaches that *"where the Spirit of the Lord is, there is liberty."* The word *"liberty"* is translated from the Greek word *eleutheria*, which means "freedom without restrictions, regulations, norms, laws, or traditions." Jesus is the Lord over the church, and the Holy Spirit is the Lord within the church. The freedom given by the Holy Spirit empowers us to do the right thing in the presence of God. It is not the freedom to do as we will.

And all of us, as with unveiled face, [because we] continued to behold [in the Word of God] as in a mirror the glory of the Lord, are constantly being transfigured into His very own image in ever increasing splendor and from one degree of glory to another. (2 Corinthians 3:18 AMP)

When God's glory was present on Moses' face, he covered it with a veil so the people would not see the glory depart from his face. (See verses 13–16; Exodus 34:29–35.) That glory was temporal, but now we have unrestricted freedom. The veil has been removed, and we can look upon the glory of God in the face of Jesus continually, as if we were looking at it through a mirror. Each time we look into the "mirror," which is His Word, a direct and positive effect is produced in our hearts and minds.

Imagine standing in front of a mirror in which the reflected image is the perfected version of you. As you look upon that image, you begin to see yourself in the Spirit, as God sees you: His completed work, created in His image and likeness. This experience causes two things to happen: (1) You begin to change and conform into the image you see in the mirror, which is Jesus. (2) You begin to reflect and manifest the glory within you in front of other people.

Seeing Jesus Face-to-Face

Can we see Jesus face-to-face today? People always want to see Him in physical form, but seeing Him means more than just a visual experience. We can see Jesus in four ways:

1. In Spiritual Visions

Some people have seen Jesus in spiritual visions as He is described in the Gospels, but they are in the minority. For example, many people have told me that, during our services, they have seen Jesus walking with me on the platform or laying His hands upon the sick. Some have seen Him during other aspects of the manifestation of His glory, as well. People in the Bible, such as John in the book of Revelation, experienced spiritual visions of Jesus. (See Revelation 1:9–31.)

2. In the Biblical Record

If you have not seen Jesus in a spiritual vision, you can see Him in the Bible, which records how He walked among men through the streets of Jerusalem and the hills of Judea. There we see Jesus preaching the gospel of the kingdom, healing the sick, delivering those who were oppressed by the devil, restoring sight to the blind and hearing to the deaf, healing lepers, and raising the dead. Knowing that Jesus did these things should effect a change in our hearts that leads us to do the same.

In addition, "seeing" Jesus rise from the dead, in power and authority, and be seated with God on His heavenly throne will produce an internal transformation that will lead you to feel as much a child of God as Jesus is and to take the authority that

He executes from the throne. When I see Jesus operating in the supernatural, I can see myself doing the same. If I can see Him and do it, then you can, too!

3. Manifesting His Power Through Other People

In a similar way, when I see Jesus using other people—especially people who are weak and unknown and have shortcomings but who are willing and full of faith—to do miracles, signs, and wonders, I experience a transformation in my heart that inspires me to do the same. Witnessing Jesus healing or delivering people through others encourages me to believe in His resurrection power, which is real and for today.

4. Manifesting His Glory Through Us!

By His grace, God has used me to do some of the same things that Jesus did when He walked the earth, things that other men and women have also been able to do. Each time He uses me, I see Jesus raised from the dead and alive through me, which also leads me to have a fresh and deeper transformation.

What changes a person is not time spent in church but time spent in God's presence.

We do not change into the likeness of Jesus because we are disciplined people, because we pray a lot, because we give tithes, or because we attend church every week. All these things are good, and we should continue to practice them. However, what really changes us is seeing God face-to-face in His manifest glory! It is in His presence that we are transformed.

If we were to expose a new believer to the presence of God for one hour and compare him to a Christian who has known Jesus for ten years but has never experienced the presence of God beyond salvation, who do you think will look more like Jesus—the new believer or the more "mature" believer? Of course, the answer is the new believer, because he has been exposed to the presence of God for a longer period of time.

Entering Into the Glory

The glory enables us to reach nations, continents, and even the whole world because, as we have seen, in the realm of glory, it is no longer the faith, gifting, or measure of anointing of men or women in operation; it is God Himself doing the work. In addition, it is because the glory operates in dimensions. A spiritual dimension has great "coverage"; it consists of width, length, depth, and height:

> ...that you, being rooted and grounded in love, may be able to comprehend with all the saints what is the width and length and depth and height....
> (Ephesians 3:18)

To use a human illustration, the movie industry is constantly seeking to increase the level of realism in its films to enable audiences to have a unique experience each time they go to the theater. A few years ago, 3-D movies started becoming more popular. Using special glasses, a movie watcher can feel like an active participant in each scene, as if he or she is able to "touch" the people and objects in the movie. In other words, the movie experience has greater depth, height, and width.

Spiritually, the glory of God is like a 3-D movie, in the sense that it opens up a spiritual place to us. To know God's love means to know and experience Him by entering into His presence and becoming a part of Him. It is more than just studying Him from afar or even looking at Him; it means to be an active participant in His life. God cannot be understood with just our intellects; we will truly understand Him only when we experience Him. Even if our minds are unable to understand Him, we will feel as if we are inside Him—that we are in Him—and are becoming a part of Him. Then we will not only run but also jump from one dimension to another!

The anointing operates in levels or measures, but the glory operates in dimensions.

Width and length: expand your spiritual sight and see stadiums full of people seeking God. See thousands of young people running toward Jesus. *Depth and height*: extend your hands and reach...and then touch Him!

When the church operates in the glory, a spiritual acceleration takes place in quality and quantity—there is a transformation in people's character, the ministry grows, finances increase, and time is redeemed. Everything accelerates, and waiting time decreases. This happens because God is at work from a dimension that lacks the variables of time, space, and matter. This means that what used to take us ten years to accomplish under the anointing will now take only a year, a month, or maybe even one day in the glory. From one day to the next, He can make the righteous wealthy; in turn, these men and women can invest that wealth into the kingdom. Remember that a multitude of Hebrew slaves who had lived in Egypt for four hundred years—much of that time poor and without land— were liberated and made wealthy in only one day. God granted them grace and favor with the Egyptians, so that their former captors gave them their wealth of gold, silver, and clothing. (See Exodus 12:35–36.) If it takes a pastor, under the anointing, five years to have a two-hundred-member congregation, then, under the glory, it will take him one day to reach one thousand or more members. This is what happened at Pentecost. In one day, three thousand were added to the church. (See Acts 2.)

God will do the same for His people today. The time is now. You can enter into a new dimension of glory! As you do, realize that the glory is not just an "experience" for us to bask in but a transformation that allows us to minister to others in remarkable ways. Jesus taught us to pray saying "Our Father," not "My Father." He came to earth to show us how to reach out to others in salvation, healing, and deliverance, just as He did. Let us be transformed into His image *"in ever increasing splendor"* (2 Corinthians 3:18 AMP).

EXPERIENCES WITH GOD

- Make a list of the areas in your life where you feel spiritually stagnant, where you have conformed to the world, and where you feel there are obstacles to transformation in your life. Yield them to the Lord in prayer. Then, ask for His glory to manifest—and expect to be transformed.

- In what ways have you "seen" Jesus (1) in a spiritual vision, (2) in the Bible, (3) working through other people, and (4) working through your own life? Write down these ways and ask God to inspire you through them to do what Jesus did and to seek His glory and power to carry them out.

9

The Process of Our Transformation

When you enter into the presence of God, you are changed and transformed. You are ignited with spiritual passion to do His work, spreading His kingdom throughout this world. Let us continue to look at the process of our transformation by returning to the verse we looked at in the previous chapter:

> ...[because we] are constantly being transfigured ["transformed" NKJV] into His very own image in ever increasing splendor and from one degree of glory to another; [for this comes] from the Lord [Who is] the Spirit. (2 Corinthians 3:18 AMP)

The verb "transfigured," or "transformed," occurs in the continuous present, which indicates that we are constantly being transformed and moving from glory to glory. We can therefore ask, "What dimensions or realms of glory exist that we do not even know about and have not yet entered?" It's an exciting thought! I perceive in my spirit that there are various dimensions of revealed knowledge, such as creative miracles, signs, and wonders, that the church as a whole has not known. However, I also perceive that the day is coming when, for example, an "average" believer will enter a hospital and all the sick people will be healed.

How can I say this? I have been in a spiritual dimension in which all sick people are healed. I have entered that dimension only once, when I was in Cuba. We had organized a meeting that drew eight hundred people, and all who were sick walked away healed. God allowed me to have a taste of that dimension, and I will continue seeking it until it happens again.

Dimensions of Glory

How do we enter a dimension we have never known before? By revelation! God's prophets are carriers of His revelation, and they open up to us the knowledge of these realms of God's glory. For instance, there are dimensions of spiritual warfare and intercession that we have yet to understand, but I believe the day will come when only one word will be sufficient to win a city for Christ. I believe there are dimensions that will allow us to have dominion over the forces of nature, such as weather and fire. I hunger for those dimensions.

I dare to believe there are dimensions of creative miracles in the area of the mind, in which children and adults will be instantly healed of mental conditions. In due time, we will see body parts grow where there were none—arms and legs that were amputated or that were missing due to birth defects. Another dimension involves the area of being raised from the dead. Although resurrections have taken place in isolated incidents, I believe we will enter a time when this dimension of glory will seem normal to any believer. I tell you these things because I want to stir you up to seek the glory!

Pastor Félix Orquera, from Iquique, Chile, is associated with our ministry, and he has seen the membership of his church triple in the last three years. He is also experiencing a significant breakthrough in his congregation regarding healing, miracles, and wonders. Not long ago, he shared the following with me:

> A sister in Christ in our congregation received a call from a family member informing her that her brother had suffered a fatal heart attack. She instantly remembered the words of boldness I had imparted, after having received them from Apostle Maldonado. The man had been declared clinically dead two hours earlier. However, she asked the family member who called

her to place the phone to the ear of her dead brother. She then proceeded to pray with boldness and courage, "I order you to rise up and live, right now, in the name of Jesus!" Suddenly, she began to hear shouting from the people who were with her brother. The man began to move. He sat on the bed as if nothing had happened. The doctors are still baffled as to what transpired there. After performing new tests to check out his heart, their surprise was even greater because they could not find any trace that could prove he had suffered a cardiac arrest. From the medical standpoint, they could not understand how he could be alive *and* healthy.

This man is alive today—praise God—because there are people who have experienced intimacy with Him and learned to use boldness to work incredible acts such as this.

Another realm of the glory is what I call "open heaven." When we are under an open heaven, we can go to public places and know the specific conditions of certain people, cities, or nations. Then, there is the dimension of supernatural provision, in which God releases wealth from one day to the next, as I mentioned earlier. In this dimension, there will be transferences of wealth from the "Gentiles" to the children of God. (See Proverbs 13:22.) And there is a dimension that has to do with the salvation of souls, in which lost people will run to individual believers, as well as to churches and ministries. They will come by the thousands to give their lives to the Lord. In just one day, we will see even millions surrender to Christ.

Many years ago, Apostle Ronald Short—a man whom I greatly admire and who was my spiritual father at the beginning of my ministry—had an astonishing experience with the glory of God. Here is what he said about that experience:

> When I received Jesus as my Savior, I became passionate about the Word, and Hebrews 6:5 captivated my attention: "*...and have tasted the good word of God and the powers of the age to come.*" And the

Lord said to me, "I will show you how this can be possible." In the two weeks that followed, I walked in an incredible realm of the supernatural. The gifts of the Holy Spirit (1 Corinthians 12) began to operate at a higher level. My prayers were answered even before I finished them. I would be in a tall building, and I would know if a certain person was there. When someone would stand before me, I could immediately perceive everything that had happened to that person and be able to minister to him or her. I was able to read the entire New Testament in one afternoon and completely understand it. When I visited a Christian bookstore, I could touch the books and know which were written by people who knew about Jesus and which were written by those who knew Jesus because from the latter would flow a continuous anointing. I knew the spiritual thoughts of the people. Any thought related to Jesus and the Word was clear and distinguishable—the rest were like static. After two weeks, the curtain began to close, and, to this day, except for sporadic moments, I have never been able to experience that realm at that level again.

I believe we are now entering into a dimension of glory that is to become commonplace to the children of God: walking in the supernatural in a continuous, daily manner.

The will of God must be revealed; otherwise, it cannot be done on earth.

"Transformed...from glory to glory" (2 Corinthians 3:18). The Word enables us to understand that we are transformed from "one place to another," or that we advance from one dimension to another. The beginning is not set; it is something that already was—a constant activity that goes from one point

to another and from one dimension to another. This is why the glory of God is a movement. The Bible confirms this when it mentions the *shekinah* cloud of the Lord continually moving in the desert. This activity is produced by the Holy Spirit. As a matter of fact, every manifestation of the glory is attributed to Him.

When we walk under the cloud of glory, we are in continuous movement, without getting tired. The people of Israel continually walked through the desert, but no one ever complained of getting tired. The cloud provided a shadow of protection from the sun by day and a column of fire, light, and warmth by night. (See Exodus 13:21.) God told Moses to construct a movable tabernacle in the desert. This tells us that if we want to move with the glory of God, we cannot do so with a mentality of settling, of putting down roots, and of having "arrived." Rather, we are to have a mind-set of constant movement, so we can go from one dimension of glory to another.

Moving from One Dimension of Glory to a Higher Dimension

God has different ways of leading us from one dimension to another. Let us look at two of these avenues:

1. God Allows Tribulations, Trials, and Persecutions

> *For our light affliction, which is but for a moment, **is working for us a far more exceeding and eternal weight of glory**.*　　　　(2 Corinthians 4:17)

God works in the midst of tribulations, trials, and persecutions to lead us into new dimensions of glory. I am not saying that God sends tribulations, but, when they come, He uses them to manifest His glory. Remember that one meaning of the word *kabowd* (glory) is "weight." I have ministered in services where the presence or the *kabowd* of God manifests, and even the thinnest person there appears to gain three times his weight in a fraction of a second. This explains why the ushers are sometimes unable to hold up a person who falls under the power of the Holy Spirit—it is because of His *kabowd*. Some people have reported that their hands, head, or legs felt very heavy. The weight of God's presence is felt in different ways.

Each dimension of glory contains a measure of weight of the essence of God.

Temporal tribulation, therefore, produces a greater weight of glory in us. Consider the following illustration: if we enter a trial with "ten pounds" of weight in glory (keep in mind that this is only an example because the glory cannot be measured in pounds) and we learn to rejoice through that trial, we will make it to the other side of the difficulty weighing "twenty pounds" in weight of glory. During crisis times, we need to die to self—the ego—and humble ourselves; however, above all, this is the time when we must learn to depend more on God. This process liberates us from self, rebellion, and religious striving, thus allowing God to be Lord in our circumstances. We must rejoice in our tribulations because they produce in us a "greater, more excellent, and eternal weight of glory." This is how God manifests His glory, which is in us. In contrast, if we complain or sink into self-pity, we will go backward and never reach that new dimension of His glory.

2. God Uses Revelation or Revealed Knowledge

For in [the gospel of Christ] *the righteousness of God is revealed from faith to faith.* (Romans 1:17)

Notice that movement is depicted in the above verse. It is revelation, or revealed knowledge, that takes us *"from faith to faith"* and from glory to glory. The inherent characteristic of all movements is that they transport us from one place to another.

In this way, neither our faith nor the glory can become stagnant. If that happens, it is because there is no revelation to move us forward.

As we discussed earlier, our faith remains at the level where revealed knowledge ends. Other dimensions of faith, glory, and miracles await us. And yet, when we lack revealed knowledge, we become "stuck," not knowing where to go or where our paths will lead us. Even though we know God has new territories, revelations, and manifestations for us, we lack the ability to reach them.

In what dimension of glory are you in right now? Are you "stuck" there, desiring to enter a new dimension? Is the growth of your church or ministry at a standstill? Has your business stopped growing? Today, God invites you to enter into His cloud—into a new dimension of His glory. He wants to give you a greater weight of His *kabowd*, one you have never before experienced. Liberate yourself from all rigidness and begin to move. Cast out religion, shake off apathy and formality, and decide to enter the cloud of His presence so that you can experience a new dimension of His glory. I challenge you to earnestly seek various dimension of the glory of God as you receive the revelation of them.

Our measure of faith will always be determined by the degree of revelation we have.

A number of years ago, our ministry was located in a building in a shopping center. However, we were suddenly faced with the need to find a new location because it became too small for the number of people attending our services. Then, through prophecy came the revelation that we would purchase a synagogue in which to hold services. We had to take a leap into a greater dimension of faith to purchase that synagogue, which had the capacity for one thousand people.

But the growth did not end there. We multiplied so quickly that, only a short time later, we were faced with a greater challenge—we had to take another leap of faith to buy land and construct a building that cost twenty-seven million dollars. A prophet friend of mine released a specific word concerning the location of the land and the miracles God would do; and so, we began to take action according to the word we received. She said the land was near an airport and that it had a man-made lake behind it. Together with my wife and other ministers of the church, we searched the city for such a place, in preparation to take the leap, and we finally found the land. The revelation led us to take that leap of faith, which was humanly impossible, but when the Holy Spirit confirmed it was the place, we began to walk around it, taking possession of the land in the Spirit.

Leaping into other dimensions of faith is not a theory. I have done it—not through my ability, faith, or power but by the revelation, faith, and power of God. Experiences such as we had with our church buildings are the things that raise us up and encourage us to take the next supernatural leap. We took leaps from one dimension of faith into a greater one. The revelation is what leads us to believe—and receive.

Revelation induces, activates, and accelerates spiritual motion.

God will never lead His people into another dimension until He gives both the revelation and the provision. We purchased the land and began to build according to God's word to us, which was progressively released through His prophets. Today, we worship God in a building that has a current market value of close to fifty million dollars. As I stated earlier, the manifestation of the glory of God accelerates things. We witnessed that acceleration when we built the church in only twenty-eight months—an unusual feat in the secular realm, and even more unusual in the Christian realm. We also know that the vision of God brings His provision; as I wrote earlier, we constructed the building debt free. Every expense was paid for in cash—supernaturally!

Now, we are ready to leap once more into a new dimension of faith and glory. We are in the planning stages of building a stadium with the capacity for twenty thousand people, and we are doing it debt free, also. One day, while in the presence of the Lord, I received a divine revelation in which the Lord said to me, "I want you to look for land for the new arena." He also said there was a piece of real estate for which I would pay half its value. Only a short time later, a prophet of God confirmed the same word I had received from God in the intimacy of my communion with Him. I immediately began to look for the land in preparation to take the leap, and I found 102 acres in an excellent location. The land was valued at 19 million dollars, but we purchased it for only 6.2 million—which is actually about *one-third* of the original price! As the Scriptures say, the Lord *"is able to do exceedingly abundantly above all that we ask or think"* (Ephesians 3:20).

A Weight of Glory Not Appropriate for Everyone

And the Lord said to Moses, "Behold, I come to you in the thick cloud, that the people may hear when I speak with you, and believe you forever." (Exodus 19:9)

God spoke to Moses from a thick cloud. The people could hear but not enter the cloud because, if they did, they would immediately die. Only Moses could enter it; hence, he had to build a small tent in which to meet with God. (See Exodus 33:7–11.) I can imagine Moses falling on his knees because of the weight of the *kabowd.* It is likely that he had a hard time breathing in the presence of such weight. However, when he exited the tent, his face glowed with the fire of God's presence. His energy was renewed and his body revitalized because the weight of the glory of God always strengthens, never exhausts.

Few people have access to this atmosphere because they are not suited for it. Most of the Israelites in Moses' day wanted the works of God but not the ways of God. They wanted the benefits of God—health, deliverance, and so forth—but not God Himself. They didn't want to pay the price to live in the fire, because, to do so, one has to be holy. Isn't that sad? Instead, they told Moses, in effect, "*You* go talk to God for us." (See Exodus 20:18–21.) The atmosphere of glory is only for those who hunger and thirst for God, for those who continuously enter into His presence, sanctifying and purifying their hearts with the blood of Jesus. It is interesting to note that Moses' right-hand man, Joshua, remained in the tent with the presence of God even after Moses had left it. His experiences in the presence must have had a lasting impact on him, shaping him as the next leader of the Israelites, who would bring them into the Promised Land. (See Exodus 33:11.)

There are dimensions of the glory of God that few humans can stand.

Smith Wigglesworth, a British evangelist in the first half of the twentieth century, was known as the Apostle of Faith. He invited several pastors and friends to pray with him. When they were together, they began to worship the Lord, and His presence was so powerful that the atmosphere began to feel heavy. One by one, the others left because they could not withstand it; only one pastor decided to stay. This man stayed a while longer, but when the weight got to be too much for him, also, he left, though not before asking Wigglesworth to invite him again. The next time the meeting took place, the same thing happened. The glory of God filled that place, and the pastor felt like he was going to explode. He said, in effect, "Very few men can withstand this type of atmosphere."[2]

---

[2] See George Stormont, *Smith Wigglesworth: A Man Who Walked with God* (Tulsa, OK: Harrison House, 2009), 70, and Peter J. Madden, *The Keys to Wigglesworth's Power* (New Kensington, PA: Whitaker House, 2000), 130–32.

I yearn for a *"far more exceeding and eternal weight of glory"* (2 Corinthians 4:17) because that alone can change families, cities, and nations. Some time ago, I was invited to minister in Cochabamba, Bolivia, where approximately 3,500 pastors and leaders gathered together. On the last day of the meetings, the Holy Spirit led me to teach and guide the people to have an encounter with His glory. After the teaching, the presence of God manifested, and everyone began to cry out. Each person there was touched by the presence of God. I heard some people cry out for forgiveness of their sins and ask God how to move in the supernatural, while others simply expressed that they wanted to serve Him. Everyone cried out according to the desire of his or her heart.

In the midst of this movement, God transformed the hearts of every leader present. The proof is that they took everything they received and shared it with their own congregations. Furthermore, miracles and amazing healings took place. A woman diagnosed with terminal cancer had been carried in on a stretcher. When she was exposed to the glory of God, she got up, completely healed! Another indigenous woman, who did not speak Spanish, had a type of rash. She had terrible boils that covered her entire face. This woman had already consulted all the witches and sorcerers in the region. She had desperately searched for a solution, but no one was able to heal her. Then, the presence of God fell upon her—without anyone touching her or translating anything we were saying—and, suddenly, every boil disappeared, and she received her healing. On the platform, she was yelling in Quechua, which is the dialect of her region, "Thank You, Daddy! What the witches and sorcerers were unable to do in years, You have done!" The weight of glory was so strong that my entire team began to cry. The musicians fell under the weight of the presence of God. No one could stand. I lasted on my feet the longest, until I, too, had to kneel because it was impossible for me to remain standing. The 3,500 leaders gathered in that building were deeply impacted by His glory.

The glory of God releases and produces something in the hearts of people that cannot be received directly through hearing teachings, reading books, listening to messages on CD, or receiving an anointing through the laying on of hands—even though these are good things to do and can point us to the glory. What the glory of God releases can be received only in His presence; there, people's spiritual DNA is enlivened. Their vision is enlarged, and a passion for the kingdom and souls is ignited within them. The glory of God releases empathy and love for others, as it generates zeal to do His will. Above all, a thirst for seeking the face of God and knowing Him intimately increases exponentially in people. If we sincerely want to be changed and transformed, we must dare to enter into His presence and stay in His movement, from glory to glory, without stopping or becoming stagnant.

How Should We Respond to God's Glory?

To experience continuous transformation, we also need to know how to respond when the glory of God manifests. There is no formula, method, or manual regarding how to do this. However, I can tell you what I have learned and testify of what has taken place in my own life when I have entered into His presence.

The most effective way to respond when God's presence manifests is to worship and totally surrender to Him.

If we refuse to respond when God visits us, we will be judged. Sometimes, His presence comes to heal or deliver, and people are aware of it, but they do nothing about it; they don't respond in faith. Even though God acts according to His sovereign will, our part is to worship Him, or to say, "Lord, I receive my healing. I receive my deliverance." We have to respond to Him when His presence comes. Sometimes, our faulty attitudes are reflected in our body language. For example, we may cross our arms when we choose to be mere spectators and seek only to observe what is happening around us rather than entering into it; our expressions may appear indifferent or lack reverence; we may talk to others in a casual manner and distract them from the ways in which God is working. On such occasions, we grieve the Holy Spirit, because His presence is a gift to us that we have chosen to ignore or even reject. God doesn't come where He is "tolerated"; He comes where He is celebrated.

> *Then Jacob awoke from his sleep and said, "Surely the LORD is in this place, and I did not know it."*
> (Genesis 28:16)

Jacob had not been aware that the presence of God was there with him. He had not perceived it. The same thing happens today with many believers. I have been in services where the presence of God was so powerful that people all over the church were crying, lying prostrate on the floor, and humbled under the weight of His glory, while others seemed totally unaware of what was taking place. They did not even realize the glory of God was present.

Is it possible for us to be in the same place where the glory of God is present and not realize it? Yes, it is possible. As we saw, it happened to Jacob. Why is this the case? There are many reasons, but, most often, it is sin, such as bitterness, resentment, and a lack of forgiveness. Or, it may be that we are totally absorbed in our own problems, so that our spiritual perception is completely turned off. We need to remain sensitive to how the Spirit of God is moving. The next time we recognize His presence, we can respond in faith and worship. When Jacob did realize that God was with him, he set up a pillar, marking the place, and anointed it with oil. (See verse 18.)

Let me share what I have experienced in God's presence: sometimes, I cry; at other times, I want to run out into the congregation and lay hands on people for healing. On occasion, I want to preach or prophesy, deliver people from demonic oppression, or minister miracles. Again, preachers almost always tend to carry out an agenda, a predetermined program, during a church service. However, that should not be our attitude when we are in the glory of His presence. Since God alone takes the initiative, our response should be to worship, worship, and continue to worship, and to obey whatever He wants us to do. We must learn to rest in His sovereignty, follow the leading of His presence, and permit Him to work. Our priority should always be to allow His glory to manifest. Again, if God, in His sovereignty, chooses not to take action, then—and only then—we must take hold of faith and the anointing and do what we already know He has called us to do: preach the kingdom, heal the sick, and deliver the demon possessed.

God will anoint you for everything He wants you to do, but in the cloud of His glory, He will do His own works.

God is raising up a new generation of men and women of all ages who will know how to respond to His presence. This generation will thirst for His glory to manifest on earth. The darkness in the world will become denser each day, and wickedness will multiply, but the manifestation of God on earth will also become more powerful and weighty with each passing moment. I believe I will witness this with my own eyes. This is a glorious generation that will impact the world and gather the greatest harvest of souls ever seen. Entire cities and nations will be shaken by His glory and will recognize Jesus as Lord and Savior. The most remarkable manifestations of His presence—through miracles, signs, and wonders—will take place before millions around the world, in an instant.

Are you willing to be transformed and join this new generation? If your answer is yes, God will take care of everything because He does not want you to waste your time following religious norms. He wants you to enjoy the highest dimension of His glory.

Surely, no change is easy; it is usually difficult and painful. But if that is what it takes to enter into a new and greater dimension of God's *kabowd*, then I want it. Do you want to be changed under the glory of God? Decide right now, and dare to be transformed so you can begin to leap from glory to glory!

EXPERIENCES WITH GOD

- Prepare your body and spirit, through fasting and prayer, to be changed by God. Do not conform to the world or to your circumstances.

- What revelation of the dimensions of God's glory has stood out to you most in this chapter? Begin to ask God to reveal it to you so you can enter into it.

- Allow your friends, family, and brothers and sisters at church to see your transformation, but, most of all, let your transformation be seen by the unbelievers.

10

Creating an Atmosphere of Worship to Bring His Presence

One of the greatest obstacles to seeing a demonstration of the supernatural power of God that I have found in the diverse places around the world where I have preached is that a spiritual atmosphere does not exist for the glory or His presence to manifest. On these occasions, it is difficult for me to preach the Word because the hearts of the people are not sensitive to receive it. If the spiritual atmosphere is hard, the glory does not descend, and, consequently, few healings and miracles take place.

A hard spiritual atmosphere may be the result of poor praise and worship. When people are not worshipping God in spirit and in truth on a continuous basis, they are not able to create the environment to bring His presence. In this chapter, I want to show you how to invite a spiritual atmosphere of worship for the glory to manifest and for miracles, signs, and wonders to take place. We will learn how we can become what the Bible calls *"true worshippers"* (John 4:23)—something that cannot be accomplished by just singing well. We need a revelation of what genuine worship is.

Let us begin by looking at the nature of praise and worship in welcoming our Lord and King into our midst. Many people do not understand the difference between praise and worship. It is all just music and songs to them; they think of praise as fast-paced songs and worship as slow-paced songs that are presented as a prelude to the preaching of the Word. Yet praise and worship are much more than this.

What Is Praise?

We will focus on two main aspects of praise in defining it: (1) praise is proclamation, and (2) praise is sacrifice.

1. Praise Is Proclamation

Praise is the declaration of the great and powerful works of God. It is expressed by singing, playing musical instruments, and giving shouts of joy, as well as by different postures of the body, including clapping, raising the hands, and dancing. The chronicles of King David's reign relate his extravagant way of praising the Lord. (See, for example, 2 Samuel 6:12–23.) The problem with our praise today is that we have not ascended high enough.

2. Praise Is Sacrifice

> *Therefore by Him let us continually offer the sacrifice of praise to God, that is, the fruit of our lips, giving thanks to His name.* (Hebrews 13:15)

The Greek word for *"sacrifice"* is *thysia*, which actually refers to a victim—a killing. Every sacrifice implies death. In this case, the victim for the sacrifice is the flesh, or the ego. Praising God always requires a sacrifice because it is something that goes beyond our strength, convenience, desire, and comfort. To praise God, we must kill something ungodly within us, such as apathy, pride, selfishness, worry, fear, bad thoughts, or anything else that keeps us from wholeheartedly expressing His greatness. Our sacrifice releases a movement of the Holy Spirit, who comes to our aid. Then, when the spirit of praise comes, praising ceases to be a sacrifice, as it was in the beginning. By this time, no one has to force us to praise Him; our praise becomes spontaneous.

Many people prefer to have a man or woman of God lay hands on them for healing or deliverance because they do not want to pay the price of praise and worship or of sacrificing the flesh until God touches them. Yet, if we want to live at the forefront of what God is saying and doing, and if we desire to live in constant blessings and to be permanently on fire for Him, the sacrifice of praise should become an intrinsic part of our lifestyle. When we experience difficult periods in our lives—when life seems full of setbacks, financial troubles, or sickness—we may not have the desire to praise God. And yet, this is precisely the time when God will ask us to present our sacrifice of praise—the fruit of lips that confess His name. (See Hebrews 13:15.) I challenge you to take a step in your Christian walk and begin to present such sacrifices of praise to your King and Lord.

What Is Worship?

Worship is more than a declaration; it is a sincere attitude of humility, reverence, respect, and fear of the Lord. In our worship, Jesus must be crowned. He must occupy the throne of our lives—the Holy of Holies within us. We know that faith is a muscle that grows when exercised. Worship works in a similar way; there is always room to go deeper in it.

Worship may also be expressed by a physical posture, such as bowing the head or body, kneeling, or falling prostrate before the Lord. If we worship in a sincere and humble way, it becomes something that goes well beyond singing or talking to God—it becomes an attitude that can be expressed even through physical contact with others, such as an embrace, through which we transmit everything that flows out of our relationship of worship with the Father.

The level of worship in a church determines its level of revelation and manifestation of the glory of God.

People who worship in spirit and truth break through to the atmosphere of eternity, where the center of attention is no longer self but God. In His presence, they are not concerned with what they feel or what they are experiencing. They know God requires worship, and this conviction surpasses every temporal situation. Worship is not a feeling but an attitude expressed by one who knows that, without God, he is nothing.

Praise is an exuberant, clamorous, enthusiastic expression that often includes many words and a physical display. Worship, on the other hand, involves fewer words—at times, no words are needed at all and there is total silence, because it has more to do with inwardly pouring out our hearts before God and asking His sovereign presence to manifest. From deep worship will come guidance for the future for an individual, a family, a city, or a nation.

Differences Between Praise and Worship

To further help us distinguish between these two ways of coming before God, let us look at some of their major differences:

- Praise focuses on proclaiming the works of God, but worship focuses on the person of God.

- Praise is initiated by us. Worship is God's answer to our praise.

- To praise is to seek God. To worship is to be found by Him.

- Praise increases the anointing, but worship brings the glory.

- Praise is like building a house for God. Worship is God moving into that house.

- In praise we talk *about* God. In worship we speak *to* God, and He answers us.

- In praise we are keenly aware of God's love and greatness. In worship, we are keenly aware of His holiness.

- Praise is the parade of the King. Worship is His coronation.

The Transition from Praise to Worship

If we want to produce truly deep and heartfelt worship, we often need to first ascend in vibrant, loud, and powerful praise. Then, it is important to discern when the spirit of praise has receded in order to allow the spirit of worship to lead. Our praise and worship should be done in accordance with the One whom we desire to please—God Himself. That is the only way to follow the leading of the Spirit and avoid getting lost in our human efforts. I have visited places where the spirit of worship is waiting to manifest, but the people continue to praise. This causes the move of the Holy Spirit to be lost. Because many leaders have not learned to recognize and respond to the impulses or leading of the Spirit, they keep people from having encounters with depths of the glory of God through worship.

We can enter into His presence only through both praise *and* worship; they work hand in hand. Therefore, regardless of whether we worship alone or alongside other people, our approach should always be this: praise until the spirit of worship comes, and worship until God's glory descends.

> **Worship will be as deep and profound as praise is high, exuberant, and powerful.**

When you continuously worship the Lord in spirit and in truth, you can expect great miracles, such as the following, which took place in a miracle and healing service in Argentina. Glorious testimonies were heard from among the twenty-two thousand people who gathered. A couple came forward with their three-year-old son, Jeremiah, who was born with spina bifida. This condition affected the boy's muscles, causing his legs to be twisted. He was unable to place his feet on the floor or to stand on his own, even if he was held by the hands. In addition, his condition caused hydrocephalus (increased fluid around the brain), and the need for diapers because he had no bladder control. To get him to the healing service, his parents had to travel north two thousand kilometers, believing the Lord would do a miracle.

During the worship, the child began to be healed. When his parents realized what was taking place, they ran from the back of the stadium, where they were seated, to the platform. With the help of doctors and pastors, they began to test Jeremiah. The parents removed the equipment the doctors had placed on his legs to straighten them out, and he began to take his first steps, just like any child who is first learning to walk. When they saw that he was able to plant his feet on the floor, they knew his legs were straight. A doctor explained that this was a creative miracle because the fact that Jeremiah was able to stand on his own and straighten up to walk was a sign that his nerves had recovered life and movement. God corrected the defects in his spine and nerves, restoring the normal functioning of his lower limbs and bladder. Jeremiah's parents were deeply moved to see their son healed before their eyes! They cried and thanked God because they had waited for so long for a miracle. They had come from so far away, believing that God would hear their cry, and they were not disappointed. It all took place in His manifest presence. When we are full of God's presence, the creative miracles manifest everywhere; there is nothing His glory cannot do.

Revelations of True Worship

With this as background, let us now begin to look more deeply at the nature of worship through seven revelations of true worship, so that we can create an atmosphere that will draw God's presence into our midst.

1. True Worship Reveals the Existence of God

First, no one can know or experience genuine worship apart from the one true God because He alone can reveal it to us. It is beyond the realm of natural knowledge. Whenever true worship occurs, therefore, it is evidence that God is manifesting Himself to us. Our worship reveals the living God; it testifies of His existence.

> *The heavens declare* [God's] *righteousness, and all the peoples see His glory.*　　　　　　(Psalm 97:6)

2. True Worship Focuses on God, Not Self

Sadly, in many Christian circles today, genuine worship has been replaced by entertainment and talent. There are many "worshippers" whose musical productions are directed toward people's desires to promote themselves rather than God. They do not exalt His name and His majesty. They have the power merely to make the flesh feel good or to mobilize the emotions. This is why we often hear songs with words such as "Touch me; bless me; heal me; deliver me." These songs are out of purpose and focus.

We cannot fake worship or communion with God.

Some people create these songs so their music can be commercialized, but they don't realize that, in doing so, they are setting God aside and turning the needs of people into an idol. They forget or ignore the fact that they were created for a higher purpose than to generate a commercial product or to write music that cradles the human emotions. They were created to worship the true God and to lead others into the same.

3. True Worship Brings the Presence of God

The primary purpose of worship is to bring the glory of God in the midst of His people. When the worship leader of a local church loses this objective, the next thing we can expect is that the attention will become focused on him or her. This type of situation is very dangerous because it means a *"spirit of* error" (1 John 4:8) is in operation. The music produced by such worship leaders is like *"strange fire"* burning on the altar. (See Leviticus 10:1–2.) This is an offering God has not authorized and that doesn't honor Him but rather offends Him. It entertains only the senses; it never involves the spirit. It may display musical talent, but the glory or presence of God is absent from it.

It is easier to find talented musicians than pure and anointed worshippers who have excellent musical ability. Do not misunderstand. I seek and believe in professional musicians, but, more than this, I seek those who are anointed by God! In our ministry, we have raised up worshippers in spirit and in truth who are pure in heart and are also very talented professional musicians.

When a person stops worshipping God, he or she also stops knowing Him.

Worshippers should have only one agenda: furthering the kingdom of God. They should have only one mission: to form and manifest the cloud of His presence. When the atmosphere is created, everything becomes possible in an instant. Observe how intricate this ministry is. During a conference in Chaco, Argentina, we met Marcos, a young man who had suffered a serious infection in his right ear due to a severe case of flu when he was eight years old. His condition became so bad that the doctors had to surgically remove portions of the inner workings of his ear, and so Marcos grew up without any hearing in that ear. Thirteen years later, Marcos came to the stadium where we were holding the conference. The worship manifested the presence of God, and when I began to declare the word of healing, the glory of God descended upon him, right where he was. Immediately, he went forward to the platform to share what had taken place. He reported that he had felt heat in his right ear. He'd then asked a friend to speak to him, in order to test if he could hear, and he could! My doctors had also tested him before he went on the platform, and he could hear perfectly well. Once he was up on the platform, his legs shook under the presence of the glory that had healed him. I asked him, "Did God create a new eardrum?" He answered, "I have no idea what happened. I only know that I could not hear anything, and now I do." The glory of the Lord had restored everything that had been damaged by the infection, as well as what had been surgically removed, enabling Marcos to hear again. God did a creative miracle!

Miracles, signs, and wonders happen supernaturally and continuously at King Jesus Ministry. We see cancers dry up, AIDS disappear, and new organs created. Above all, lives are transformed and become living testimonies of the power of God. This happens because we have cultivated His presence, and it is permanently among us. Our greatest desire should always be to experience new and deeper moments in God's glory because only His presence will transform the human heart. Our efforts cannot accomplish this. The Bible says that our works are as *"filthy rags"* (Isaiah 64:6) before the holiness of God.

When we have cultivated His presence in our lives, we will be His instruments to work in others' lives. For instance, after I've been in God's presence, whether I've been worshipping at home or in a service where the glory of the Lord was strongly felt, people notice a tangible presence on me. I can be at my office, in a restaurant, or at a hotel, and people around me will begin to cry or laugh or be touched by the power of God on the spot in healing or deliverance. The power that touches them is not mine; it just flows through me after I have been in His presence. This is why I firmly believe that our purpose in worship is to invite His presence to descend. Only in His presence will we be transformed so that we can take the same power of transformation to others.

4. True Worship Receives and Sends Forth Heavenly Sounds

Worship that resonates from God's throne will include the spoken declaration of His Word, as well as various sounds that reflect the manifestation of His glory and the spirit of that worship.

The Power of the Spoken Word

Remember that the spoken words of God were vital to the creation of the heavens and earth. When He made various declarations in creation, such as *"Let there be light"* (Genesis 1:3), each aspect of His creation responded to the sound of His voice and to the authority behind the words, and it became a physical reality. The crown of God's creation was humanity, made in His image and likeness. And, as we express our worship to God, declaring His own Word back to Him, His will is carried out by the words of our mouths.

When you are anointed by the power of God, therefore, miracles will naturally materialize. His Word in our mouths is the same as if it was spoken by Him. (See, for example, John 15:7–8.) The Word of God has the power to bring what is in eternity into the realm of time. The Bible says that the power of life and death is in our tongues. (See Proverbs 18:21.) We must learn to use the voice of authority we have in Christ to establish the power, the glory, and the will of the Father, rather than to release curses or judgment.

Our level of ascension into the presence of God is determined by the sound of the worship we release.

How much of God's Word is in our hearts and spoken by our mouths in faith? Do we have enough of it to speak to the elements of nature, to sickness, and to demons and have them obey our decrees? The voice of a person anointed by the Holy Spirit can break bondage, sickness, depression, curses, spells, demonic oppression, and much more. The command of Jesus' voice was so anointed that demons ran away when they heard it, the eyes of the blind were opened, storms ceased, the dead came forth from the grave, and the sick were healed—some without even being within hearing range of that voice. Why was this the case? It is because what the Father was saying in heaven, Jesus was saying on earth. We can do the same as we worship our all-powerful God.

The Power of Heavenly Sounds

Heaven-given sounds, as well as words, have a significant role in our worship of God and in carrying out His will in the world, especially in a new season of God's plan for His people. For example, in the book of Joshua, we read about the fall of the walls of Jericho as the Israelites took possession of the Promised Land. God gave His people two instructions: blow trumpets and shout. He commanded them to release sounds. When the people obeyed, the sound called forth such power and glory from God that the walls of Jericho fell flat, just as He had promised. (See Joshua 6.)

In the Upper Room, on the day of Pentecost, *"a sound from heaven, as of a rushing mighty wind"* (Acts 2:2) was heard. The word *"sound"* is translated from the Greek word *echos*, which means "a loud, strong sound; an echo." The Holy Spirit, whom Jesus had promised would come to help His followers, presented Himself to the 120 believers gathered there with a strong sound. The outpouring of the Holy Spirit also manifested before them in the form of tongues of fire over their heads. Instantly, everyone began to speak tongues (languages) of heaven—another manifestation of sound—which, up to that day, had been unknown to human beings. (See verses 3–4.)

The Bible also tells us that the second coming of Jesus— the time when He returns for His church—will be announced with *"a shout, with the voice of an archangel, and with the trumpet of God"* (1 Thessalonians 4:16). Jesus will announce His return with sounds! The shout and trumpet are reminiscent of the sounds of the shout and trumpets that the Israelites were instructed by God to make in conquering Jericho.

Today, God is releasing new sounds through worshippers in the body of Christ. He is raising up prophetic worshippers who

176 ⌒ *The Glory of God*

worship Him in spirit and in truth, with the ability to interpret and bring down divine sounds from His throne that have a part in fulfilling His plans. The sound that releases God's vision may be the voice of a prophet who proclaims the revelation of His divine determination for the future. When it is difficult for people to understand or believe a revelation from God through words or explanations, then music and prophetic worship can become the means by which they are able to spiritually understand or receive what God is saying and doing.

God is releasing new sounds on earth that initiate angelic activities.

In light of the above, we can understand why Satan's attacks are directed mostly at the ministry of praise and worship. He knows that if he can stop our worship of God, he can also stop heavenly revelation and sounds from being released on the earth, and therefore hinder God's movement in this generation. We must be alert to his schemes, covering and surrounding the ministry of worship with prayer and intercession. We cannot allow the enemy to corrupt or destroy worshippers—we need them!

Satan is interested in our worship because he knows that God's spiritual power will manifest on earth through it. Because of his background, he understands well the power of music and other sounds in worship. The Bible says of him:

> *You were in Eden, the garden of God; every precious stone was your covering: the sardius, topaz, and diamond, beryl, onyx, and jasper, sapphire, turquoise, and emerald with gold. The workmanship of your timbrels and pipes was prepared for you on the day you were created.* (Ezekiel 28:13)

Satan had been created by God as a powerful cherub (see verses 14–15) named Lucifer (see Isaiah 14:12), whom many believe was responsible for directing the worship in heaven. The Bible describes his creation in detail, stating how his coverings were made of precious stones. We can infer from this passage that his interior was created with a dimension of sound, since there is the reference to musical instruments—*"timbrels and pipes."* The name *Lucifer* means "morning star." He was therefore a carrier of light; when he worshipped God, light reflected off him, and his whole being shined. Though he was created to worship, he became vain and full of pride and corrupted his purpose. He rebelled against his Creator and dragged a third of the angels down with him in that rebellion. (See Revelation 12:3–4.)

After he fell, he was called Satan. The Hebrew word for Satan means "adversary" and the Greek word means "accuser." As the adversary and accuser of God and man, he distorts his gifts and musical knowledge to destroy humanity. He is no longer the carrier of light but the carrier of darkness. While heavenly sounds release divine angelic activity, satanic sounds release demonic activity. In the present generation, Satan has purposely encouraged musicians and singers capable of releasing sounds of death. He uses various words, music, and rhythms to spread his messages of sin and death, releasing dark sounds over the earth to cause confusion, rebellion, and destruction. This is why we must monitor what our children are listening to and protect them from any demonic powers that may be released over them through the sounds they receive.

One obvious characteristic of satanic sound in today's generation is violence, along with alcohol and drug abuse, alienation, wildness, and suicide. Demonic philosophies are running wild, spread through every means of communication—television, radio, movies, magazines, and the Internet. This is a violent generation because of the sounds it is hearing. We cannot remain ignorant of these principles, because the enemy is using them to bring destruction and rob this generation of purpose.

> *Each time a new sound overflows in a church, the atmosphere changes and old structures are broken.*

Through worship, demonic strongholds can be broken. The anointed human voice is powerful! When we emit heaven-inspired sounds in the Spirit, with our delegated authority from Jesus (see, for example, Luke 10:17–19; Matthew 28:18), God's angels respond and begin to operate because they obey His instructions. As God's children, we can produce sounds that release love for God, salvation, revival, deliverance, peace, restoration, unity, health, prosperity, purpose, productivity, and life on the earth.

We were given the ministry of worship to the one true God in order to release the sounds of heaven to the present generation. Worship is not just about singing or feeling good about a nice melody. This is a war of worshippers. If we settle for just singing nice songs and sweet melodies, we will not fulfill the main purpose of our ministry as worshippers.

When we understand these principles, our worship will change forever. We need to learn how to identify the sounds that God is releasing today to be in harmony with heaven's worship. This is how we will birth His will for our lives, families, churches, cities, nations, and continents in this generation.

5. True Worship Exalts the Name of Jesus and the Word of God

Today, many "worship" songs used in churches or played on Christian radio stations lack power because they are not based on the Word of God. I know ministries in which most of the worship is really idol worship because the songs minister only to the flesh. We must write scriptural songs—songs that can take the sounds of heaven and truly minister who God is, as many of David's psalms do—songs that pour out constant worship and revealed knowledge. True worship is based on the Word of God and flows from an understanding of that Word.

This causes God to back it up—His power and manifestations will confirm it. The Scriptures say,

Take words with you, and return to the LORD.
(Hosea 14:2)

Although the context of the above verse is words of confession of sin, the overall principle we can gain from it is that we need to know what God's Word says about any matter, agree with it, and then bring it back to Him—in repentance, in prayer for healing, in trusting Him for provision, and so forth.

If our worship lacks the Word, God will not honor it or release His power through it.

When I listen to songs whose words are not based on Scripture, I do not sing them because I know that Jesus is not being exalted by them. Rather, I sing in spiritual tongues. When I travel, I choose to take my worship team with me so that I can minister from an atmosphere of glory. The members of this team know the sound of heaven and how to flow with me. They have learned how to break through a heavy atmosphere and how to release the sound that worships God. I take them with me because they recognize that the purpose of their worship is not to display their gifts as musicians or singers but to bring His presence to win souls, deliver the captives, and heal the sick with the power released from the cloud of His glory. They are not artists or stars. They are worshippers; they are a royal priesthood who serve to worship God and guide His people into His presence. Of course, they are not unique. I know many psalmists, singers, and musical groups who know how to manifest the presence of God.

6. True Worship Transforms the Worshipper

They have hands, but they do not handle; feet they have, but they do not walk; nor do they mutter through

their throat. **Those who make them are like them;**
so is everyone who trusts in them.   (Psalm 115:7–8)

In the above passage, we see—in a secondhand way—the reason why the Lord wants our worship: He wants us to be like Him. Human beings become the image they worship. This psalm describes individuals who create and worship idols, placing all their trust in them. The result of this is that they become like the object of their worship—lifeless. In contrast, when we worship the true God in spirit and in truth, we receive new life in Jesus! No one can remain in God's presence and not change or be transformed, because His light exposes our true condition and His fire purifies us. Something of Him will come upon us! This happened to Mary, the woman who poured the very expensive perfume upon the head of Jesus. (See, for example, John 11:2.) Even though her only purpose was to worship Jesus, she left permeated with the perfume of His presence.

The same thing happens when we pour out our hearts in worship to God, and His presence descends: we walk away with the aroma of Jesus. This causes other people to want to know Him more because His essence in us will attract others! Our hearts are the most expensive perfume we can pour out in His presence.

The highest level of worship is when we become worship.

As Christians, we do not just worship at church; we *are* worship, and this is true eternal life. As we die to self and offer God love, reverence, and honor, we experience a radical transformation because we are made into new creations.

The Lord created humanity to adore Him, and when we fail to do so, we do not function properly. We have lost our identity, because we have not become who we really are: worship. We know we have become worship when God plays us like an instrument, in the same way that an expert musician plays his instrument. We must allow the Lord to pull from us the most beautiful melodies of worship to Him, which will happen when we make ourselves available only to our Lord and our whole being is in a state of continuous adoration.

7. True Worship Is Intimacy with God

This leads us to our final and perhaps greatest revelation of worship: In Scripture, worship is considered intimacy. People with carnal minds do not understand the purity of this comparison (see Titus 1:15), but sexual intimacy between a man and a woman who have been joined in marriage is the human representation of the spiritual intimacy we can have with God. (See, for example, Ephesians 5:28–32.) In this perfect unity, we become one with His heart, His plans, His sufferings, His vision, His struggle, and His victory. This is why worship cannot be quick or mechanical. Think about it: If something quick and mechanical does not sexually please a woman, how will our dead worship satisfy the heart of God?

> *When God does not manifest His glory,*
> *it is usually because He is not satisfied with the worship.*

When God touches us through our worship, His glory will manifest in us, but how can we expect His glory to manifest when we offer Him something mechanical by singing tired songs and engaging in dead worship directed toward meeting our needs? This will not lead to a romance with God in which He can reveal Himself and become one with us.

Some people believe they enter into the presence of God according to the number of songs they sing. But let me tell you, regardless of how many songs we sing, if they are not of the Spirit, God will be grieved, and nothing will happen. In my experience, a *rhema* song given by the Spirit can be sufficient to enter into His glory, and this does not depend on our condition before entering the service. In some instances, there are those who continue to sing a song when the presence of God is no longer there. To avoid this, we need to know God in such a way that we understand how to keep the manifestation of His presence in our services. When the *rhema* song, inspired by the Spirit, is being sung, the worship leader no longer needs to push or encourage the people to worship. The song will appeal to their spirits and mobilize them, and they will respond. If we know our Father, it will not take long to enter His presence because the distance between our ascension and entrance into His glory is shortened each time thanks to the permanent relationship we have built with Him.

> **Worship is the revelation of God,**
> **and man is His image and likeness; therefore,**
> **man was created to worship and reveal God.**

The day is coming when worship will not be merely a service starter in our churches but the most important part of the service because it is what manifests God's glory, which will become our greatest passion. If we want to live in His presence, we will always have a new song in the Spirit playing inside of us. Corporate worship in churches will also become the longest part of the service because the people will enter into His presence and stay there. God will speak to His people, to each person, as a Friend. Then the transformations of the heart will accelerate, and, among other things, it will not take years for believers to develop spiritual maturity.

When God is satisfied with our worship, His presence goes with us everywhere and intervenes in every situation. Pastor Guillermo Jiménez and his wife are being trained by our ministry to take great leaps of faith. Some time ago, they purchased land in Las Vegas at a price of three million dollars. They gave one million as a down payment and financed the rest. After making their monthly payments for a year, they faced a hard financial situation and were tempted to let the land go—along with everything they had invested—because they could no longer make their payments. However, the pastor's wife decided to fight the situation through prayer, praise, and worship. She dared to speak with the owner of the land and ask that he forgive the debt. That businessman had the opportunity and the right to keep the million dollars they had given as a down payment, but God touched his heart, and he decided to fully forgive their debt. Praise God! When His presence is with us, we can rest in Him because He cares for us and everything that pertains to us.

Right now, the signature or seal of God on earth is worship.

I believe we will see unusual miracles, signs, wonders, and transformations that have never before been seen. We are already seeing the power of God come through worship. Let me give you another example. Aneth was a forty-eight-year-old Cuban woman who had been deaf-mute from birth. During a healing and miracle crusade held at our church, she came forward, claiming her miracle. I asked the congregation to join together in prayer for her, and I declared her healed. When I laid hands on her, she testified that she felt a "pop" in her ears, and, to the glory of God, she began to hear and speak for the first time in her life! I tested her by standing behind her so she could not see me, and I began to clap and had her repeat the same beat she heard. If I clapped once, she clapped once. If I clapped twice, she clapped twice, and so on. It was evident that a miracle had taken place! She was so emotional that she cried, because her dream of hearing and speaking had become a reality.

The saturation of the presence of God, in an atmosphere created by praise and worship, produced the miracle that transformed Aneth's life and then that of her family. You can experience the same if you change the way you worship and generate an atmosphere of worship to the true God—an atmosphere where everything is possible!

Where Our Lifestyle of Worship Begins

I will bless the LORD at all times; His praise shall continually be in my mouth.   (Psalm 34:1)

Some people have the impression that worship as a lifestyle is created from the pulpit, but this is not true. It can be developed only in our time of intimacy when we are alone with the Lord. Afterward, it is translated to the church, to the congregation of all the saints. (See Psalm 149:1 KJV.) Each Christian is therefore responsible for taking his or her worship to church. In other words, our worship begins at home—in our prayer closet, office, or car, in our secret place with Jesus—and it follows us everywhere we go and at all times. In my private prayer time, I invest at least two hours daily seeking the presence of God—one of which I spend worshipping Him. If I pray for three hours, then I spend ninety minutes worshipping Him.

This does not mean that I watch the clock or that I think this is a rule everyone must follow. I just want to say that I spend half of my prayer time in worship. For example, I give God thanks, praising Him for His faithfulness and for what He's done in my life. I worship Him as my Lord and King. I talk to Him as my heavenly Father. I commune with Him—declaring my love for Him, telling Him of my willingness to obey whatever He tells me to do. I wait on Him, listening to hear what He wants to speak to me at that moment. I have learned to seek His presence when no one is watching because my worship is for Him alone, not for others to see.

One of the questions I ask believers is, "How is your private life of prayer, when no one is watching you?" I like to know because their Christian experience depends on it. Herein lies the reason why many worship leaders are ineffective when it comes to entering the presence of God themselves and guiding the people into it: they do not have a life of private worship with Him. If they do not know God, do not know how to enter into His presence, or do not know how to have spiritual intimacy with Him, how can they lead people into that same presence? You cannot really guide anyone to where you have not been. It is not as if you can point it out on a map. If the Holy Spirit has not led you during your intimate time with Him, then you will not have any idea how to get there.

> But David said to Saul, "Your servant used to keep his father's sheep, and when a lion or a bear came and took a lamb out of the flock, I went out after it and struck it, and delivered the lamb from its mouth."
> (1 Samuel 17:34–35)

David developed his courage and fighting skills in the vastness of the fields, in the loneliness of the mountains, and in the darkness of the caves while he took care of his father's sheep. There, where no one could see him, he killed bears and lions. This is how he trained to kill the giant Goliath in the presence of many. Likewise, God wants His people to seek His presence in secret because that is the place from which they will emerge strengthened and equipped to win the private and public spiritual battles.

One reason we have not seen God's glory descend upon our lives is that we do not have a continuous and effective private life with Him, which is what allows His presence to be seen in public. Worshipping God in private is an attitude that flows forth, spontaneously and from the heart, when no one sees us, when the responsibility to minister to people is not there, when we do it simply out of love, without seeking any rewards. Those special, private moments cause God to powerfully manifest His presence and speak and minister directly to our hearts.

Principles for Creating a Spiritual Atmosphere

I consider it a necessity for believers to know how to create a spiritual atmosphere of worship so God's glory can descend during their personal times of prayer or during corporate worship at their churches. Here are three principles for inviting God's glory to manifest.

1. A Throne Must Be Built for the King

But You are holy, enthroned in the praises of Israel.
(Psalm 22:3)

In the spiritual realm, we "build God's throne" when we worship Him—His presence will always manifest when the throne is built. Therefore, the sign that indicates the throne is complete is when we experience the outpouring of His glory. We cannot stop our worship before this happens. Let us always remember this principle: Praise until the spirit of worship comes, and worship until the glory descends. There is no formula for how long we need to praise and worship God; it should always be *until* His spiritual throne is built. The Holy Spirit is our Helper, and He stands by our side to receive the worship and take it to the Father. He teaches us to worship God in spirit and in truth.

2. A Cloud of His Presence Must Be Formed

In the Scriptures, clouds represent the glory of God, and the Lord always speaks from a cloud. (See, for example, Exodus 16:10–11.) When Jesus was transfigured on the mountain, God the Father spoke from a cloud. (See, for example, Matthew 17:1–5.) When Jesus ascended to heaven after His resurrection, *"a cloud received Him out of their sight"* (Acts 1:9). The day Jesus returns, it will be *"coming on the clouds of heaven with power and great glory"* (Matthew 24:30). When we worship, we form a spiritual cloud that is the glory or presence of God. Spiritual clouds create the right atmosphere for God to speak and do creative miracles.

The formation of a spiritual cloud depends on the depth of our worship. For example, during a service in a local church, the Holy Spirit will stand by the true worshippers. If He passes by anyone who is not worshipping as he should, He will go on to the next person. He stops by each person, takes in the substance of his worship, and with it forms the cloud for that service, which allows the presence of God to descend. Everyone who contributed worship to form that cloud will receive what is in it. For example, in our church, I have often witnessed that the move of the Holy Spirit begins from the front to the back, while at other times, it begins in the center. The reason is that the people in those areas formed the cloud.

3. The Spiritual Atmosphere Must Be Perceived and Released

Once the cloud and throne are edified, we can perceive the spiritual atmosphere of glory. In the natural, atmosphere is a gaseous substance surrounding a celestial body, formed by ingredients in the environment. In the spiritual realm, it works basically the same way. The ingredients in the atmosphere of glory are continuous prayer, offerings, intercession, praise, worship, obedience, and honor. In the Bible, we often find that when these ingredients exist in an environment, they produce an open heaven and build a divine spiritual atmosphere.

Perceiving the Atmosphere

When I travel to places where a good spiritual atmosphere to preach, teach, and minister miracles has not been built, the first thing I do is begin to break down the bad atmosphere—charged with religiosity, doubt, and egocentricity—through praise. I then worship until the presence or glory of God descends. When I feel it descend, I begin to preach, teach, or release miracles. Sometimes, this takes a long time, but we cannot force God to adjust to our programs. We must worship until the atmosphere of His glory is formed. If we want what is true, we must yield to true worship.

The ingredients in the atmosphere of glory are continuous prayer, offerings, intercession, praise, worship, obedience, and honor.

As I wrote earlier, before moving into our current church, we had purchased a former synagogue as a church building.

From day one, we built a spiritual atmosphere of continuous praise, thanksgiving, prayer, intercession, offerings, and worship there. In that building, we went from one service to five services on Sunday for almost five years, in addition to the Thursday service, the youth service, early-morning prayer, worship team practices, discipleship groups, the leadership institute, retreats, conferences, and much more. Today, this building is used for other activities and for services on special occasions. Every time we gather there, the people quickly feel the presence of God. It is easy to preach, teach, minister miracles, or do deliverances in that place because the atmosphere that was continually built remains. I've noticed the same thing in the room in my house where I pray each day. I have raised a spiritual throne there for my Lord. I have formed a cloud of His presence and a spiritual atmosphere where the glory of God permanently dwells. This is why it takes me only seconds to enter into His presence when I pray in that room. You can do the same, if you worship God continually at home or in church.

Releasing the Atmosphere

> *If the clouds are full of rain, they empty themselves upon the earth.* (Ecclesiastes 11:3)

In the natural, there can be no rain without clouds. Likewise, worship creates a cloud so that the manifestations of the glory of God can shower down upon us. But what would happen if physical clouds were formed and full of water, and it still did not rain? In order to create and encourage rainfall, some researchers, public officials, and businessmen favor using one or more of several techniques called "cloud seeding":

> A rainstorm happens after moisture collects around naturally occurring particles in the air, causing the air to reach a level of saturation at which point it can no longer hold in that moisture. Cloud seeding essentially helps that process along, providing additional "nuclei" around which water condenses. These

nuclei can be salts, calcium chloride, dry ice or silver iodide.[3]

A similar thing happens in the Spirit. Sometimes, the cloud is formed, but there is no visible manifestation of God's presence. For instance, I have ministered in services where the atmosphere is charged with the glory or presence of God, but, to my surprise, nothing has happened. I knew there was potential in that atmosphere, that God was ready to heal, save, and do miracles, but something stopped Him. What had occurred?

As I wrote earlier, God is sovereign, and He may decide not to speak at a given time. It is not that anyone has a hard heart that is blocking Him from speaking; it's according to His sovereignty. Yet I have also found that it is equally as important to learn how to release what is in a cloud of glory as it is to know how to form one. Sometimes, we need to "sprinkle" the cloud with more seeds of worship, until His glory descends, but, at other times, God will show us something specific to do. For example, one day God showed me that in the service there was a woman covered in sores caused by a spirit of fear. She was afraid of getting cancer. When she went forward, we prayed for her, and she was instantly delivered. The Lord also revealed the name of a woman, Maria, who had a large goiter in her neck. A goiter is the enlargement of the thyroid gland. When she came forward, I asked my team to pray for her, and God healed her instantly! The goiter disappeared! Maria cried uncontrollably. She kept touching her neck and yelling, "It disappeared! It disappeared!"

Let me make clear that when God's presence descends in our corporate worship, He is the One who takes the initiative. If we participate, it is because He ordains it. Sometimes, He tells me to declare a word; other times, He gives me a vision of someone specific, with the person's name and the type of illness from which he is suffering. In the glory, I do not move

---

[3] Jacob Silverman and Robert Lamb, "Can China control the weather?" 19 July 2007. HowStuffWorks.com. <http://science.howstuffworks.com/nature/climate-weather/meteorologists/cloud-seeding.htm> 10 January 2012.

unless He gives the order. The essential thing to know is that when we operate from an atmosphere of worship, we do what God tells us to do, when He tells us to do it—no more, no less, just as Jesus did.

In addition, to receive what the cloud contains, we must discern what is in it. The cloud will sometimes have healing, deliverance, or provision, but it will always bring transformation and growth in our lives. We must worship continuously and form a cloud for the present, because God always moves in the "now."

Another reason why the contents of a divine cloud may not be released is that we have not learned to pull from that atmosphere. When the glory of God manifests, we must "take" our miracles. How? By declaring them and doing corresponding actions. We must begin to do what we could not do before, and, when we can, we have to run to testify what God has done; this seals the miracle.

A spiritual atmosphere is created through worship, but the cloud must be discerned to release its contents.

God is ready and anxious to manifest Himself, and all He needs is for us to build the throne. We must give God and His worship priority. We must take all the time we need to worship Him *until* His presence manifests, regardless of how long it takes.

In my experience, when people do not participate in the corporal ascension of praise into the presence of God, they become obstacles in the service. This includes the pastor. When people arrive late and miss worshipping with the rest of the believers, they have no idea what is happening and have a difficult time joining in. Furthermore, the moment they enter, they can hinder or kill the atmosphere—not because they are bad people but because they did not partake of the corporal ascension. This is why I always exhort people to arrive early to church and be present from the beginning. There are also those who, for various reasons, take longer to enter into the worship, while others enter more quickly. The atmosphere, then, must be created from the bottom up by praising until the spirit of worship comes and by worshipping until the glory of God descends. When this happens, everyone can ascend to the throne and enter into worship in harmony, as one body.

In due course, the hearts of the people must be ready to hear the Word, and God must be satisfied with the worship to manifest His glory through the cloud formed in that place so the people can be reached and touched.

The Ultimate Purpose of the Presence of God

Everything we have discussed so far—raising a throne, forming a cloud, and creating an atmosphere—are necessary steps for God's glory or presence to descend. However, what is the reason we need the glory of God to descend? Again, the primary purpose is to have continuous experiences with His presence in order to be transformed into the image of Christ and to manifest His power. In this way, we can take His glory to people who need to be saved, healed, and delivered.

I have met many people who were led supernaturally by God to our church. He spoke to them in dreams and gave them my name or the name of our ministry, and as soon as they entered the parking area, they could feel the presence of God so strongly that they began to cry. Right there, they repented of their sins, and many were healed or delivered instantly. This is similar to what happened to Dr. Coradin and his family, whose testimony was included in chapter 1. It is not uncommon for us to hear this type of testimony. The spiritual atmosphere of continual worship, prayer, intercession, obedience, and submission maintains our church under the constant cloud of His presence.

In the presence of God, there is healing, deliverance, transformation, visions, dreams, prophecy, revelation, impartation, and activation. We will hear His voice and be fired up to go and give to others what we have received. The objective is to take His glory to a lost world—to people without God, faith, or hope. Our experiences in His presence must be taken to our workplaces, schools, and community organizations; they must be taken wherever we go: restaurants, department stores, supermarkets, and the streets. They must be shared with our entire circle of influence. His glory will give us the boldness we need to preach His Word, speak of Jesus, heal the sick, deliver the captives, and do miracles. Let us make the decision right now to take His glory to all the nations of the earth!

EXPERIENCES WITH GOD

- Begin to build an atmosphere of worship in the place where you usually pray. For seven consecutive days, of your own free will, approach God with thanksgiving, praise, and worship, learning to discern the moment in which you must make the transition from praise to worship. Then, let this become a regular practice in your life.

- Examine your attitude as a worshipper and make the necessary adjustments until you are able to worship God in spirit and in truth.

- Begin to be a carrier of God's glory, manifesting what the cloud of His presence contains to the people around you in salvation, healing, and deliverance.

11

Ignited by the Fire of God's Presence

In the world today, spiritual darkness is becoming thicker and opposition to the spirit of Christ stronger; challenges are intensifying, and we have to be ready to meet these circumstances. We must be Christians who walk in the fire of God's presence so that we will know how to alleviate human suffering and bring people to Christ in the midst of these momentous last days.

In this chapter, we will receive the revelation of what it means that God is an all-consuming fire. Furthermore, we will learn what it means for us to be full of the Holy Spirit and His fire. We will come to understand the purpose for the fire of His presence, what it produces in us, and how to keep it burning. This will encourage us to go and gather the great and final harvest of souls prepared by the Lord before His coming.

God Is a Consuming Fire

For the LORD your God is a consuming fire, a jealous God. (Deuteronomy 4:24)

We have seen that the glory of God is His essence—what He is within. We have also learned that His nature has many facets and that only He, in His absolute sovereignty, can decide which aspect He will reveal or manifest to His children—and when. One aspect of His glory is *"a consuming fire,"* which can descend to bring judgment on earth and on those who do not repent of their sins. But His fire also purifies and sanctifies His people, who have turned from their wicked ways and yearn to live in righteousness and justice, filled with the Holy Spirit.

What Is the Appearance of His Glory?

> *The sight of the glory of the LORD was like a consuming fire on the top of the mountain in the eyes of the children of Israel.* (Exodus 24:17)

God's glory is a consuming fire that burns everything that is not holy. His fire also affects the hearts of people in powerful ways. But be careful! This fire is not for those who do not desire to live holy and pure lives. Remember that the people of Israel were afraid of this fire, and the root of that fear was their unwillingness to pay the price demanded by it.

Many people want to be holy but do not want to pay the price of being sanctified.

This attitude can be seen today among believers in the church of Christ. Many people reject the revivals, the power, the glory, and the miracles because they are afraid of the presence of God and because they do not want to pay the price required to keep it burning.

Who Can Live Under the Fire of His Presence?

> *Who among us shall dwell with the devouring fire?*
> *Who among us shall dwell with everlasting burnings?*
> *He who walks righteously and speaks uprightly.*
> (Isaiah 33:14–15)

In simple terms, these verses show us the conditions for walking under God's fire. The Lord is saying, in effect, "I want you to enter My presence, where I will release the fire, but these are the requisites for the fire not to fall upon you as judgment."

Are we willing to pay the price to live in justice and holiness? I personally consider that no price is comparable to the high value of the manifestation of the fire of His presence.

The Israelites were a stiff-necked people who refused to enter into these conditions; hence the reason Moses had to raise the Tent of Meeting outside the camp in the desert in which to meet with the Lord. (See Exodus 33:7.) Had he not done that, the fire would have destroyed the people. In Hebrew, the word for "stiff-necked" is *qasheh*. Among its meanings are the concepts "hard," "cruel," "severe," and "obstinate." (See, for example, verse 3.) Only Moses and Joshua were able to enter the cloud of God's glory and dwell in the fire without being burned or dying. If we carefully read the accounts of the Israelites in the desert, we can see that the cloud of God always accompanied the people during their trajectory through the desert—as He had promised—but He did not dwell in their midst.

Moses' Experiences with the Fire of God's Presence

What was Moses' first experience with God's fire? When he was a shepherd in Midian before God called him back to Egypt to deliver His people, it was likely a common occurrence for him to see a thorn bush burning in the desert. One day, he saw such a bush on fire, but he discerned that the fire in this bush was not common—it did not consume the shrub. Why? Eternity was invading the natural dimension with a supernatural manifestation. Moses was able to discern the supernatural from the natural. The bush did not burn because the fire of God never burns out. This was a manifestation of the eternity of the Lord and of the passion for God that would continually burn in the heart of Moses until the end of his days.

It was from that fire that God spoke to him:

So when the LORD saw that he turned aside to look, God called to him from the midst of the bush and said,

"Moses, Moses!" And he said, "Here I am."

(Exodus 3:4)

The Lord manifested Himself before Moses through fire not only in this incident but also throughout Moses' life. The first time, God told him to remove his sandals because the ground he was standing on was holy—this symbolized that Moses would no longer walk in the natural but would walk in the supernatural. (See verse 5.) When Moses approached God, what he saw from below was a consuming fire. He lived under the fire of the presence of God, and from there he released some of the most amazing miracles recorded in the Bible.

What Happened to Moses After His Experience with the Burning Bush?

The heart of Moses was changed—transformed—forever in his experience with the burning bush. God released in him the same passion He had to deliver the people of Israel, who were being held captive in Egypt. It is interesting to note that for the first forty years of his life, Moses had been totally submerged in the Egyptian culture as the adopted son of Pharaoh, which had shaped him into an arrogant and self-sufficient individual. This is why, when he saw the suffering of his people, he tried to deliver them in his own strength. He could not do it because this was not God's plan or method for freeing His people. (See Exodus 2:1–15.)

Then, Moses fled Egypt and spent forty years in the desert, where God removed the Egyptian culture from him and killed his ego. By the time He was done, Moses said, *"'Who am I that I should go to Pharaoh, and that I should bring the children of Israel out of Egypt'* (Exodus 3:11), if I can't even speak?" (See Exodus 4:10.)

Last, Moses spent forty more years like the burning bush in the desert, ignited with the fire of the Lord, blazing continuously and passionately to lead Israel to the Promised Land and to know the Lord intimately. One moment in the fire of God led him to deliver a people he had not delivered in the course of eighty years. Moses became a faithful friend of God, a leader of millions, a man zealous to do the will of his Lord—performing miracles, signs, and wonders by God's hand and speaking with Him face-to-face.

None of this would have taken place, or would have been even remotely imaginable, without the burning-bush experience. It was only after this encounter that he was able to believe, rise, and lead an entire nation to receive its inheritance in the Promised Land. This change was caused by the fire of the presence of God!

When Moses had the experience with the burning bush, he received the fire of God's presence.

Through these pages, God has commissioned me to say that you, too, can have the same experience. He is the living God who continues to do miracles among His people. He has a special mission for you to carry out—the reason why you were created—and He will give you His fire to empower you to see it through, a fire that will never burn out. Whatever you have been unable to do up to now, you will do with the fire of God.

Every believer needs to have a burning-bush experience. Without it, we will have only an *opinion* about supernatural power—pure theory. However, once we experience the fire, we will ignite in a never-ending passion that will lead to the demonstration of supernatural power. We will also be able to transfer that power to others, in order to release revivals, healings, miracles, signs, and wonders that can deliver individual people, cities, and nations from the bondage of sin, sickness, and curses.

You might ask, "Will I be ready for an experience with the fire of His presence?" or "Is it possible, in this day and age, to have an experience similar to what Moses had?" My answer to these questions is, "Of course!" The process of formation and development you have endured in the "desert" of your own life has not been in vain; it has prepared you for this experience. Around the world, thousands of men and women like me, as well as others I have trained, are experiencing the fire of God's presence every day. The evidence is that they are igniting churches, cities, and nations with this holy fire.

The fire of God is included in the *"restoration of all things"* (Acts 3:21), which we talked about earlier, and this is the time for its manifestation. You and I are living in the time of the restoration of all things! For this to take place, it is necessary for the fire to burn the *"wood, hay,* [and] *straw"* (1 Corinthians 3:12) and purify the gold in the church. (See verses 12–15.) Only then will we see what is true shine through.

My Personal Experience with the Fire

When I received Jesus as my personal Lord and Savior, I was immediately filled with the Holy Spirit with the evidence of speaking in other tongues. The Bible refers to this experience as being filled with *"power from on high"* (Luke 24:49) to be an effective witness of Jesus. (See verses 46–49.) But I noticed that even though I had been filled with God's power, I still did not have the fire of the Spirit for bringing souls into the kingdom. Yes, I was happy and full of joy that I knew Him and had His power. I rejoiced in His presence, in experiencing Him, and in knowing Him, but I had not been submerged in His fire.

The Greek word translated *"power"* in Luke 24:49 is *dunamis* and refers to "explosive power." This is the word from which we derive the terms *dynamite* and *dynamic*. In the natural, a stick of dynamite cannot be made to explode without fire. Therefore, I can say that, at the beginning of my Christian walk, I had the dynamite of the power of God, but it had not yet exploded because the wick had not been lighted. I needed the fire!

How was the wick lighted? One day, when I was alone in my room and enjoying the presence of God, He baptized me with the fire of His presence. This baptism released an uncontrollable passion in me to save souls, to know the face of God, to be holy, to extend His kingdom, to raise a radical generation for Christ, and to manifest His supernatural power. From that moment until now, the fire has continued to burn inside me like an eternal flame. Everything I do is done with great passion. I pray, praise, worship, preach, cast out demons, minister healing to the sick, and preach the gospel throughout the world with passion because the fire of the Spirit burns in me.

> ### *You cannot impart the fire until you have a burning-bush experience.*

This same experience has happened to many others. A young man named Andy came to our church about ten years ago. He had grown up in a dysfunctional family. His grandfather had lost his father at the age of two, and his father hadn't met his own father until the age of eighteen. A generational curse of broken homes, divorce, and adultery was afflicting the lives of this young man and his family members. Andy's father was physically and verbally violent; this caused Andy to feel strong hate and rejection toward him. Later, this hate turned into rebelliousness. As a teenager, he entered the world of drugs and gangs, where he met people who felt the same way he did. Instead of finding answers to his pain, what he found was a faster way to deepen the depression, sense of lost identity, and lack of paternal love he felt inside. Life meant nothing to him. Finally, he decided to commit suicide.

Yet, on the night he had chosen to take his life, he heard a voice say, "Don't do it. I have a purpose for you." The voice brought such deep conviction to his heart that he fell to his knees and began to cry—after years of not being able to shed a single tear due to his hardened heart. That night, he asked God to enter his heart and change his life. He had never felt a love so true and so pure as the love of the heavenly Father, and he was never the same again. Andy completely fell in love with God. He left behind the drugs, illicit sex, gangs, delinquency, and unforgiveness. In place of these things, he began to attend the early-morning prayer sessions at our church and was trained in prayer under my wife's guidance.

One day, the Holy Spirit led me to commission Andy as a youth pastor in our church. Today, he faithfully serves God, and his fruit has been abundant and supernatural. He is producing a spiritual revolution among the youth, activating them in the gifts of words of knowledge, prophecy, and deliverance to evangelize the streets of Miami with signs, wonders, and tremendous fruit. He has multiplied himself in others who are also on fire for Christ—young people who provide pastoral care and who witness as he does, under the slogan "Street Glory." This group goes out every Saturday to evangelize the streets, invading the entire city—including the dangerous zones. In the first fifteen weeks of Street Glory, these young people harvested over six thousand professions of faith. Street Glory is now expanding into Washington, D.C., New York, Mexico, Venezuela, Argentina, Guatemala, Spain, and England. At twenty-six years old, Andy imparts the fire of heaven to youth leaders who are under the spiritual covering of our church. Yes, God is raising up the fire generation!

Jesus Came to Bring Power and Fire

I came to send fire on the earth, and how I wish it were already kindled! (Luke 12:49)

While Jesus ministered on earth, His greatest passion was to release the fire of God's presence so that, after His resurrection, multitudes of people around the world could reproduce His miracles and lead men and women to know the Father with the same passion. In addition to providing for our salvation, this is the reason He went to the cross and died. He knew what He was doing! When He was resurrected, that fire was released over the disciples in the Upper Room, and they shook up the world. This is why John the Baptist said,

> *I indeed baptize you with water unto repentance, but*
> *He who is coming after me is mightier than I, whose*
> *sandals I am not worthy to carry. He will baptize you*
> *with the Holy Spirit and fire.* (Matthew 3:11)

In this passage, we see that there is a difference between being baptized with the Holy Spirit and being baptized with fire. John uses the conjunction *"and"* between the terms *"Holy Spirit"* and *"fire"*—indicating two baptisms that are different but equally necessary.

To understand what it means to be baptized with fire, let us first look at the Greek word for *"to baptize."* This word is *baptizo*, which means "to dip" and "to make fully wet." This word was used to describe the event of a boat being covered or submerged by a great wave, and this is essentially what happens when we are baptized in water by immersion. We are completely covered, totally submerged underwater. The same experience occurs when we are baptized with the Holy Spirit and fire. We are submerged in the consuming fire of the presence of God so that it affects our whole being.

Two Essentials for Being an Effective Witness of Jesus

Undergoing these baptisms is fundamental for making our testimonies effective. Most Christians want to be witnesses of Jesus. However, many believers do not witness, while others do the best they can but are ineffective. Why? They haven't fully entered into the baptisms of the Holy Spirit and fire. Therefore, let us look more closely at these two essentials:

1. Be Filled with the *Dunamis* ("Dynamite") Power of the Holy Spirit

> *But you shall receive power....*   (Acts 1:8)

The first thing we need is the power of God's Holy Spirit. This power goes beyond the ability to speak in other tongues. It is also more than just an opportunity for creating a "social club" where people can prophesy to each other. The power of the Spirit has to do with winning the lost for Christ! To be filled with the Holy Spirit and fire is to have the ability to shake up the world with the good news of the kingdom. (See Acts 17:6.) It helps us to produce supernatural evidence proving that Jesus indeed lives. We should take the gospel everywhere we go—healing the sick, freeing the captives, and testifying of Jesus' redeeming work.

Being baptized with the Holy Spirit has nothing to do with testifying about a church, a ministry, or an individual believer. It is about Jesus of Nazareth—the Son of God. Since Jesus' death and resurrection, many people have abandoned that central purpose. We need to return to being true witnesses of Him. We can testify of all that God does, but the main purpose for doing so is to glorify the protagonist of our testimonies: the resurrected Christ. Jesus needs to be the center of our witness! And, to testify effectively, we must have a personal experience with the Holy Spirit—provided by Jesus Himself—because the Spirit is the One who will convict sinners of their need for salvation.

The individual with an experience is no longer at the mercy of anyone's opinion.

Some of us are really good at discussing theology, but we often lose our arguments because we cannot prove what we say. The point is that God did not call us to argue but to testify of what we have seen, heard, and experienced. It is not a science. It is an experience! Then, there is nothing to argue about because, in general, the veracity of an experience cannot be refuted.

2. Be Filled with the Fire of God's Presence

There are believers who have received the infilling of the Holy Spirit with the evidence of speaking in other tongues and who have been filled with power from heaven, yet they never testify of Jesus. Neither do they pray for the sick or cast out demons. To return to our earlier analogy, they have the dynamite, but it has not been lighted with fire.

Baptism with fire takes place when we go before God so that He can set us ablaze with passion—the same kind of passion that burns in the heart of the Father—the passion to be witnesses of Jesus, to bring the truth of the dominion, lordship, and will of the King on earth by doing miracles in His name and by His hand.

The fire of the presence of God releases the passion that is in Him.

Remember that the lampstand in the Old Testament tabernacle represents the church—all believers. The lampstand was kept filled with oil, the substance used to keep the light going continually. The oil symbolizes the Holy Spirit, who today is the "fuel" that keeps the light of His glory ablaze in us. And yet, there was another condition for the lampstand to shine. Its wicks had to be lighted with fire. When the fire no longer burns, regardless of how much oil there is, the lampstand will not shine. Likewise, we cannot be powerful, effective witnesses of Jesus if our lamps have not been lit with the fire of the glory of God.

This is the reason why many believers speak in tongues and are full of the power but, instead of being on fire, are passive and indifferent. They either lost the fire or never received it to begin with. The answer, of course, is to be lighted by the fire of His presence. Let us now look at ten results the fire brings about in believers' lives.

Ten Results of the Fire of God's Presence

In numerous passages throughout Scripture, we see when, how, and why God released the fire of His presence. He continues to do the same today for the same purposes.

1. The Fire Produces a Passion for Saving Souls

The greatest harvest of souls the church has ever seen is about to take place, and it will be the result of the fire of the Holy Spirit burning in believers. Many revivals have taken place throughout the world, but few people seem to have recognized their purpose. Some people have thought of them as a means for feeling good, dancing, crying, and having times of rest. These things are beneficial and are part of the divine manifestations that bring revival. Yet God's main purpose for sending revivals is for people to encounter Jesus and be saved.

> *He was the burning and shining lamp, and you were willing for a time to rejoice in his light.* (John 5:35)

John the Baptist was like a torch that burned and gave light, but that light was only for the purpose of helping others to see *the* Light—Jesus. His role was to announce the Messiah's coming and what He would do on the earth. In those days, many people rejoiced in the light of John and followed him yet did not progress much farther than that in their faith. Similarly, many believers today rejoice in the light of others but stop short of having the fire of the passion of God within themselves. Their fire has gone out. They need the Holy Spirit to light them up again.

We cannot be light if we are not on fire.

Jesus said that believers are to be the *"light of the world"*:

> *You are the light of the world. A city that is set on a hill cannot be hidden. Nor do they light a lamp and put it under a basket, but on a lampstand, and it gives light to all who are in the house. Let your light so shine before men, that they may see your good works and glorify your Father in heaven.* (Matthew 5:14–16)

We are lighted by the fire of God. No other light, other than the light we received from the Holy Spirit through Jesus, can disperse the spiritual darkness. There is no other source of light to bring His presence, miracles, and everything else He wants to do for people through us. Jesus has returned to heaven, and now we are the light of the world. Without the fire of the Spirit of God, the light of His glory will not shine.

Javier Va Hoje, a disciple in our ministry, is a professional Cuban singer with an impressive musical background. He watched our television program, *Tiempo de Cambio [Time for Change]*, from Las Vegas, where he lived and attended church with his family. His wife became pregnant, but in her fourth month, the doctors diagnosed that the baby would be born with Down syndrome. Javier and his wife faced the same challenge as the woman I talked about at the beginning of this book, and their response ignited the fire of God in their lives. While the doctor advised it would be wise to abort the baby, they did not accept the diagnosis. Instead, they decided to protect the life of their child.

Javier appropriated the word he had heard through my teaching that truth is the highest level of reality. He recognized that the doctors had based their opinion on a real diagnosis, but he also knew the higher truth—Jesus had paid the price for the healing of their child. The doctors did not understand the decision of Javier and his wife not to abort the fetus and said they would not be responsible for the pregnancy. The couple was made to sign a document certifying they had been informed of the baby's condition.

At the time, Javier was witnessing to a friend who was addicted to drugs, and he shared with him the battle of faith they were fighting for their son. He told his friend, "You will see that my child will be born without any medical problems. He will be born perfectly normal and healthy." He made a pact with God for the gospel to be confirmed in his friend through the miracle healing of his son.

God kept His Word. Javier's son was born completely healthy! The glory of God created a miracle, restoring the normal chromosomal count and bringing the pregnancy to a healthy conclusion. Thanks to this miracle, Javier's friend accepted Jesus and was delivered from his addiction.

Later, Javier decided to move his family to Miami so they could attend our church. They were hungry to know more of God. Today, trained, equipped, and filled with the fire of God, Javier preaches when he is on tour; he declares healing over the sick, and they get healed; he prays for the deliverance of young people, and they stop using drugs; he preaches to witches and sorcerers and wins them for Christ. He has a fire in his heart that never dies down.

Jesus comes for a church that is not only experiencing revival but also is on fire for the harvest.

If the experience of the baptism with the Holy Spirit, through which we receive the power of God, does not push us to reach the lost, it remains inconclusive. The baptism in fire is necessary to ignite us to go and evangelize. A revival is an injection of new life through which we are empowered—completely filled with God's power—to gather the great harvest. We should be aware that millions of people are going to hell while the church continues to operate behind four walls, singing, dancing, and ministering to each other but never going out to seek the lost. Let us pray that a passion for the lost will be released in every one of us!

2. The Fire Brings Judgment

> *Then...the sons of Aaron, each took his censer and put fire in it, put incense on it, and offered profane ["strange" KJV] fire before the LORD, which He had not commanded them. So fire went out from the LORD and devoured them, and they died before the LORD.*
>
> (Leviticus 10:1–2)

This passage includes the term *"profane fire"* or *"strange fire,"* which I mentioned briefly in the previous chapter. It refers to incense that symbolizes worship but originates from a wrong motive and consequently activates the judgment of God over those who offer it. The fire of judgment discerns between the holy and the profane, between the pure and the wicked. This truth enables us to understand why many people are sick and others die inexplicably. (See 1 Corinthians 11:27–30.) Some men and women of God are being judged by His fire because of immorality, misuse of finances, pride, commercializing the anointing, and other transgressions of His law. As the Scriptures say, *"For if we would judge ourselves, we would not be judged. But when we are judged, we are chastened by the Lord, that we may not be condemned with the world"* (verses 31–32).

Each time the earth fills with corruption and violence, God brings His judgment to purify it—usually through fire.

We do not want to be condemned with the world. The world is experiencing crisis times in which sin, iniquity, and wickedness abound. The planet is under a curse due to acts of vengeance, homicides, and other types of crime and violence that cause the constant shedding of innocent blood—including the approximately fifty million children in the United States alone who have been killed while still in their mothers' wombs since abortion became legal in 1973.[4] We also have curses such

---

[4] http://www.nrlc.org/Factsheets/FS03_AbortionInTheUS.pdf.

as suicide, poverty, sterility, divorce, and incurable diseases, which originate in past and present sin. God must judge the inhabitants of the world. A clear biblical example of this state of affairs is the destruction of the cities of Sodom and Gomorrah. (See Genesis 13:12–13; 18:17–19:28.) God destroyed them with fire because of their multiple transgressions and iniquity. The same will happen to the earth in the end times.

Isaiah 24 is very clear about the judgment of the Lord upon the earth, affirming that its inhabitants have violated the *"laws," "ordinance,"* and *"everlasting covenant"* (verse 5). Because of these things, the curse consumes the world, and its inhabitants are devastated. (See verses 4–6.)

> *For thus says the L*ORD *of hosts: "Once more (it is a little while) I will shake heaven and earth, the sea and dry land."*
> (Haggai 2:6)

I believe that, at this time in human history, God is shaking the inhabitants of the world. He is shaking people's personal lives and families. He is shaking the banking system, large companies and other businesses, governments, religious institutions, and even physical constructions. The continents and the oceans have been shaken through natural disasters. In the midst of the chaos and uncertainty caused by this shaking, the only unshakeable One is Jesus, along with His Word and His kingdom. We must remain in Him.

3. The Fire Purifies and Sanctifies

God desires to bring His fire in our lives not to judge us but to cleanse us. When we have a personal experience with the fire, we are purified and sanctified because it burns and destroys the impurities in the various areas in our lives. It burns and destroys everything not pleasing to God! Again, *"if we would judge ourselves, we would not be judged"* (1 Corinthians 11:31). Do not fear the fire of His presence, because it makes holy those who respond in submission, humility, faith, and obedience. If we love God and want to please Him, we do not have to be afraid of His fire. It will not consume us. Instead, it will bring us closer to Him and fill us with His passion. Knowing this, we must seek to live exposed to an atmosphere where this fire is always ministering. We can no longer live in the same way we have been. It is time to seek His fire! This will take sacrifice on our part.

> *Then the fire of the LORD fell and consumed the burnt sacrifice, and the wood and the stones and the dust, and it licked up the water that was in the trench.*
> (1 Kings 18:38)

For many believers, *sacrifice* has become a bad word. They go to all lengths to avoid losing their comfort and conveniences. The sacrifice is the demand, the persecution, the rejection that comes with revival. A sacrifice cannot exist without inconveniences. This is why we must cross over the line of convenience.

God's fire falls only where there is sacrifice because it proves that what was offered to God is real.

But yesterday's sacrifice is today's convenience. It is easy to measure our sacrifice by how strong our past has been, but we are not willing to look at our future in the same way. We are not looking for more to sacrifice, yet we do want to live in a permanent state of reward for what we have already sacrificed. This is why we stop growing, maturing, and entering into higher dimensions; it is why we are not willing to invest our time and, much less, our finances, in God's work. I have never read a Bible verse that says the fire fell upon the altar empty of a sacrifice. We must always look for new levels of sacrifice.

4. The Fire Reveals the Motives of Our Hearts

> *...it will be revealed by fire; and the fire will test each one's work, of what sort it is.* (1 Corinthians 3:13)

We need to ask ourselves periodically, "What is the true purpose of what I am doing? Do I want to serve God and use the gifts He's given me to the fullest extent, having a love for others and a desire to manifest His glory?" If our motives are right, there is nothing for us to fear, and if we have gone off course, we can make the necessary corrections. Then, we will desire the revival God brings to our lives and ministries.

This constantly happens in the New Believers Retreats sponsored by our church. Our motivation is to save, heal, and restore the lost, and God supports His Word with life-changing transformations. The people find themselves with His fire, and the entire work of Satan in their lives is consumed. In one New Believers Retreat that we hosted outside Miami, a thirty-year-old man named Kendris testified that he had been set free from mental problems. His condition had been so severe that the doctors had hospitalized him several times, leaving him with no memory of those situations. The doctors could not find a cure for what plagued him because his condition was spiritual; it was a generational curse that came from his grandmother.

In addition, from the age of nine until the age of twenty-four, he had been an alcoholic without hope of recovery; no rehabilitation program had worked for him. At thirteen, he had started using marijuana. At seventeen, he had not only used cocaine and ecstasy, but had also sold them. Yet, the first time he visited our church, he accepted the Lord into his heart, and his life began to undergo a complete turnaround. His marriage was restored. He was delivered from the sin of adultery and from his addictions, and his mind was restored to normal. Before he was saved, his family did not believe in him; they considered him to be a phony and a liar. However, his transformation was so radical that his parents, too, came to know Christ.

Kendris found a job as a kitchen helper and later was promoted to chef. Today, he is the executive chef at a corporation. He serves God as a House of Peace leader and preaches to everyone he meets, testifying and demonstrating what God has done in him. He is on fire for Jesus!

5. The Fire Produces a Passion to Fulfill Our Callings

Then I said, "I will not make mention of Him, nor speak anymore in His name." But His word was in my heart like a burning fire shut up in my bones; I was weary of holding it back, and I could not. (Jeremiah 20:9)

This is how the prophet Jeremiah described his experience with the calling and the fire of God. In my personal experience, when I preach in other nations, I return home happy with the harvest and with everything God did, but I cannot deny the physical exhaustion it produces. When I feel exhausted, I often purpose in my heart to wait one or two months before traveling again, but this decision does not last. After a few days, the passion and fire to take His glory to the nations, to see people run to Jesus for salvation, and to extend His kingdom, revives in me; it begins to burn me once more, and I want to return to the nations. The same happens when I do not preach or minister in the local church. I miss it! The passion that burns within activates me. It is a fire to preach and minister, to be with the people and see them transformed—this fire never ends.

That is what happens when there is a genuine call from God within us. It is a fire that burns down to the bones. It cannot be extinguished! This is the purpose for which we were created. Regardless of the diverse and wonderful ways in which believers manifest His purposes, our callings are like an eternal flame that never burns out.

6. The Fire Produces a Passion to Overcome Opposition

I will know that you stand firm in one spirit, contending as one man for the faith of the gospel without being frightened in any way by those who oppose you. (Philippians 1:27–28 NIV)

The word *passion* describes a fervor—an obsession, an extreme pursuit or search for something. It can also refer to suffering and martyrdom. That is why the journey of Jesus toward

Calvary is known as the "passion of Christ." His ardent desire to save humanity led Him to suffer and die on the cross. Likewise, the passion of the fire of God's presence enables us to withstand all suffering and to overcome all opposition for His sake.

For passionate men and women ablaze with divine fire, everything develops around the vision of God; from their simplest conversations to their highest priorities, they are aligned with carrying out this objective. Sadly, some believers—and, worse yet, Christian leaders—have little desire for the things of God. A simple desire is not enough. When you have divine passion, you will be spiritually on fire, and no opposition to God's purposes can defeat you.

7. The Fire Produces a Passion to Know God Intimately

I find that whenever I spend a long period of time in God's presence, I walk away from the experience with an even greater passion to remain in the cloud of His glory. Entering the presence of God releases greater zeal in me to seek Him and to know Him more intimately; it also often creates the same passion in those around me.

Discipline produces the admiration of others,
but passion is contagious.

Passion is like a forest fire: a small flame is all that is needed to set a forest ablaze to the point that it cannot be extinguished.

8. The Fire Produces Supernatural Boldness

Now, Lord, look on their threats, and grant to Your servants that with all boldness they may speak Your word.... (Acts 4:29)

Peter and John had been taken before the religious council in Jerusalem and then imprisoned because they had caused an additional multitude to believe in Jesus by preaching the resurrected Christ. Their teachings were a menace to the religious leaders because thousands of people heard them, exercised faith, and were saved, causing them to leave religiosity and tradition. Furthermore, the sick were being healed, and they testified of Jesus to everyone they knew. The wick of the gospel had been lit, and its flame was spreading like wildfire!

When they were released from prison, Peter and John met with their companions and prayed to the Lord with them, asking for a greater level of boldness to preach the Word and to continue doing miracles in the name of Jesus. They were not satisfied with what they had been doing. They wanted more, and God granted their request! (See, for example, Acts 4:31; 5:12.)

I can attest to the fact that each time I enter His presence, I receive supernatural courage to believe and to do what is humanly impossible. When someone exercises supernatural boldness, he or she assumes great risks, and this, undoubtedly, inspires others to do the same—in addition to bringing about God's support. God loves people who are bold!

There are people in our church who are ablaze with the fire of God. They do not fear taking risks, suffering, or paying the price to preach about Jesus. A woman named Caroline has testified that she was a teacher in a Christian school until she was let go for coming to our church, speaking in other tongues, and believing that God performs miracles today. Yet, instead of becoming discouraged, her faith was strengthened, and she knew that God would provide another job for her. During her search, she came upon an opportunity to work for an orthodontist. She was not sure she should take the job because the office was full of Buddhist images, but she finally accepted.

One day, the orthodontist called her into her office to talk. Caroline believed she was about to lose her job because she was a Christian, so she boldly entered the office and began to prophesy to her boss. She had said only two or three things when the woman started to cry and shout. Her shouts were so loud that Caroline had to close the office door. The orthodontist then began to feel the love of God. At this point, Caroline said, "The Lord says you will have no other gods but Me." This impacted her boss so much that she immediately called in her secretary and gave her fifteen minutes to get rid of every image and statue in the office. Since that day, Caroline—lighted by the fire of the passion of God to save souls—has preached in the office openly and freely. The orthodontist was convicted by the Holy Spirit, opened up her heart to Jesus, and made a complete turnaround in her life. Caroline continues to win souls for Jesus at her workplace. She is on fire! God transformed her so that she could become a deliverer.

9. The Fire Produces Passion to See Miracles, Signs, and Wonders

Everywhere I go, my prayer is always the same: that God would do miracles, signs, and wonders for the purpose of sensitizing people's hearts to receive Jesus as their Lord and Savior. I have a passion to see these wonders take place because many of God's people are sick and in need of divine healing. They also need to see a demonstration of God's power and to develop a hunger for the fire so they can reproduce the same miracles, signs, and wonders in their own families, communities, cities, and nations. Again, believers have been chosen and anointed to shake up the world, not with theory and reasoning but with God's supernatural power.

During a miracle service in Miami, the people in one of our Houses of Peace in Caracas, Venezuela, met to watch it via satellite. In attendance was a forty-five-year-old doctor named Betty who had been operated on for cancer of the thyroid gland, which had spread to her lymph nodes. She had also suffered a heart attack. After chemotherapy, the cancer reappeared in her neck; the nodes were so large that they could be felt easily. She was invited to the meeting by friends, and she arrived desperate for a miracle. She did not want any more chemotherapy or radiation because she understood all too well the destruction such treatments can cause.

When I began to curse the seed of cancer and death, Betty felt the fire of God on her neck. She was asked by those present to do what she could not do before, in order to confirm her miracle. She touched her neck and could not find any inflammation. The cancer had disappeared from her body supernaturally! When she realized she had received her miracle, Betty began to cry and to scream, testifying of what God had done. Because she was a doctor, she knew more than anyone else that, scientifically speaking, there was no explanation for what had happened to her. She was so happy that she began to celebrate in such a way that the police showed up at their meeting place. The leaders took advantage of the opportunity and shared the gospel with the police officers. All received Jesus as their Lord and Savior. Days later, Dr. Betty had tests done to check on the cancerous cells. The results confirmed that she was completely healed. The Lord had removed all of the cancerous cells that had invaded her body.

A passion for miracles had led these believers in Venezuela to connect to our program via satellite and to believe that what took place in Miami could also take place where they were. They were not wrong! God has the passion to do miracles everywhere!

10. The Fire Produces Revival

The Spirit of the LORD is upon Me, because He has anointed Me to preach the gospel to the poor; He has sent Me to heal the brokenhearted, to proclaim liberty to the captives and recovery of sight to the blind, to set at liberty those who are oppressed, to proclaim the acceptable year of the LORD. (Luke 4:18–19)

This passage describes the ministry of Jesus when He was anointed by the Holy Spirit to bring transformation in every area of His society.

"Preach the gospel to the poor." This phrase describes the purpose for the revival that came with Jesus. It refers to the economically impoverished, as well as to the poor in spirit. In

the revivals I've personally been involved with, both the United States and in other countries, I've noticed that prosperity is a common denominator; the economy of the entire region involved greatly improves.

"Heal the brokenhearted." The brokenhearted are those whose souls are wounded and full of pain, bitterness, unforgiveness, guilt, rejection, low self-esteem, and more. As previously explained, one of the manifestations brought about by a revival is laughter or joy in the Spirit because it has healing power. (See, for example, Psalm 126:1–2.) One of the most renowned pioneers of the "laughter" movement is my great friend Apostle Rodney Howard-Browne. A revival of joy and laughter resolves more problems than hours of therapy and counseling.

"Proclaim liberty to the captives." The captives are individuals who remain in bondage to addictions—alcohol, drugs, nicotine, gambling, pornography, illicit sex, and so forth. They are also those who are chained by the enemy in prisons of witchcraft, sorcery, and other practices of the occult that keep them in bondage to depression and suicidal thoughts. When the fire of God comes upon them, it destroys every shackle of slavery in their lives.

"Proclaim...recovery of sight to the blind." This aspect of divine healing is often produced when the fire of God falls, as a sign that it is also opening up spiritual eyes, enabling people to see God and His ways clearly.

"Set at liberty those who are oppressed." People who are depressed are being tortured by the enemy with thoughts of guilt, rejection, and insecurity, and they need deliverance in their minds. The revival of the Holy Spirit breaks demonic strongholds that keep people in bondage to oppression.

"Proclaim the acceptable year of the Lord." This phrase refers to proclaiming liberty to the earth and its people. In the Old Testament, God instructed the Israelites to have a Year of Jubilee every fifty years. (See Leviticus 25:10–19.) In this year, people were to have restored to them any property they had been forced to sell due to poverty and were to be set free from bondage if they had sold themselves into slavery to pay their debts. Also, no work was to be done in the fields during this year, so that both people and fields could be renewed.[5]

Spiritually, we experience Jubilee when we hear the good news of the gospel and receive God's forgiveness for all our sins. Since Jesus' resurrection, the church has been announcing the "Year of Jubilee" to the world—proclaiming that Jesus forgives sin and sets us free. Now, during the end-time "Year of Jubilee," believers will evangelize and proclaim the season of God's good-will both inside the churches and outside them: in the market-place, schools, hospitals, and prisons. The gospel of the king-dom will be announced throughout the earth. So, again, it is imperative that we go and preach in order to gather the great harvest of souls promised for the end times.

From the passage in Luke 4, therefore, we can conclude that a revival embraces all aspects of people's lives: physical, emotional, mental, social, and spiritual. It brings transforma-tion for all of humanity's needs. This knowledge should confirm in us an urgency to cry out to God for His fire to be released. In my own ministry, I have seen lives transformed in each of these areas by the fire of God. Let me tell you the story of one of our pastors, Tommy Acosta.

Tommy was born in Cuba and grew up without a father. When he moved to Miami as a child, he had a great void in his heart, which led him to seek refuge in bad relationships, alco-hol, and drugs from the time he was fourteen. At twenty-one, tired of his life and hoping to leave his addictions to drug and alcohol behind, he decided to look for his father. Sadly, that encounter proved a disappointment because he did not receive the love he was looking for. This caused him to fall deeper into his addictions to LSD, hallucinogens, pills, crack—anything he could get his hands on. When he returned to Miami, he was in even more distress, and his hopes for his life were all but destroyed.

---

[5] See Merrill F. Unger, *The New Unger's Bible Dictionary*, R. K. Harrison, ed., "Festivals: Jubilee" (Chicago: Moody Press, 1988), 408–09.

Even with all these things working against him, Tommy managed to graduate from school with the title of electronics engineer and open his own business. He also met his wife, Sarahi, and they were married six months later. Yet financial prosperity only enabled him to spend more on his addictions. Sarahi knew about his drinking but did not know the extent of his addiction to alcohol or the fact that he used drugs. When she discovered his drug addiction, their marriage began to suffer. They argued all the time, and their family life was chaotic; there was no peace. They had a son, but Tommy's addictions kept him from spending much time with him. Later, they had a baby girl.

Sarahi, too, had experienced a difficult childhood. Her father had abandoned her mother and her, and now she was in her own private marital hell. She was drowning in bitterness and wanted to burn down the house and take her own life.

Tommy began to hate his wife until there was no relationship between them. He kept drinking, but he did not accept help from anyone because he believed he could stop using alcohol anytime he wanted to. Eventually, he decided to attend Alcoholics Anonymous, but he did not change. He was now drinking every day. On a typical day, he would start with vodka and then smoke a cigar and marijuana. His addictions finally led him to the point of vomiting blood and receiving the diagnosis that he had cirrhosis of the liver—a condition that causes the liver to deteriorate and malfunction.

Even this knowledge did not change his lifestyle. Yet, one day, something happened that shook him forever. He arrived home, drunk as always, and went to bed, only to be awakened by his wife's horrific screams. She had discovered their two-year-old daughter dead! The little girl had been put to sleep in her crib, but, minutes later, her older brother had found her. Their daughter had tried to climb out of her crib and had somehow gotten herself caught in the cord of the vertical blinds and accidentally hung herself.

Tommy ran to the room. He desperately untangled the cord from his daughter's neck and rushed her to the hospital. When they arrived, the doctors were able to restart her heart, but they had little hope of saving her life. Tommy and Sarahi spent the next four days in torture. He felt guilty, and both of them were thinking of taking their own lives. The second day in the hospital, someone spoke to them about Jesus, but they made no decision at that time.

The day their daughter was disconnected from the machines that had been keeping her alive—she was already dead—both Tommy and Sarahi accepted Jesus as their Lord and Savior. As he repeated the "sinner's prayer," Tommy experienced what felt like an electric current pierce his back and exit through his chest. He felt as if he would explode from anguish, but, in an instant, he was born again and completely delivered from twenty-two years of addiction. He was also completely healed of hypertension and cirrhosis. He had a new liver—something that can be accomplished in the natural only by a liver transplant.

Tommy's past was buried the same week he buried his daughter. From that point, his relationship with his wife completely changed. They began to love each other deeply once more. As their relationships with God intensified, both were led to serve Him in the ministry. Today, Tommy is a pastor and Sarahi is a prophet. They rescue lost souls, restore marriages, and deliver people from addiction and pain. If you are experiencing the same oppression that Tommy was—or something even worse—the fire of God is your answer. Pastor Tommy and Sarahi Acosta praise God every day for the fire that transformed them forever. This same fire can transform you.

"Revive Your Work!"

O Lord, revive Your work in the midst of the years! In the midst of the years make it known. (Habakkuk 3:2)

The Israelites asked God to *"revive"* His work. The word *"revive"* is translated from the Hebrew word *chayah*, and some additional meanings of this word are "quicken," "restore to life," "save," and "give life." They wanted God to renew or revitalize His work.

I believe that every new believer experiences a "reviving" when he or she first meets the Lord; the Bible refers to this as the *"first love"* (Revelation 2:4). In our first love, we experience so much passion for Jesus that we tell everyone about Him, His love, and His power. We are so on fire for Him that we want to share it with the entire world. But, after a while, for different reasons, we lose that passion. This is why the prophet Habakkuk prayed to God to revive His work *"in the midst of the years."* Today, there are thousands of believers who have lost their fire and passion for God. If this is your situation, I believe that as you read this book, the Holy Spirit will release that fire and passion in you once more.

When the church loses the fire, God's revival is interrupted. As we have seen, this circumstance leads to people's search for religious substitutes, new methods, rules, and structures in an effort to raise up what is dead. The worst part of this result is that the substitutes do not allow the new wine of the Holy Spirit to flow. The new wineskins that carry the new wine of revival are flexible men and women who understand that a genuine, living relationship with the Father is higher than a religious structure, that life is more important than tradition, regulations, and order. Please do not misunderstand me. I am in total agreement with the need for order in the church, but only as long as we continue to be flexible and willing to move according to the leading of the Holy Spirit. The new wine—the revival—is life, not law. It is a relationship with the living God and the experience of the fire of His presence.

Essential Steps to Walk in Revival

To walk in either personal or ministerial revival, we must follow these five fundamental steps:

1. Cry Out to God to Be Ignited

Hear the word of the LORD! Thus says the Lord GOD:
"Behold, I will kindle a fire in you...." (Ezekiel 20:47)

Even though God is talking about judgment by fire in this verse, we can apply it to the other purpose of the fire, which is to ignite passion in us as we are purified by Him. If we recognize our passive spiritual condition, lack of commitment, lukewarm attitude, and complacency, God will kindle a fire in us that will burn up all these hindrances and transform our lives, thus making us into instruments that will light up others who are in the same state of indifference. When we recognize our spiritual condition and cry out for revival, we will receive the fire of His presence.

2. Break Down the Old Atmosphere in the Local Church

In the previous chapter, I explained how and why we need to break through the hard atmosphere of oppression and doubt to create another atmosphere of glory and the presence of God. If this is not done, it will be very difficult for revival to come and even more difficult for it to remain. To accomplish this breakthrough, let us remember that our praise should be high and our worship deep.

When the old atmosphere is changed by an atmosphere of glory, then hunger and thirst for God are produced in people's spirits.

---

3. Be Willing to Pay the Price for Revival

Our ministry is a living testimony that it is worth paying the price for the fire. From the beginning, we have had a continuous revival. What do I mean by this? We have witnessed or heard about the salvation of thousands of people at the altar of the church and thousands more in the nations in which we have ministered. Thousands have been filled by the Holy Spirit and baptized in water to become faithful disciples of the Lord and have been filled with the Holy Spirit. We have witnessed countless healings, deliverances, and restored marriages and families; thousands of young people have been delivered from drug addiction, and there have been miracles, signs, wonders, and incidents of supernatural provision. Thousands receive and are filled with joy and fire, and thousands are ignited by the fire of the passion of God and go out to preach Jesus everywhere. I could continue listing the fruits of this continuous revival, but I believe that the key has been the constant manifestation of the glory of God in our congregation, as well as the churches under our spiritual covering, which are spread throughout thirty nations of the world and manifest the same revival and evidence the same fruit.

How often have we seen these things? Every time I have preached the Word of God—for more than twenty years, locally and internationally. I believe this is due to the fact that we have made ourselves available to God, that we are committed and ready to pay the price to have a continuous revival of the Spirit in our midst. Likewise, we have taken this revival of miracles, salvations, and deliverances to over fifty nations around the globe, with the same glorious results. And we plan to continue expanding and bringing the fire to every country and continent where the Lord will take us.

4. Decide to Seek and to Have an Experience with God's Fire

> *I know your works, that you are neither cold nor hot. I could wish you were cold or hot. So then, because you are lukewarm, and neither cold nor hot, I will vomit you out of My mouth.* (Revelation 3:15–16)

The city of Laodicea was on an important trade route and was very prosperous. It was also a growing banking center.

Laodicea had many industries and was famous for producing an eye ointment called *collyrium*.[6] But the arrogant atmosphere of that city had been taken into the church there, and the Lord had to call His people to repentance. The city's financial prosperity caused the believers to feel self-sufficient. Jesus told them to acquire from Him *"gold refined in the fire"* to be truly wealthy and special ointment to heal their spiritual blindness. (See verses 17–18.)

Unfortunately, the attitude of the Laodiceans is the state of mind of a good part of the church of Christ today. We essentially have self-satisfied congregations full of "secret agents"—agents undercover—who never speak to anyone about Jesus and who are not a voice in their communities to express the values of the kingdom and to confront the moral issues. They are people who have chosen to conform to dead religious systems, having the appearance of being Christians without the power (see 2 Timothy 3:5); they have been absolutely neutralized by the enemy. These believers do not take into account that their condition displeases God. Because of their lukewarm attitudes, they expose themselves to being vomited from His mouth and to being consumed by His fire of judgment. It is time to decide to be on fire for God. This decision will certainly appall some people and make others uncomfortable. Yet, as long as we please God, we should not worry about other people's attitudes and opinions.

5. Revive the Gifts Within Us

Therefore I remind you to stir up the gift of God which is in you through the laying on of my hands.

(2 Timothy 1:6)

The church is full of believers who have received special gifts from God but have completely shut them down. Many have

---

[6] *The Zondervan Pictorial Bible Dictionary*, Merrill C. Tenney, gen. ed., "Laodicea" (Grand Rapids, MI: Zondervan Publishing House, 1967), 476, and Simon J. Kistemaker, *Comentario al Nuevo Testamento: Apocalipsis* (Grand Rapids, MI: Libros Desafío, 2004), http://cofccasanova.files.wordpress.com/2009/05/apocalipsis-simon-j.pdf.

received gifts for music, ministerial gifts (see Ephesians 4:11–12), and motivational gifts (see Romans 12:6–8), while others have received the grace to prophesy, teach the Word, or move in the area of leadership, or government (see 1 Corinthians 12:27–28), but they are wasting their gifts because their fire has been extinguished. If this is your situation, God will call you to account for that! Revive the fire of the gift!

In 2 Timothy 1:6, the apostle Paul urged Timothy to stir up the fire of the gift he had imparted to him. The Greek word translated *"stir up"* is *anazopureo*, which means "to rekindle." This is the only time this word is used in the New Testament. Paul did not say to resurrect or revive it, as in Habakkuk 3:2, but he exhorted Timothy to stir up—to rekindle—the fire of the gift of God that he had already received and that had been active in the beginning. One major function of the apostolic ministry is to impart gifts and to lead people to reignite the gifts God has already given. This is exactly what I am doing with you right now! First, we must stir up our personal gifts so that, later, with the same fire, we can help others stir up their gifts. This demands a decision on our part to seek to be ignited by His fire, now!

Dear friend, allow me the opportunity to pray for your life, so that the fire of the presence of God can come upon you, and you can begin to seek His face and His fire.

Heavenly Father, thank You for each person reading this book. I ask that those who have never been filled with power through the baptism of the Holy Spirit with the evidence of speaking in other tongues be filled right now. In Jesus' name, amen.

Dear reader, my advice to you is to open your mouth now and begin to speak the words the Holy Spirit gives you in other tongues. And, in the name of Jesus, I release the fire of the presence of God to everyone who hungers for it. I declare that you are submerged and ignited this instant. Receive it now and be filled with the power and fire! Have absolute faith and conviction that His fire is burning your interior at this instant. Once you are ignited—on fire—go as an instrument of the Lord and be a witness of Jesus. Call the lost to salvation, heal the sick, cast out demons, and deliver the captives. Amen!

EXPERIENCES WITH GOD

- The time you've spent in intimacy with God as you've read this book will begin to produce fruit. Pray for the fire of God to purify and sanctify your life and to release in you a passion for saving souls.

- Once you are ignited by His fire and passion, do as I urged at the end of this chapter and gather the great harvest! God will give you supernatural boldness to preach His Word, confirming it with miracles, signs, and wonders.

12

Earthen Vessels Chosen to Manifest His Glory

From the beginning of creation, God intended men and women to live and walk in His glory—to be carriers of His presence. As we have seen, His purpose has always been to dwell in us. That is why He deposited in us His breath of life and why He regards us as the supreme beings among His creation, crowning us with glory.

> *You have made* [man] *a little lower than the angels, and You have crowned him with glory and honor.*
> (Psalm 8:5)

Human beings were the first tabernacle of the presence of God. Yet, from the moment man sinned and fell away from God's glory, He no longer had a physical dwelling place in which to reside. We can see a symbol of this reality in the account of the great flood, from which Noah and his family were saved through the shelter of the ark. After forty days and nights, the rain finally stopped, and

> [Noah] *also sent out from himself a dove, to see if the waters had receded from the face of the ground.*
> (Genesis 8:8)

In the Bible, a dove is usually emblematic of the Holy Spirit. When the dove first flew out of the ark, it could not find a place to rest. This symbolizes God's desire for a permanent place in which to dwell. He could not return to live within human beings until Jesus paid the price for humanity's sin, resulting in the spirits of humans being made new to receive the gift of the Holy Spirit.

Jesus Became the Dwelling Place of God's Glory

In the Old Testament, God's Spirit rested on people who fulfilled various leadership roles—kings, priests, prophets, and judges—but He did not remain with them. When the Spirit descended on someone, that person would prophesy or receive a special boldness to do something, but once he finished what he'd been led to do, the Spirit would leave. His presence was only temporary. In some additional examples, the glory of God *"descended and stood at"* the door of the Tent of Meeting, allowing Moses to speak with the Lord (see Exodus 33:9–11); it descended upon and filled the tabernacle (see, for example, Exodus 40:34); and it filled Solomon's temple (see 1 Kings 8:10–11). But all of these visitations were temporal, as well. Then came the unfolding of God's plan of restoration:

> *And the Word became flesh and dwelt among us, and we beheld His glory, the glory as of the only begotten of the Father, full of grace and truth.* (John 1:14)

This is a beautiful verse to reflect on because we see here, for the first time since the fall of humanity, the revelation of God dwelling in a Man. He made Jesus—who was fully human as well as fully God—a dwelling place, a home, a tabernacle for Himself. Jesus walked on earth as *"Immanuel,"* which means *"God with us"* (Matthew 1:23). God the Father dwelled in His Son, who came to heal the sick and deliver those who were oppressed by the devil. When Jesus went to the cross, He surrendered His life to redeem humanity from the wages of sin, was raised on the third day, and later ascended into heaven. However, before this took place, He prayed to the Father in a way that no other man had done before. Let us return to the verse we began with in chapter 1:

And the glory which You gave Me I have given them,
that they may be one just as We are one. (John 17:22)

Jesus' declaration is extraordinary, regardless of how we look at it! His mission was to restore the glory we had lost. We are the dwelling place of His presence, and we carry His glory inside of us. Can you imagine human beings walking in the same dimension of glory that raised Jesus from the dead? That is the essence of Jesus' prayer to the Father. The Son of God, through His death on the cross, paid the price to restore the glory of the Father to all of humanity. Today, every believer, as a member of His body, is responsible for carrying, protecting, and manifesting that glory on earth. Finally, God has found a permanent dwelling place. We are the temple built not by men but by God's hand, where His presence dwells by the Holy Spirit. (See 1 Corinthians 6:19.) This is wonderful!

What Is Your Relationship with the Glory?

Yet people in the church today have different relationships with the glory that is within them. We have looked at several of these relationships at various points throughout this book. Let us review them here so we can gain a clear understanding of people's perspectives on this most remarkable gift to us.

- **People who oppose the glory.** There are those who criticize and persecute the revelation of the glory, as well as its manifestations. As we have seen, some do so because they do not understand it, others because they are afraid of anything that is new or that is beyond what they have already experienced, and still others because they have been blinded by traditions and the spirit of religiosity.

- **People who follow the glory.** There are those who are satisfied with watching from afar what the glory of God is doing through others; they never dare to enter the river of the Spirit in order to do the same.

Some people might hold back out of fear of the unknown, fear of commitment, or fear of the fire of God, which exposes their spiritual condition; others might hold back because they have made decisions that have led them away from this river. Still others might choose to watch the glory from afar because they lack sufficient knowledge or revelation about it.

- **People who carry the glory.** In essence, each believer is a carrier of the glory of God. Nevertheless, just being a carrier is not enough. We must also receive the revelation of His presence. In this way, Jesus can become a reality in our lives and in the lives of people in all nations of the earth, and He can manifest His presence to bless others. One of the reasons I wrote this book was to encourage believers to become active carriers of His glory!

- **People who bring the revelation of the glory.** God raises up men and women to teach others the revelation and knowledge of His glory—there can be no manifestation without first having the revelation. However, though these teachers bring the revelation, they do not necessarily manifest it.

- **People who manifest the glory.** Those who manifest the glory of God on earth have received the revelation of it and are putting their knowledge into practice through visible demonstrations. The Lord is raising up a bold and different generation in this season to display His glory from among those who are willing to pay the price to manifest it.

- **People who protect or guard the glory.** When a move of God—in this case the glory—comes upon the earth, the Lord raises up people to protect and safeguard it from being taken to the extremes, thus protecting the revelation of the glory from losing its original purpose. Every time God reveals a truth to the body of Christ, the enemy raises a parallel lie to discredit it; his goal is to prevent people from believing it. God has restored the ministry of the apostle as a custodian of the truths He is revealing to the church in these last days. In accordance with this protection and safeguarding, all teachings from such movements should be weighed, as the words of prophets and others exercising spiritual gifts should be, to make sure they are consistent with the Scriptures. (See 1 Corinthians 14:32; 2 Timothy 2:16–17.)

What is your relationship with the glory? Are you someone who manifests the presence of God, or are you content to watch others do so? Here is what the glory can do:

During one of our church services, a man named José Luis shared his testimony with us. A blood test had revealed that he was HIV positive. When he was diagnosed, the doctors immediately put him on antiretroviral medications, which made him nauseous and dizzy. Even so, he took these medications for four years. At the time, José Luis was an unbeliever, a non-practicing Catholic.

One day, while watching television, he came across our program, *Tiempo de Cambio*, exactly when I said, "Do not turn your television off!" José said that these words impacted him, and he continued to listen. His sister-in-law had invited him to come to the church several times, but he'd never gone. However, when he saw the program, he decided to visit and, when he did, he received the Lord. Little by little, his life began to change. He attended a House of Peace meeting where the leader prayed for the power of God to heal him. José began to believe he could be healed. He decided, by faith, to stop taking the medications, in spite of the fact that the doctors had told him that if he did so, he would quickly die.

A year later, he got tested again, and the results were negative. The AIDS virus had disappeared! The Lord had healed him. Today, José Luis is a happy and changed man. He used to be harsh and coldhearted with his employees—so much so that no one wanted to work with him. Now, that situation has changed because of the miracle that took place in his heart, as well as his body. God used a House of Peace leader to be the instrument of José Luis's healing and salvation. He can use you in the same way! Will you move from revelation to manifestation?

The Former Glory and the Latter Glory

As we manifest God's presence in our times, we must understand what the Bible means by the "former glory" and the "latter glory."

> *"The glory of this latter temple shall be greater than the former," says the* LORD *of hosts.* (Haggai 2:9)

What Is the Former Glory?

The former glory includes all the events and supernatural acts that took place from *"the law and the prophets"* in the Old Testament through John the Baptist in the New Testament. Jesus said,

> *The law and the prophets were until John. Since that time the kingdom of God has been preached, and everyone is pressing into it.* (Luke 16:16)

The following are some of the spectacular manifestations of the former glory: the calling of Moses through the burning bush; Aaron's rod turning into a serpent and eating the rods/snakes of Pharaoh's servants; the ten plagues of Egypt (water turned to blood; frogs; lice; flies; livestock dying of disease; boils; hail; locusts; darkness; and the death of the firstborn); the deliverance of the Israelites from Egypt and their instant wealth and health; the Israelites crossing the Red Sea on dry land; the bitter waters of Marah sweetened; manna from heaven and quail provided as food; Moses drawing water from the rock; the pillar of fire that led the Israelites by night, and the pillar of cloud that led them by day; the Israelites' sandals not wearing out (the children's sandals must have miraculously grown as the children grew); the cloud of glory resting upon and filling the tabernacle; Joshua dividing the waters of the Jordan River and conquering the Promised Land with the new generation of Israelites; the walls of Jericho falling and the defeat of the city; Gideon conquering the Midianites with only a small remnant of men; Elisha causing the ax to float on the Jordan River; Samson tearing apart a lion and killing thousands of Philistines in their temple through his supernatural strength; the widow in Zarephath being provided for by the multiplication of the oil and flour, and then having her son raised from the dead, both through the ministry of Elijah; Elijah's sacrifice on Mount Carmel being consumed with fire from heaven; the return of rain in Israel after a three-and-a-half-year drought; Elisha's bones reviving a dead man; David killing the Philistine giant Goliath, becoming king, and defeating Israel's enemies; Daniel's friends surviving the fiery furnace; and Daniel being preserved from the lions' den by the powerful hand of God. And then, before initiating the new covenant through His death and resurrection, Jesus gave sight to the blind; hearing to the deaf; health to the lame, the lepers, and the paralytics; and even life to the dead. He walked on water, calmed storms, and fed thousands through the multiplication of only a few loaves and fish. All these things took place under the old covenant. If they represent the former glory, imagine what the latter glory will be like!

What Is the Latter Glory?

Jesus was the bridge between the former glory and the latter glory. He participated in the former glory since He both lived under the law and fulfilled it while He was on earth. (See Matthew 5:17.) Then, He ushered in the latter glory after His resurrection. This glorious movement was released in the Upper Room on Pentecost. Again, if everything we read above (and much more) took place according to the former glory, which was under the lesser covenant—the law and the blood of sacrificed animals—how much more we can expect with the latter glory, which is under a *"better covenant,...established on better promises"* (Hebrews 8:6) and comes through faith in the blood of Jesus, the perfect Lamb! This is why Jesus said that we would do *"greater works"* (John 14:12) than He did while on the earth.

What manifestations can we expect to see in the latter glory? We can expect to see an acceleration of God's work in every area, as well as radical transformations, miracles, signs, wonders, the casting out of demons, millions of souls won for Christ, dominion over nature, supernatural provision and protection, the shaking of cities, nations, and continents by revivals produced by the glory of God, and other phenomena we cannot fathom.

Recently, I was invited to preach to more than twelve thousand church leaders in Lima, Peru, by Pastor Peter Hornung, a dear friend who has one of the largest congregations in Latin America. The Lord gave me specific instructions for what I was to tell them:

- Impart a clear understanding that He is our Father and we are His beloved children (a spiritual reality many people have difficulty accepting because of dysfunctional family backgrounds).

- Teach that He desires to restore His supernatural power in our generation to fulfill His purposes.

As these leaders received the above biblical truths, God stirred up what was latent within them: their ability to hear His voice through the Holy Spirit and their anointing to move in the supernatural, so they could go and win souls for Jesus.

At the end of the service, the leaders went to the malls in Lima and presented the gospel to every person they encountered. The glory upon them was so great that Pastor Peter and his son asked me to stay one more day. I accepted the invitation because the Lord confirmed that it was His will for me to do so. The next day, God led me to show these twelve thousand Peruvian leaders how to have an experience with His glory. We praised and worshipped God passionately until the atmosphere was ready for God to speak. Seven minutes into the teaching, the cloud of the glory of God descended, deeply touching the leaders. Everyone was crying uncontrollably. The presence of God could be felt in every corner of the church. As this was taking place, people were healed, fractured relationships were restored, and a true understanding of God as Father and us as His children was established in their hearts.

I believe the latter glory is the union of the two glories; it magnifies the power that is released and the wonders of which we testify. The manifestations of this new glory are taking place right now, in the present, and we will see them in their fullness in the future. Let us note an important fact: every manifestation of the former glory that took place while Israel walked in the desert was a sovereign act of God because the people lacked faith—they knew only how to murmur and complain. Yet, through Christ, we can live within the dimensions of faith and glory, having the ability to experience the manifestations of God's glory in the *now*! All because Jesus conquered the cross and was raised from the dead!

The latter glory will be the joint manifestation of the latter and former glories.

I want to relate two additional miracles that I believe belong to the manifestations of the latter glory. On one of my trips to Argentina, I met a twenty-one-year-old man named Matias who was no taller than a ten-year-old boy. Matias was born with achondroplasia, which is "a genetic disorder disturbing normal growth of cartilage, resulting in a form of dwarfism characterized by a usually normal torso and shortened limbs."[7]

The doctors explained to Matias's mother that a lack of amniotic fluid had stunted her son's growth in the womb. The medical resources in the area where they live are limited. Even

---

[7] *Merriam-Webster's 11th Collegiate Dictionary*, 2003, electronic version, s.v. "achondroplasia."

so, they consulted several doctors, but none could give them any hope. Matias was unable to rotate his arms. He also could not walk steadily, and he underwent surgery to correct the curvature in his legs—they were in danger of crossing over into an X—but without positive results.

This young man was also dealing with severe guilt and low self-esteem because he considered himself a burden to his parents. He sought relief in alcohol and drugs, and he stopped going to school because he felt rejected by his fellow students. He desperately needed a miracle! Then, he attended one of our healing services, and after I declared a word for creative miracles, he came forward to testify. He said he felt the fire of God touch him, and he was able to move his arms normally. Matias cried so much that it was plain to see that the powerful presence of God was upon him. When I saw how small he was, my heart was moved with compassion, and the Holy Spirit guided me to declare that in twenty-four hours, his body would begin to grow. Then, he fell under the power of God.

The event ended, and I returned home. The following day, Matias's pastor—who is also a doctor—called to tell me that Matias was growing! After I declared that word over him, Matias had grown a little over two centimeters (about three quarters of an inch) in the first twenty-four hours. Forty-eight hours later, he had grown three more centimeters (a little more than an inch); seventy-two hours later, three additional centimeters. He grew until his clothing no longer fit him properly. In three days, he grew a total of eight centimeters (a little more than three inches)! And he continues to grow!

Matias started to complain of muscle aches—especially in the muscles between his hips and legs, as well as his quadriceps—so he returned to the doctor to see what was happening. The doctor explained that since his bones had grown so much, all of his muscles, tendons, tissues, and so forth had to adjust to it. This miracle transformed the life of a young man, his family, and all who know him. Matias returned to school, and he shares his testimony everywhere he goes, using it to increase the faith of others, who also need healing. What happened to him was impossible in the natural. I have never seen such a miracle.

In Lima, Peru, one of my spiritual sons, Pastor César Augusto Atoche, was rushed to the hospital due to an obstruction in his coronary artery. He underwent a double bypass. Immediately after the surgery, he suffered a fatal heart attack. The doctors did all that was humanly possible to resuscitate him, but to no avail. They left the operating room disheartened and informed his wife that he had died. Pastor Atoche's body was left in the operating room for a little over an hour. His loved ones were broken, crying at the death of their father, pastor, and leader. It was a very painful time of grief.

While this was occurring, I was in Dallas, Texas—over 3,200 miles away—doing a telethon for Enlace, a TBN affiliate. Pastor Atoche's wife had sent an offering to Enlace, and it was my turn to touch and pray for the offerings that had been called in. I had no idea what was happening to the pastor, but the Lord showed me something, and, in obedience, I gave the order: "Rise! In the name of Jesus, I order you to rise!" At that precise moment, Pastor Atoche came back to life—he resurrected! Imagine the commotion in the hospital! This is the power of the resurrection in Christ. God raised him from clinical death, and he went on to live with a perfectly healthy heart. Today, Pastor Atoche is an exceptional witness of what it means to move in the glory of God. He prays for the sick, and the power of the resurrection continues to manifest through him in Peru, healing, delivering, saving, and restoring life. The latter glory is manifesting!

You have no idea what God can do through you if you will only allow yourself to be used by Him in the latter glory. He is truly manifesting Himself in unique ways. We have seen phenomena such as people experiencing instant weight loss—some have immediately gone down several clothing sizes. Money has appeared in people's wallets or bank accounts that was not there before and for which there was no rational explanation. In addition, debts have been canceled supernaturally and mortgages have been paid in full without human intervention. Creative miracles are a common occurrence. For example, God has created kidneys, hips, and muscle tissue. He has created and elongated bones, given new teeth where they were missing, and caused hair to grow on the heads of those who were bald. And, He has delivered people from demonic bondage. However, the most important aspect is this: when the glory or presence of God manifests, radical transformations take place in people's lives. Jesus has not changed. He continues to transform lives and do miracles. (See Hebrews 13:8.)

I want to relate another testimony of a young man in Honduras named Sergio who belongs to a church under our spiritual covering:

> My older brother gave me the book *How to Walk in the Supernatural Power of God* as a gift. Many things have been revealed to me through the book, one being that faith is the first dimension of the supernatural and that faith is for "now" and not for the future— faith is now! In the book, Apostle Maldonado explains that when we declare something through prayer, we must also establish a time for the manifestation in the natural. That word hit me like lightning in the spirit. At the time, I needed money to fulfill my financial obligations at the university so I could graduate, but my bank account was negative. So I made the decision and prayed, saying, "Father, I am Your son, and I have served You. This revelation is mine today. I declare that by the end of this month, the money I need will appear in my bank account supernaturally." I continued in the spirit of worship with the full conviction that God would meet my need and answer my prayer. Two days later, I began to call the bank every day to check if a deposit had been made. Nothing happened until the last day I had declared in my prayer. On that day, I called the bank and, to my surprise and amazement, I was told that a deposit had been entered into

my account, and it was for an amount greater than what I needed! That was humanly impossible! I never told anyone that I needed money, and no one owed me money; that meant that only God could have made that miracle happen. I am amazed! I have never before experienced something of that sort. That day, I shared my testimony in church, and the entire congregation was touched. To seal the miracle, I continue to share the testimony with anyone willing to hear me—as Apostle Maldonado teaches in the book.

The eyes of your understanding being enlightened; that you may know what is the hope of His calling, what are the riches of the glory of His inheritance in the saints. (Ephesians 1:18)

The prayer that Jesus lifted before the Father in John 17:22, affirming that He had given His glory to His followers, is being realized in our times. The glory of God is the inheritance of every believer. And we must manifest it to others, so they can be saved, healed, and delivered, because they are heirs of God, just as we are. We need to understand that the glory is not for us to "store up" for our personal benefit alone.

But we have this treasure in earthen vessels, that the excellence of the power may be of God and not of us. (2 Corinthians 4:7)

In chapter 1, we learned that the Hebrew word for "glory," *kabowd*, can carry the idea of "abundance" and "wealth"—in other words, "treasure." And, the term *"earthen vessels"* in the above verse refers to human beings (Adam was formed from the dust of the earth), who are fragile and full of weaknesses, insecurities, shortcomings, and imperfections. How is it possible for this treasure, this glory, to be manifested through us? There is only one answer: it is possible when God, not man, is continually glorified in our lives.

We are chosen vessels that carry the "treasure of light" within us to the world, which consists in taking and manifesting the realities of heaven where there is need. When people see the supernatural things that take place through us, they will realize that this remarkable power comes from God. At this realization, they will begin to glorify Him. It is wonderful to know that, wherever we go, this treasure that dwells in us has the ability to save, heal, deliver, and transform hearts. The only requisite to having this treasure is to make ourselves available to manifest His glory.

In the Old Testament, only the Levites—purified and sanctified—were allowed to carry that presence. That is why some people think that miracles, signs, and wonders are not for today—or, if they take place, it is only in the churches, during the services, and exclusively through pastors and other ministers. This perspective causes people to set their eyes on men because they believe only these leaders can give us something from God. But Jesus prayed to the Father for *all* vessels of clay—all those who confess Him as Lord and Savior of their lives—to become carriers who manifest His glory. I want to emphasize again that the glory that manifests is not demonstrated only in the churches; it is revealed wherever the vessels of clay go: restaurants, workplaces, schools, sports arenas—basically, anywhere.

God Ordains Us to Demonstrate His Glory on Earth

Isaiah 60 includes a striking description of how we are to demonstrate God's glory in the world:

> *Arise [from the depression and prostration in which circumstances have kept you—rise to a new life]! Shine (be radiant with the glory of the Lord), for your light has come, and the glory of the Lord has risen upon you!* (Isaiah 60:1 AMP)

"Arise!" This is a calling, but it is also an order to make the decision and take action. Sadly, indifference is the condition of many believers today when faced with the great challenges imposed by the world. They are passive—waiting and not taking action. They are stuck in a worldly, atheistic system that keeps people without Jesus and His love and power—drowning in depression, confusion, and insecurities; sick and wounded. But today, God has given us an order: "Arise! Arise from that depression! Arise and set aside discouragement! Arise from failure! Arise from death! Arise into a new life!"

"Shine...." The word *"shine"* is translated from the Hebrew word *owr*, whose definitions include "to be or become light," "to be luminous," "to give, show light," and even "to set on fire." This shining occurs when we *"arise"* from that spiritual condition of passivity and conformity. To shine, we have to arise! God is ready to manifest His glory, but for this to happen, we need to take action.

"...for your light has come." God gives us His light to make us shine; this light is life and prosperity, as well as knowledge and guidance to carry out what He ordains. His light shining through us removes all traces of darkness around us; therefore, wherever we go, that light will transform our surroundings. Since each of us, as Christians, has God's light, we can determine what dimension of glory, or what portion of His light, we will allow to manifest on earth. Will the light we radiate be like the light of a lamp that shines over a desk, or will it be like an overhead light that brightens an entire room? Will it be like the light of the moon—only a reflection of solar light? Or will it be like the sun that shines brightly on the earth? The amount of God's light you choose to shine will determine the range of your influence and dominion.

In what degree of light are you operating? To impact the whole world with the gospel of the kingdom, we must shine fully with the glory of God. You were born to make history! It is time to shine in the midst of darkness!

Darkness is the terrifying influence of Satan's kingdom on earth. Light is the glory of God that removes the darkness.

God's light overcame the darkness when I was ministering in East London, South Africa. The Lord revealed through a word of knowledge that a woman in attendance at the meeting had AIDS. When I prayed for her, the demon oppressing her manifested by using her vocal cords. It screamed out, "I know who you are. I know you, and I hate you. I hate everyone." I took authority immediately in the name of Jesus and ordered the demonic spirit to leave her. Instantly, the woman fell on the floor under the power of God and began to tremble and shake. Then, she started to cry like someone who had spent a very long time being tormented and had finally been given relief. It was plain from the expression on her face that she was now free. Two days later, the same woman returned to the conference happy and accompanied by her family to testify that she had gone to the doctor for testing. She had the documents certifying that she was healed. I just did what God told me to do—arise and make His light shine in the midst of darkness—and He was glorified!

"...the glory of the Lord has risen upon you!" We always expect the glory of God to "fall" from above, because that is how it happened in the Old Testament. Today, the glory can still come *upon* us, the same as it did upon the early Christians (see, for example, Acts 11:15; 19:6), but it is also *within* us, just as it was for them—the former and the latter glory together. It is a treasure that is birthed in us, and revealed knowledge will bring about its manifestation. Earlier, we discussed what happened to Jesus at the Mount of Transfiguration, noting that using the term *transfigured* is like saying that whatever was inside has come out. The true essence has been expressed. And the same glory that Jesus had is in *us* today! God does not want to be limited. He wants us to allow Him to shine out from us to a lost world.

For behold, the darkness shall cover the earth, and deep darkness the people; but the LORD will arise over you, and His glory will be seen upon you. (Isaiah 60:2)

"His glory will be seen upon you." The glory of the Lord will manifest in a visible and tangible way when we *"arise."* The world will see the glory in us, but how will it manifest? God will do such things as attract multitudes to the church, speak to the hearts of people through words of knowledge and prophecy, and heal the brokenhearted through the embraces of believers.

This is the glory of God! It is not just theory, a pretty concept, or mere theology that is impossible to demonstrate in this natural realm. No! We will see the glory with our own eyes! But, again, for this to take place, we have to be willing to seek the lost, to testify of Jesus, and to demonstrate the gifts of the Holy Spirit; we must be prepared to *go* where there is need, manifesting His glory where people are struggling with depression, loneliness, sickness, and poverty. The question is: Are you willing to go? Are you willing to be used by God for His glory?

"The darkness shall cover the earth, and deep darkness the people." Spiritual darkness covers the earth, and that darkness is getting thicker, while the people have no idea what to do about it. The strongest evidences of this state of affairs include the escalating natural disasters taking place today—earthquakes, hurricanes, tsunamis, and so forth—as well as the constant shedding of blood, the multitudes dying of hunger, the endless wars among the nations, the increase of evil, and even the global economic crisis. What should believers do in the midst of this darkness? We can remain calm because the glory we carry has the power to alleviate the darkness and—ultimately—end it.

The glory of God can manifest in any of His aspects—visible and invisible—here and now.

We must decide which we love more: the glory or darkness. The Bible teaches us to expose the darkness but to have nothing to do with it. (See Ephesians 5:11.) If we love the light, we will run toward it, but if we love the darkness, we will flee from the light. There is no middle ground or room for being lukewarm or holding onto tradition. What side will you run to?

I had an opportunity to expose and defeat the darkness in the same meeting in East London, South Africa, in which the woman was healed of AIDS. The service had almost concluded when the Lord gave me a word of knowledge. By the Spirit, I knew there was a "witch doctor" who had come to perform some witchcraft against me and the service. I shared this with the people and then said, "I know you are here and that your god has no power. My God is greater than yours; this is why you are now shaking in your seat."

I made another call for the lost to receive salvation, and no one came forward. The Spirit of God revealed that this "witch doctor" was a woman. Immediately, a woman came forward, and I asked her if she was the witch. She nodded. Then, I said, "Do you know that God loves you? If you repent tonight, He will deliver you from witchcraft." I quickly led her to pray the "sinner's prayer" and receive Jesus as her Lord. When I stepped off the platform to pray for her, the demon manifested violently, challenging me. With boldness in the Spirit and with authority, I said, "By the finger of God, let her go!" The demon instantly left her. The next day, she returned to the service with her husband and other family members, completely transformed by the Holy Spirit. What had happened? The presence of God had shone in the midst of her darkness and rescued her life.

God's miracles in these days of the latter glory are taking place in the lives of individuals, but they are also manifesting in society. A few years ago, during our annual Apostolic and Prophetic Conference (CAP), something truly amazing happened. It was October, and together with the other guest speakers, we welcomed over twelve thousand people to the American Airlines Arena in Miami—more than six thousand of them were leaders representing the fivefold ministry from over fifty nations around the globe. Our purpose was to train and equip them to walk in the supernatural power of God and to take spiritual dominion over the areas where they lived. While we prayed for the conference, the Holy Spirit guided me to decree to the heavenlies over the city that no crimes would take place in the streets of Miami during the conference. (See Ephesians 6:12.) I took authority and dominion in the name of Jesus over the principalities and strongholds, prohibiting all criminal activity during those three days.

The conference was glorious. God did amazing wonders and miracles. In November, the police report was published for October. We were amazed to read that for the first time in forty-two years, no homicides were registered in Miami during the course of an entire month.[8] This is an example of how believers can exercise dominion over the forces of evil in their communities.

The Gentiles shall come to your light, and kings to the brightness of your rising.　　　　　　(Isaiah 60:3)

"...kings to the brightness of your rising." As I stated earlier in this book, I believe that for God's glory to descend, divine order must be established in the church through the fivefold ministry of apostles, prophets, evangelists, pastors, and teachers. If we receive and honor this fivefold ministry, the promise in the above verse will come to pass. Once God manifests His glory over us and it becomes visible to the world, then the world's leaders—presidents, prime ministers, governors, mayors, senators, congresspeople—will seek our guidance and direction. They will understand that they do not have the answers for the people whom they govern in the midst of such dense darkness. Many of those leaders have already consulted witches, sorcerers, and soothsayers but have found no answers. When God manifests His glory upon us, we will not give them answers based on human understanding or natural reasoning but on the revelation of the Holy Spirit. We will give them supernatural prophetic words that will speak specifically to their lives, cities,

---

[8] http://articles.sun-sentinel.com/2008-11-03/news/0811020215_1_homicide-miami-lt-girlfriend-s-brother.

and nations, as Joseph did for the pharaoh of Egypt and Daniel for the king of Babylon. (See Genesis 41; Daniel 2, 4.)

> *...they come to you; your sons shall come from afar, and your daughters shall be nursed at your side.*
> (Isaiah 60:4)

"...*your sons shall come from afar.*" God is bringing home a generation of prodigal sons and daughters to save them and raise them up in this movement of His glory. He is bringing them *"from afar,"* releasing them from alcohol abuse, drug addiction, immorality, depression, and more. This generation yearns for the supernatural and is running toward the light. It is being transformed in His glory to deliver others who are held captive to the same bondages and strongholds.

Peter, one of my spiritual sons, is a living testimony of this remnant. Here is his story:

> My father died of AIDS when I was fourteen years old; that was when I began to use drugs and alcohol. At seventeen, I was diagnosed with schizophrenia and obsessive-compulsive behavior. The doctors told me I had no cure and that I would have to live the rest of my life on medication. I felt empty and did not want to live.
>
> One day, I was invited by a friend to visit his church. When the evangelist made the call to receive Jesus as Lord, I felt that something was pulling me to the altar. I went forward and accepted Jesus and was even baptized on the same day. After that service, I felt like a whole new person. God showed me that Jesus was the only way. He delivered me from schizophrenia, and I was able to stop using drugs. My psychiatrist said that I could not go without these drugs, but nine years later, I am still free and not on medication!
>
> God gave me a passion for souls....Sometime later, our spiritual father activated us to evangelize

with words of knowledge and prophecy, activating others to do the same. The fruit was even greater than before. Evangelism has become a way to prove that God is real and to manifest Him....I approach large groups of people and say that I can prove God is real. I pray for healing, and they receive healing. We are seeing multitudes come to Christ! While evangelizing outside of a school in Miami, the students made a line waiting for us to give them a word from God. Almost everyone was in tears. Three students who were saved that day are already mentors in the church: Sandra, a seventeen-year-old girl, who said she would have committed suicide if she had not been saved on that day, is now an evangelist who flows in the supernatural and has led many to the feet of Christ. Yosselyn, twenty-one years old, has won over one hundred souls from the day of her salvation. She prays for healing and miracles. And Joel, eighteen years old—full of piercings—was touched by the prophetic word he received. He began to attend church and lead his professors to Christ—prophesying and producing supernatural healings. Some time ago, the Lord used me to evangelize a young man named Victor who was sixteen years old. I found him outside of the school gathered with a few of his friends, all of whom were high on marijuana. I gave them a word of knowledge, and right there they received the Lord. Victor was shocked! Also, he was waiting to be sentenced to years in prison for four crimes he had committed. We prayed for him and, miraculously, they let him go. Less than a year after his salvation, he was already a House of Peace leader, leading many lost souls to Christ. He has delivered other young people and brought his entire family to Christ. He is a carrier of the glory and manifests it through miracles and healing. God reveals to him words of knowledge— names and dates—to lead the lost to Christ. Since the day we started to activate others in the gifts, approximately forty of those we have led to Christ are now House of Peace leaders and mentors who do the same for others. This is a chain reaction that never ceases to grow!

Church leaders need an answer for everyone, especially the young people who are coming to their services not in search of religion but to see the power and glory of God. These young people want to have a personal experience with the living Christ who can answer their questions. The main reason many young adults refuse to attend church today is that all they see is religion, formalities, rules, and an appearance of power. They are able to identify the hypocrisy in the traditions, and they flee from them. They want to see the manifest power of God! We cannot give them just theology. It is urgent that we give them a demonstration of the palpable power of God. It is time to break the empty rites, religious structures, molds, and appearances; it is time to stop being an institutional church so we can become living temples where the glory of God can be constantly witnessed. Then, God will raise a generation of young people who will shake the world.

...the wealth of the Gentiles shall come to you.

(Isaiah 60:5)

"...the wealth of the Gentiles" will be transferred to the righteous. (See also Proverbs 13:22.) Remember that one aspect of the glory—the *kabowd*—of God is wealth. The wealth of the gentiles—the unbelievers—will come to the righteous in the manifestation of His glory, just as the Israelites received wealth from the Egyptians when they left Egypt by the powerful hand of the Lord. Now is the time for God to release unusual favor over His sons and daughters so we can receive the wealth of the unrighteous by His grace.

Our heavenly Father delights in providing for His children. I am reminded of the testimony of Luisa and Margarita, two sisters who moved to Miami from the nation of Colombia. They were successful professionals but were living their lives independent of God. One day, they decided to restore their relationships with Him. This recommitment was followed by strong persecution from the enemy. In the process, they lost their business, wealth, contacts, and lifestyle, and they were in grave financial distress, to the point where they were bankrupt. And yet, through all of this, they never turned their backs on God. They continued to tithe, to give offerings, and to give their firstfruit to the Lord. (See Proverbs 3:9.) They also learned to seize their miracles.

When they thought they were about to become homeless, God opened a door, and they were welcomed into a home where they did not have to pay rent, electricity, or water for six months. They knew that God was in control. During their crisis, the Lord began to give them divine connections and covered them with supernatural grace and favor. One day, a prosperous Christian businessman visited Margarita at her place of employment and said, "God spoke to me, saying that my wife and I had to help and provide for you, and we both agreed to do it." Margarita did not understand, but they insisted on knowing how much money she and her sister needed because they were going to pay off their debts. And they have! Every month, for the past two years, they have deposited $3,500 into the sisters' account. As if this were not enough, a few months later, this couple called and invited them to look at a house that was for sale. They did, and as they were leaving, the husband and wife asked their opinion on the property. The sisters said it was big, beautiful, and in a good location. Then, the businessman and his wife said, "Good, I am glad you both like it, because it is yours!" Right there, they gave them a check to pay off the house. A few days later, the bank gave them the title deed to their property. The Lord provided supernaturally! Praise God! The joy and gratitude of these women was so great that it is impossible to put into words, but the impact that their testimony has caused—and continues to cause—has encouraged others to trust in God's provision.

You may still be thinking, *What can I do for these miracles to take place in me and through me?* The answer is to create an atmosphere of worship that will enable His glory to descend, miracles to take place, and souls to be won for the kingdom. Then, you will be able to discover the true purpose for which you were created, and there is nothing more satisfying than that—your life will finally make sense. You will rise each morning and live each day passionately, as you see the supernatural power of God flow through your lips and hands.

You can join the "new wine" generation of men and women whom God is raising up, whose mission is to impact cities, nations, and continents. You can become an instrument that God will use in releasing the greatest flow of miracles the world has ever seen and to gather the final harvest of souls.

We cannot see the manifest presence of God if we are not seeking it.

Again, you can decide what your relationship to the glory will be and how you will respond to it. Don't just store up information—act on it! Allow God to give you a revelation of His glory—a *rhema* word—and say, "I want to manifest His glory." Now, go out and touch others with the presence of the Lord!

EXPERIENCES WITH GOD

- Today, during your time of personal worship, commit to separating yourself for God's use, so you can become a true chosen vessel, a carrier of His glory.

- Ask the Holy Spirit to guide you to be a light in your neighborhood, city, and country.

13

Manifesting God's Glory as You Go

Wherever I go, I anticipate that God's presence will manifest. I continually live with that expectation. For example, at a Christian convention, during a book signing for one of my books, the presence of God suddenly became tangible. In front of me was a woman who had a serious back problem because one of her legs was shorter than the other. She had experienced years of continuous pain. These were symptoms of scoliosis, a deformity of the spine resulting in a curvature in some part of it. I had the woman sit down and, in the name of Jesus, I ordered the short leg to grow longer. Instantly, the leg grew longer by almost half an inch, and the pain disappeared.

I often minister in this way. I will be talking to people when, suddenly, I know God's presence is there, because my heart is constantly seeking or waiting for His presence to manifest. Every time this happens, I surrender to what the Holy Spirit wants to do at that moment, and a miracle is immediately produced.

Will you carry the presence and glory of God everywhere you go, manifesting His works? In this last chapter, I want to take you to another level of passion and boldness that will compel you to go out and win souls for Jesus, disciple believers, and be a witness who manifests God's glory through miracles, healings, and other marvels. Jesus' promise in Mark 16:17 specifies that signs will follow believers, and you are not the exception. People of all ages, races, cultures, and social and economic status are being transformed into vessels that manifest His glory.

God's Presence Is Manifesting Everywhere

I want to tell you about some additional great things God is doing through those who have made themselves available to be used by Him.

Miguel Bogaert is a young man who excels in medicine and social outreach in the Dominican Republic. He is a doctor, thoracic surgeon, and pulmonologist, as well as a former colonel in the air force. In addition, he is the only Latino to receive the Supremo de Plata award, which is given to honors students in Spain. Miguel and his wife, Montserrat de Bogaert, who is a computer engineer, are pastors of one of the fastest-growing congregations in their country—a church full of Christians on fire for Jesus. However, it all started when Miguel hit bottom in his life. Here is his testimony:

> Regardless of my professional merits, my life was in chaos because of my upbringing in a dysfunctional home. I was a rebel without a cause, a depressed alcoholic who felt rejected and who suffered unforgiveness and lack of identity. At nineteen, I tried to commit suicide but failed; instead, I hid behind the protective wall of pride and vanity, which led me to experience such a deep void in my life that I hated God. My only way to overcome what I felt was to say that I was capable of doing it all. After each surgery, the patient would say, "Thank God everything went well," to which I would answer, "Not thanks to God but to my hands, because God did not study medicine or surgery." The people used to say, "You are so coldhearted!" This continued until I operated on a lady with lung cancer. I made a mistake during the surgery, and she began to bleed out. Her death was imminent. In that instant, I felt in my chest the strongest pain and coldest sensation I have ever experienced—I was impotent in the face of death. In the midst of that crisis, I cried out, "God, if You exist, save this woman, and I will serve You for

the rest of my life." And then I heard a voice that said, "Where are your hands? Let your hands save her!" Right there, I asked God to forgive me. I cried as I opened up my heart to Jesus and made Him my personal Lord and Savior. Eight days later, that woman left the hospital alive and healthy.

A week later, I visited a Christian church and gave my life to Jesus; that was over twenty years ago. It was there where I met my wife. Fourteen years later, we began to work with the Couples Ministry. When the group grew to forty people, we heard of CAP (The Apostolic and Prophetic Conference) in Miami and attended the conference. There we were impacted by Apostle Guillermo Maldonado's message on the fatherhood of God. We returned the following year for CAP and met with him for thirty minutes, and he said, "I adopt you as my son and also your church." My answer was, "I do not have a church, just a group of forty people." His answer was, "That does not matter. I adopt you and them because God is leading me to do it." I cried as he embraced me. In one second, I could see all of my past suffering and pain, but I also never felt such deep peace. That embrace and hearing the word "son" changed my life. For the first time, I felt I had identity. The next year, the forty-member group had grown to six hundred. The congregation grew as the fatherhood of God healed our souls. Seven years later, we have over four thousand members. We are one of the fastest-growing churches in Dominican Republic, and everything that happens in El Rey Jesús is duplicated in our ministry. Furthermore, we have five churches under our spiritual covering.

...we are transmitting the gospel through five television stations and one international station, sending out the glory of God by any means. In addition, we just purchased land to build our new church debt free; one day, it will house seven thousand people.

A project has also been approved by the government to create a network that provides medical attention at low cost to pastors and their families throughout the nation who do not have medical coverage. The country has over five thousand pastors, and 98 percent of them do not have access to medical services. This project includes a hospital with eighty rooms with the highest standards at a cost of twelve million dollars, which God already provided. Also, we are close to finishing the construction of our first Children's Home for abandoned children. These children will be sponsored by companies and will eventually be adopted by Christian parents....

One woman who was thirty years old, married, and had one son visited the church after being diagnosed with schizophrenia and depression. She had already been hospitalized and treated with antidepressants and antipsychotic drugs several times....The root of her depression began with an abortion she'd had before she was married. When we prayed against the spirit of depression, there was a strong demonic manifestation in her. She went through inner healing and deliverance, and several months later, she came to see me. When I saw her, the Lord revealed that she would birth a daughter. Two months later, she was pregnant, and today she has a precious baby girl. She was completely healed and never needed psychiatric treatment again. She is now an amazing intercessor with a happy and healthy family.

Believers are common people used by a supernatural God.

Manifestations of the glory of God are being reported by many leaders and members of our congregation and the congregations under our spiritual covering. You may remember Pastors

José Luis and Rosa Margarita Lopez, whose testimony we read at the beginning of this book. They are experiencing all types of supernatural signs in their ministry. One testimony comes from a lady in their church who took her four-year-old son to the pool. She had planned to leave him for only a minute, but the next thing she knew, a half hour had passed. She ran to find her son and discovered him at the bottom of the pool! Desperate, she began to scream and to ask for help, but by the time the boy was taken out of the pool, he had turned purple, his pupils were dilated, and he had no pulse. An ambulance was called, and the paramedics tried to resuscitate him by doing CPR, but it did not work. They confirmed that the boy was dead.

While this was happening, his mother remembered the training on the supernatural that she had received from her pastors, so she never stopped praying for him. Out of respect for her pain, the paramedics said nothing. She spent an hour cradling her son in her arms, crying out to God for his life. Suddenly, an hour after the child was pronounced dead, the mother ordered him to come back to life, and he did. He opened his eyes and began to breathe and to move. The paramedics checked his pulse, and it was normal. This boy came back from the dead without neurological damage, thanks to a mother who had learned to activate the power of Jesus' resurrection. Praise God! Keep in mind that if God uses average men and women to perform miracles, then you, too, can be a chosen vessel to manifest His glory.

What Type of Church Is Jesus Coming For?

...that He might present her to Himself a glorious church, not having spot or wrinkle or any such thing, but that she should be holy and without blemish.

(Ephesians 5:27)

Jesus is coming back for a *"glorious church,"* not a church that is sick, depressed, poor, powerless, without oil for its lamp, or lost in darkness. He is not coming back for a church that does not shine His light in the world.

The word *"glorious"* in the above verse indicates the manifestation of every aspect of the essence of God. Let us remember that the Hebrew word for "glory," *kabowd*, is used figuratively in the sense of "splendor," "abundance," "honor," or "glory." In the Old Testament, *kabowd* is used variously to describe an individual's wealth, power or majesty, influential position, or great honor.

In other words, someone glorious is honorable, illustrious, esteemed, wealthy, solvent, secure, of high reputation, and splendid. Accordingly, a glorious church is one that visibly demonstrates the power of God with miracles, signs, wonders, healings, and the casting out of demons. A glorious church manifests the holiness, character, and purity of its King; it manifests His wealth on earth. It shines with the light of Christ, testifying of Him wherever it goes and removing the darkness. This glorious church continually preaches, establishes, and expands the kingdom everywhere. It manifests the resurrection life of Jesus by doing creative miracles, by raising the dead, and by taking dominion in every area of society: politics, the arts, science, medicine, business, sports, education, religion, and more.

Who Belongs to This Glorious Church?

And that He might make known the riches of His glory on the vessels of mercy, which He had prepared beforehand for glory. (Romans 9:23)

Every believer who receives and recognizes Jesus as Lord and Savior is chosen to be a vessel of mercy to manifest His glory on earth, regardless of his or her culture, age, nationality, race, or gender. If you are willing, if you will commit to God with total surrender and make yourself available to serve Him, His glory will inevitably grow in you because now is the time!

The end-time movement of God will be a movement of the manifestations of the sons of God.

*For I consider that the sufferings of this present time
are not worthy to be compared with the glory which
shall be revealed in us.* (Romans 8:18)

Perhaps you have been experiencing great tribulation in
your life. You might be feeling ready to give up and think that
this transformation of glory cannot take place in you. But the
Scripture says that our afflictions are nothing compared to the
glory that will be revealed in us when Jesus returns, and I believe
they also cannot be compared to the glory that will seen as His
presence is manifested in and through us now. Marital problems,
sickness, unemployment, or any other type of temporal attack of
the enemy that you might be facing right now cannot compare
with the following: the satisfaction of praying for the blind and
seeing the miracles as they recover their sight or praying for the
deaf and witnessing them begin to hear; of praying for the demon
possessed and watching them be delivered or testifying of Jesus
and seeing people receive salvation and be transformed; of praying for supernatural provision and witnessing it manifest; and so
on. None of the present conditions can compare with the glory
that God will cause to shine upon you. Your affliction is brief,
temporal; and it will produce in you a greater weight of His glory.
(See 2 Corinthians 4:17.) God will not let you drown in your failure. He will make you more than a conqueror! (See Romans 8:37.)

*For the earnest expectation of the creation eagerly
waits for the revealing of the sons of God.*
(Romans 8:19)

Even creation has an earnest expectation—an ardent desire—to see the manifestation of the carriers of God's glory.
While this *"revealing"* will ultimately occur at Jesus' second
coming, I believe that creation is, in effect, vigilant even now;
it is waiting for the moment when a child of God will enter a
hospital and declare a word, and all the sick will be healed. It
is waiting for a child of God to enter a funeral parlor and raise
the dead. The earth waits, with eager expectation, for a son or

daughter of God to pray for thousands of sick people and see them be healed. Do you want to be that person? Do you want to leave the comfort and convenience of your four walls and make yourself available to God? This is your moment; this is the promise of the last days for every believer!

Jesus Is Our Model for Demonstrating the Kingdom, Power, and Glory

The former account I made, O Theophilus, of all that Jesus began both to do and teach. (Acts 1:1)

In Matthew 6:13, we read, *"For Yours is the kingdom and the power and the glory forever."* Each of these aspects is distinct. In simple terms, the kingdom is the message of heaven. The power is the ability of heaven. And the glory is the atmosphere or environment of heaven. Jesus powerfully demonstrated the message of the gospel He carried and brought the environment of heaven to earth.

In today's culture, we are used to instructors who do not demonstrate or practice what they teach, because concepts, theories, and knowledge are often more highly regarded than experience. For example, people can attend business school and graduate with a master's degree in business administration, never having been taught by an active businessperson or anyone who has direct knowledge of how to manage a business. That is why society generally considers knowledge without experience to be the norm. I am a lover of knowledge, theory, and theology, but I do not settle just for them. I like to go beyond them—I want to have an experience with that knowledge, theory, or theology.

New Testament believers should teach, demonstrate, and flow in the supernatural.

In contrast to our culture, the Bible emphasizes that teachers must not only teach but also do. For example, Nicodemus told Jesus, *"Rabbi, we know You are a **teacher** come from God; for no one can **do** these signs that You do unless God is with him"* (John 3:2). Also, after the seventy disciples were sent out by Jesus to minister in various towns, they returned to Him with the report of what they had both said and done. (See Luke 10:1–17.)

I define the verb *to teach* as "to impart knowledge, information, and facts" and the verb *to do* as "to demonstrate, manifest, or realize something." What is the main reason believers who have been baptized in the Holy Spirit and with fire attend church? It is to receive knowledge, revelation, activation, and the fire of His glory to take it "all" out there. If the kingdom is not being manifested in the streets, and if the knowledge of the glory is not filling the earth at a faster pace, it is because many believers are not doing anything with what they have received. They have become addicted to knowledge and to attending conferences; this does not make them much different from an addict to any other substance. They seek only a blessing—for someone to touch their lives with healing and deliverance—but they never do anything with what they receive, and they never set anyone else afire with the glory of God.

"Do and teach" (Acts 1:1)! These two things caused Jesus to operate with a double-edged sword. He had both the Word and the works. If the theology we preach does not produce the "do," then we are just transferring information and not imparting revelation.

Let us note that, most of the time, Jesus demonstrated before teaching. If we follow His general pattern and supernatural ministry, in which He revealed first, then we will *do*—manifest the presence—and then *teach* the gospel and the glory to others, because the supernatural demonstration makes people's hearts receptive to believe and receive the Word. Without a visible manifestation, the arguments and doubts in people's minds will likely hold sway over them. Even after His resurrection, Jesus demonstrated that He was alive with unquestionable signs to each of His disciples, leaving no room for doubt.

The most important aspect of a church service is for God to manifest His presence.

What is God demanding of each believer today? Availability! Each one of us is a vessel that carries the kingdom, the power, and the presence of God. He wants to use you. These are not the days of Moses, Elijah, or David. This is your day! Until this day, people have heard of them, but they have not yet heard of you. They were common men who received a divine passion and manifested God under a lower glory than we have today. I challenge you! Dare to take hold of the boldness of the Holy Spirit!

God's glory is not limited to a specific place or situation. I want you to truly understand that He moves outside the church, as well as inside it. A primary reason He chose us to be carriers of His presence is that wherever we go, He can manifest!

Carrying the Presence of God Outside of the Church

When you are a carrier of the glory of God, the miracles, signs, and wonders will manifest wherever you go. You will not have to wait for the next church service to see a healing or miracle occur.

Many church leaders and believers think that for God to become visible and tangible, it is imperative to have a musical group and corporate worship; otherwise, God cannot flow. Corporate worship does produce the cloud of glory that makes all things possible. It fills us and renews the oil in our lamps, giving us the fire we need and bringing forth spontaneous miracles. However, it is no less true that you and I can manifest God's presence outside such a setting through "raw" authority and faith, without choirs, music, or any built-up atmosphere of glory—the Holy Spirit in us is more than enough! You can be God's instrument anywhere in the world because you are a mobile tabernacle of the glory of the Holy Spirit.

We carry with us the dominion, the lordship, and the will of the King, thereby possessing the potential to manifest the reality of His kingdom to each person and in each situation we encounter, establishing it forcefully by demonstration. *"From the days of John the Baptist until now, the kingdom of heaven has been forcefully advancing, and forceful men lay hold of it"* (Matthew 11:12 NIV).

In the move of the latter glory, the weakest believer will be like David, and the whole church united in Christ will be like God. (See Zechariah 12:8.)

In a conference held in a stadium in Argentina, the following miracle left us truly astounded. A fourteen-year-old boy named Pablo Alejandro received his miracle during the meeting. He had been suffering from a genetic condition called congenital ectodermic dysplasia, which had stunted his growth due to a lack of hormones. His mother said the condition had already taken the life of another of her children, as well as the life of her brother. As a result of his infirmity, Pablo could not sweat, even though he lived in a part of the country where the temperature climbs very high during the summer. This is a life-threatening condition due to hyperthermia. His illness had also caused him to grow without gums or teeth, so he had to use dental prosthetics. In addition, his skin stung and burned. He was desperate for healing and for deliverance from all that plagued him—and from death.

During one of the services, the glory of God poured out, making everything possible. When I began to declare creative miracles and supernatural signs, Pablo started to feel heat in his mouth; he said it felt like a "sting." So, he asked the person next to him to check his mouth, and to his surprise, gums were being formed. The person could tell that he now had bone and that his teeth were growing! His prosthetic no longer fit. Furthermore, hair started to grow all over his body. For this miracle to take place, God had to create new sweat glands. Where medical science could give no answers, the glory of God did a creative miracle!

Steps to Manifest the Glory of God Today

You can be a carrier of the type of miracle that happened to Pablo. All you have to do is believe and then make yourself available to God.

1. Believe Wholeheartedly

Jesus said to her, "Did I not say to you that if you would believe you would see the glory of God?"
(John 11:40)

Jesus gave us the key to seeing the tangible and visible glory of God: believe—above all reason and intellect and beyond all circumstances. Have you considered that, perhaps, what you are experiencing now could serve for His glory to manifest? The only requisite for it to happen is for you to believe wholeheartedly!

2. Commit to "Go"

And [Jesus] said to [His disciples], "Go into all the world and preach the gospel to every creature."
(Mark 16:15)

"Go" is translated from the Greek word *poreuomai*, which means "to go on one's way, to proceed from one place to another"; it "is more distinctly used to indicate procedure or course."[9] One grave problem—if not the worst—that the church is experiencing is that most believers have failed to understand the true meaning of this word "go." It is so simple, but it seems that

---

[9] *Vine's Complete Expository Dictionary of Old and New Testament Words* (Nashville, TN: Thomas Nelson Publishers, 1985), 269, s.v. "Go (Went), Go Onward."

many Christians still do not understand it or simply do not want to do it. We read in the book of Acts that the same thing happened in the early church. The believers were not moving; ten years after Jesus' resurrection, they continued to preach mainly within the walls of Jerusalem, receiving more revelation, praying more, and ministering to one another. They may have believed they were not ready to go, as many in the church believe today. Yet they were never ready to go until the persecution started.

In our day, believers continue to receive knowledge, pray, fast, seek more activation and impartation, and ask for another prophecy or word of knowledge, but they are never ready to *go*! I am not saying that any of these things is wrong—they are all good—but what are we doing with all that we receive? If the attitude in the body of Christ does not change, we will experience the same "prompting" as the early church. God had to allow tribulation to force them to go to the rest of the world and preach, impart healing to the sick, and cast out demons.

Each chapter in the book of Acts was written for you to receive knowledge and revelation, impartation and activation—and then immediately to go and do the same. The moment you learn something, you become responsible before God to practice it. If you merely convert it to head knowledge, you will become one more religious person who knows truth but does not live it. Therefore, before this happens, or even if it has already happened, I challenge you to make the decision to go to your "world"—your home, office, business, and city—and testify of Jesus. I assure you that the glory of God will manifest with unquestionable signs, because this is the time for the manifestation of the glory in and through believers. The signs follow those who go and obey, according to the Word of God.

You will experience the power and the glory of God only as you go.

Where should you go? You should go *"into all the world."* The Greek word translated *"world"* in Mark 16:15 is *kosmos*, which means "orderly arrangement" or "world." In its immediate sense here, it apparently refers to the physical earth as the scene of human habitation,[10] since Mark used a present participle, "as you are going about into the world." Yet, in another sense, the word *kosmos* can denote "'the present condition of human affairs,' in alienation from and opposition to God."[11] I consider that sense of *kosmos* (cosmos) to be the social order that is organized or structured in the world in which we live, and is designed to work against the system, government, or kingdom of God, because Satan is the *"ruler of this world"* (John 12:31).

What are the systems of this world? The major systems are: political, judicial, artistic (theater, movies, music, and other entertainment), economic/financial, educational, communicational, medical, and religious. Even though there are believers working in each of these areas, these systems are generally controlled by Satan and his human agents—people who serve him (knowingly or unknowingly) in maintaining the systems. We can "go" with God's power, kingdom, and presence to remove the demonic powers that control these systems, so that people will come to know Christ and so those who belong to the kingdom of God can influence these areas.

It is impossible to accomplish this in human strength! We have to use God's supernatural power, according to the measure of favor, grace, and influence He has given us. What is our cosmos? It could be a barbershop, hospital, warehouse, office, corporation, television or radio station, video production company, publishing house, bank, supermarket, movie theater, courthouse, library, university, taxicab, airport, street, parking lot, ballroom, service station, beauty salon, health center, hotel, tourist area, and so forth. We can manifest the glory that dwells in us by sharing the Word of God, laying hands on the

---

[10] See, for example, Watchman Nee, *Love Not the World: A Prophetic Call to Holy Living* (Fort Washington, PA: CLC Publications), 11.

[11] *Vine's Complete Expository Dictionary*, 685, s.v. "World," 1. (e).

sick, and casting out demons; by taking the truth and reality of heaven to those areas of our cosmos.

As We "Go," We Demonstrate the Supernatural

> *And as you go, preach, saying, The kingdom of heaven is at hand! Cure the sick, raise the dead, cleanse the lepers, drive out demons. Freely (without pay) you have received, freely (without charge) give.*
>
> (Matthew 10:7–8 AMP)

Since most of the church has failed to follow the Holy Spirit and demonstrate the supernatural, we now find ourselves trying to teach and explain what believers were originally meant to have captured—by association and by living under the divine spiritual atmosphere. For the most part, the church has not learned to move spontaneously; instead, as we have seen, it has reduced the supernatural to reason, because many people feel that if they do not understand something, it is not real.

The supernatural was designed to first be experienced and then understood.

Carnal or worldly individuals do not understand that God is supernatural; they feel there is no purpose for the spiritual realm because they are in darkness and unable to see it. It is our responsibility and task to demonstrate it, to show them the light and the miracles. No one can explain God, but when we experience Him, no further explanations are needed. If we find ourselves giving explanations, it is because religion has separated us from experience. People will believe when they can experience God.

Besides the ones I've already related in this book, I could tell you story after story of what happens through the members of our church as they go about their daily lives manifesting the revelation of the glory of God in their cosmos.

For example, a woman named Silvia went to the doctor for a routine examination. Two weeks later, the doctor called her with the results. The test had come back positive for HPV (human papillomavirus), and she was told she had cervical cancer. She immediately rejected the diagnosis and the sicknesses. She did not accept them or confess them but declared herself healed in the name of Jesus. That same week, in her discipleship group, her mentor prayed for her and prayed against the spirit of infirmity. Silvia felt a tingle in her womb, followed by a great sense of peace. When she returned to the doctor for a follow-up, no HPV or cancer cells were found. She was completely healed! The doctors could not explain what had happened.

The following month, Silvia noted that her boss seemed depressed and was always talking about dying. She learned the reason: the doctor had diagnosed her with cancer in both breasts. Immediately, Silvia shared her testimony and said, "If you believe that God can heal you, pray with me." Her supervisor accepted the invitation and confessed Jesus as Lord and Savior. Silvia prayed for her health and laid hands on her, declaring her healing. Then, she returned to work. A week later, her boss went back to the doctor, who examined her and declared her completely healed. She is no longer depressed. She has hope, joy, health, and Jesus! Before this, she would not allow Silvia to read her Bible or talk about Jesus in the office, but now she has her praying for her sick friends and believing for their healing. Silvia is carrying the kingdom to her office, while she works. God healed her, and now she is imparting healing to others.

The message of the kingdom, power, and glory irritates the religious but revives those who thirst for God.

What excuses do believers give to avoid manifesting the kingdom? Both the relaxed and comfortable Christians and the

intimidated and insecure Christians of today have countless excuses, including: "I'm shy," "I can't talk," "I have my own problems," "My finances are not going well," "I don't have the time,"
and "I am too tired." Or, they give the excuse that manifesting
the kingdom is only for apostles or evangelists. God is tired of
excuses! The time has come for you to preach, teach, and demonstrate His kingdom, beginning with your family, then your
friends, and then your wider cosmos.

Should I Wait to Be Sent Out Officially by the Church?

Jesus said, *"As you go..."* (Matthew 10:7), which means as
you are on your way, walking through life. We do not have to
wait for the pastor to call us forward to the altar and send us
out with a special title to preach and demonstrate the power of
God. Jesus already sent us to all the world, to all the strata of
society: the poor, the rich, the intellectuals, the illiterates, the
professionals, the common workers, the bosses, the employees,
the businesspeople, the artists, the athletes, the children, the
young adults, the adults, and the elderly people; to the city, to
the country, to the suburbs, to the nations.

By saying this, I do not mean that Christians should govern alone or that they are under no authority. We have already
discussed the importance of being subject to spiritual authority, and the fact that submission brings order and spiritual covering. What I am referring to is the preaching of the gospel and
the manifestation of the kingdom by each believer in his or her
sphere of influence.

No titles or special permits are required to do this.
Therefore, as you go through life, share manifestations of God's
glory. Your neighborhood is where you are called to demonstrate the glory you have within you. When you are at the hair
salon, share a word of knowledge with your hairstylist, and, if
she is ill, pray for her. When you go on vacation, pray with the
clerk behind the front desk at the hotel. Give him a prophetic

word, and win him for Jesus. When you go to a restaurant, tell your waitress about Jesus and pray for her. You get the idea. In our ministry, hundreds of young people have asked their teachers' permission to stand in front of their classes to pray for their sick classmates. God has stood by them with powerful miracles and signs, demonstrating His glory through their bold words and actions.

The believer who wants to be a chosen vessel to carry the glory of God must cross over the lines of comfort, convenience, and reason.

We are to be vessels who carry the glory of God to heal, deliver, and manifest amazing miracles as we go through life and as we go outside the church walls. I ministered in Chaco, Argentina, in an outdoor stadium, and during the worship portion of the service, many people went forward to dance and celebrate the Lord. Our photographer took several pictures of what was taking place, and among those pictures was one of a little girl, who looked no more than eight years old. She was dressed in violet and was seated on a young man's shoulders. Her hands were raised to heaven, and we could see that most of the index finger on her right hand was missing.

Later, when the glory of God descended on the more than twenty thousand people who had gathered, I prayed for the sick and ordered all shortened bones to stretch. We could feel the supernatural power of God working! The people were deeply touched. I asked for testimonies, and from the crowd came the little girl. Her mother was with her, crying and impacted by the miracle that had taken place in her daughter. God had recreated her finger! She now had an index finger of normal size on her right hand. She had lost her finger in an accident involving a bread slicer when she was only two years old, and she had suffered a lot because her school friends made fun of her all the time. But, that night, she felt the fire of God in her hand, and she turned to show her mother. Afterward, the doctors examined her and were in total shock. The before-and-after pictures clearly showed how much the finger had "grown"!

Sometimes, the demonstrations of the presence of God outside the church are more powerful than those that take place in the church. I am convinced that this is the season when great supernatural manifestations will take place not only in churches but also in coliseums, arenas, parks, theaters—anywhere a believer who is full of His presence goes and is willing to manifest it.

What Concerns You More: Your Needs or the Needs of Others?

Some people are so centered on their own needs, egos, reputations, or fear of rejection that they have a hard time getting the courage to demonstrate the glory that God has deposited in them. Yet the miracles, signs, and wonders will take place when we forget about self and become aware of and centered on the needs of others and on how to meet those needs. When you wake up in the morning, ask God to place across your path someone in need—someone who is sick, depressed, or lost. Ask Him for boldness to manifest His presence so that person can see His light. Remember that, wherever you go, God's glory is potent and ready to be manifested.

Federid was born deaf-mute due to an infection he suffered while in his mother's womb. The atmosphere in his home was one of frustration because of his condition, but his mother, Reyna, never gave up believing in the love of Jesus. Not long ago, she brought her son to one of our services where we were ministering healing and miracles. During the worship, I began to pray for the people, and when I got close to this child, I could feel his mother's faith. I laid my hands on him and ordered the deaf-mute spirit to release him, saying, "Leave him! Let him go!" Then, I told the child to repeat the word "Daddy."

In that atmosphere, which was full of the presence of God and a multitude expecting to see His power, Federid suddenly said, "Daddy." The people exploded in shouts of joy when this nine-year-old boy, who had neither heard nor spoken in his life, suddenly repeated the first sound that his ears—healed by the glory of God—registered. The boy had arrived a deaf-mute but left with a creative miracle that enabled him to hear and speak. In one instant in the glory of God, he was transformed.

Are You Willing to Commit to Demonstrate God's Presence?

If you like religion or are satisfied with it, you are not going to want to "go" and do what God is asking you to do today. You are also not going to understand what I am talking about—this is why many believers in past centuries became ineffective. For many of them, religion and formalism turned into bondage that kept them from fulfilling their commission from God. Every believer is called to make history, not to live out a routine or tradition without the supernatural power of God. This is the time to commit to become a member of the remnant of chosen vessels—the carriers *and* demonstrators—of the glory of God. Then, as you go on your way in life, beginning where you are now, make history! Preach to the lost, heal the sick, cast out demons, and remove the darkness with the light of His glory.

Be a part of this final move of the glory of God that will fill the earth in these last days. The greatest manifestations of His power will be seen in this dispensation—this revealed period of time—and you cannot be left behind. That glory is in you. Go and manifest it outside of your church with signs, miracles, and wonders. You are a carrier of light for this world! Start right now and experience the most impressive supernatural experiences you could ever imagine.

From this moment forward, begin to take leaps of faith, so that you can perhaps write your own book, filled with the same types of miracles that are found in the book of Acts. Let the generation being born today not only read the Acts of the Apostles in the Bible but also read what God did through you. Now, go and manifest His presence!

I invite you to pray with me:

Heavenly Father, right now, in the name of Jesus, I ask You to forgive me for having conformed to religion, legalism, and empty traditions. In the name of Jesus, I ask You to release upon me a hunger and thirst for Your kingdom and glory. I ask You to use me as a vessel of clay chosen to manifest Your glory as I live my life. I ask You to release the fire of Your presence in me, right now, so I will never again be a passive Christian but an active and daring one. Give me boldness, Lord. Let Your glory be upon me, every day of my life, as it was over Moses all the days of his life—and even more so in this time of the latter glory. I commit to make myself available to You, to surrender my body as a living sacrifice, and to obey Your Word. I want to be a part of the remnant You are raising to manifest the latter glory. I receive it right now, and I go to my "world," in the name of Jesus. Amen!

The movement of the glory of God will begin as a small current of water; the current will increase until it becomes a brook; the brook will grow into a great river, which will overflow and become a sea; and that sea will transform into a powerful ocean. Then, the glory of God will cover the earth as the waters cover the sea, and Jesus will come for His church!

EXPERIENCES WITH GOD

- The hour has come for believers to manifest the knowledge of the glory of God on earth! Are you available? If you are experiencing hard times, now is the time to cry out to the one true God for His help and provision. If you have never recognized the resurrected Christ—Jesus, who is the only answer to your problems—reach out to Him, right now, by repeating this prayer out loud:

Heavenly Father, I recognize that I am a sinner, and now I repent of all my sins. With my mouth I confess that Jesus is the Son of God, and I believe in my heart that the Father raised Him from the dead. In the name of Jesus, I am saved. Amen!

• Pray for the sick, testify of Jesus, and prophesy His words to others. Move in the gifts of the Holy Spirit to seek the lost; go where depression, sickness, and poverty are found. Manifest the glory of God everywhere you go.

About the Author

D r. Guillermo Maldonado is a man called to bring God's supernatural power to this generation at the local and international levels. Active in ministry for over twenty years, he is the founder and pastor of Ministerio Internacional El Rey Jesús [King Jesus International Ministry]—one of the fastest-growing multicultural churches in the United States—which has been recognized for its development of kingdom leaders and for visible manifestations of God's supernatural power.

Having earned a master's degree in practical theology from Oral Roberts University and a doctorate in divinity from Vision International University, Dr. Maldonado stands firm and focused on the vision God has given him to evangelize, affirm, disciple, and send. His mission is to teach, train, equip, and send leaders and believers to bring the supernatural power of God to their communities, in order to leave a legacy of blessings for future generations. This mission is worldwide. Dr. Maldonado is a spiritual father to more than 100 pastors and apostles of local and international churches as part of a growing association, the New Wine Apostolic Network, which he founded.

He has authored many books and manuals, a number of which have been translated into several languages, including *How to Walk in the Supernatural Power of God* (*Cómo Caminar en el Poder Sobrenatural de Dios*), and *The Kingdom of Power: How to Demonstrate It Here & Now* (*El Reino de Poder Cómo Demonstrarlo Aquí y Ahora*). In addition, he preaches the message of Jesus Christ and His redemptive power on his international television program, *Tiempo de Cambio* [*Time for Change*], which airs on several networks, thus reaching millions worldwide.

Dr. Maldonado resides in Miami, Florida, with his wife and partner in ministry, Ana, and their two sons, Bryan and Ronald.